Mission-Church
DYNAMICS

To Dr. George W. Peters

Thank you for the
very thorough and helpful
critique which you gave
on this manuscript, which
helped me in preparing the
final draft.

And thank you for all you
mean to me personally, and to
the work of the SIM as well
as missions worldwide.

W. Harold Fuller

Mission-Church
DYNAMICS

*How to change bicultural tensions
into dynamic missionary outreach*

BY W. HAROLD FULLER

William Carey Library

1705 N. SIERRA BONITA AVE. • PASADENA, CALIFORNIA 91104

Library of Congress Catalog Card Number 80-83659
International Standard Book Number 0-87808-176-3

Published by the William Carey Library
P.O. Box 128-C
Pasadena, California 91104
Telephone (213) 798-0819

In accord with some of the most recent thinking of the academic press, the William Carey Library is pleased to present this scholarly book which has been prepared from an author-edited and author-prepared camera ready copy.

PRINTED IN THE UNITED STATES OF AMERICA

Contents

ACKNOWLEDGEMENTS

The author gratefully acknowledges:

-- the permission of other authors and publishers for quotations used in this text, as noted;
-- the helpful critique of those missiologists, church leaders, and educators who read the manuscript;
-- the assistance of the SIM International Publications Department in preparing the copy for printing;
-- the creativity of Charles J. Guth, who designed the cover and prepared the artwork for it and the diagrams;
-- the infinite patience of my secretary.

        -- W.H.F.

Foreword

The more I look at church-mission relations around the world, the more I think of the relevance of what the Lord said in His prayer in John 17.

The Lord was emphasizing the unity which cuts across cultural barriers, although He recognized that there was a need to cross culture. For example, He said in His prayer that He was praying for the disciples. But He said, "Neither for these only do I pray, but for them also that believe on me through their word; that they may all be one." So you see you have the mission ("these") and the national church ("them also that believe on me through their word") "that they may all be one . . . that the world may believe."

The Lord identifies a relationship, a unity, which is patterned, if you like, on the Trinity. This is a unity which will be a significant force for local evangelism and for world missions.

The mission comes from another culture to bring the message to people whom the Lord has laid upon their hearts. The results of the work are consolidated into a church; then the mission and the church together push the frontiers of faith further. Both Christians and non-Christians see that this is not something foreign being imposed on them. The gospel is being shared by people of different cultures, and together they are taking it to the next group of people. The Lord said this is a significant part for our mission to play.

Missions have too often operated in another way. They
have brought the gospel, set up a church, appointed leaders,
and then they have unilaterally decided to leave. This has
slowed the spread of the gospel in a serious way, because
it has not been seen as something which belongs to all of
us. It has been seen as something which belonged to "them"
and now they have given it to "us." Thus the international
nature of the church is lost.

I think this is a very important basis for church-mission
relations. Obviously it is going to bring problems;
tensions are going to come. But the tensions are to be
faced in obedience to the Lord, who said things ought to be
done in this way. I'm quite sure the Lord will provide the
answers.

What is the secret of solving those tensions? I think
the secret is to realize that the determining factor is
neither the missionary's own culture nor the culture of the
people he has brought the gospel to. The determining
thing in the forward movement of the church of Jesus Christ
should be the gifts that the Holy Spirit has given to
individuals. Both the mission and the church must bring
together spiritual gifts which will make for further advance. That is not based on culture, but it may mean
crossing culture. For the local church it may be among
people of similar culture, and for the missionary it may be
among very different cultures. But the mission and the
church will need to cross cultures with the gospel, if
other than their own people are to hear.

Let us go forward in obedience to the Word of God, and
bring together the spiritual gifts the Lord has given to
both missionary and the national churches, and use these
gifts for further advance in missionary outreach.

                              G. Osei-Mensah
                              Nairobi, Kenya
                              June, 1979

Introduction

We obviously have a live issue before us.

"The problem of too frequent failure to reach true brotherly interdependence and biblical relationship between the 'younger churches' and 'missionary agencies' was viewed as a painful reality of 'ecclesiological crisis.'" W.E. Mulwa of Kenya quotes René Padilla of Latin America in this statement, and goes on to say that the same holds true in Africa.[1]

Such tensions are not only universal, but they also span the ages from the days of missionary Paul. The theological seminary of the Association of Evangelical Churches of West Africa (ECWA) at Igbaja, Nigeria, asked me to give a series of lectures putting these tensions into historical perspective and current context. ECWA and the Sudan Interior Mission were in the process of developing a new relationship. It was fitting that the lectures were to be the first in the Byang Kato Memorial series, for shortly before Kato died in a drowning accident, he and I had discussed the topic. To me, Byang Kato had been a true friend and wise counselor; students at Igbaja also valued him as a visiting professor. His position as General Secretary of the Association of Evangelicals of Africa and Madagascar gave him wide knowledge of the church-mission situation across the continent.

As I did research for the lectures, I realized the need
for a more comprehensive analysis of several assumptions
concerning missions, and their effect on church-mission
relations. As Vergil Gerber of the Evangelical Missions
Information Service points out, evangelicals have not
written much on this topic.[2] Orlando Costas, Latin-American
theologian, notes that "in evangelical circles the church-
mission issue is just beginning to attract the attention of
missionary leaders and theorists."[3]

Africa provides a fitting locale for our study, because
it has been a microcosm of missionary activity and church
growth over the past two centuries. Nigeria, the most
populous African nation, provides us with the main case
study. However, we have kept Africa in a world context by
referring to the experiences of church and mission in other
continents and worldwide trends which affect us all.

There are other major issues which need pursuing further,
such as the true nature of the church, the apostleship, the
mission. Although these affect church-mission dynamics,
in-depth study of them is outside the immediate scope of
this volume. We have touched on these other topics only
enough to give perspective and significance to our theme.[4]

I contemplated deleting some of the early historical
material in chapters one and two, but several respected
educators and missiologists felt that this brief review
adds to the teaching value of the book, since it highlights
events relevant to the topic.

Many missiologists have written about the need to change
relationships. I hope that this book may go further and
help us to see *how* to do so. No book can give a formula
suitable for all situations, and this one does not pretend
to. However, perhaps our analysis can help bring about
understanding of the tensions, and change them into dynamic
relations.

When Igbaja Seminary asked me to give these lectures, I
thought back on the mission-church tensions of my own
forefathers. They were animists, polygamists, and slaves.
In fact, the Roman imperialists were of the opinion that
English slaves were among the most stupid.[5] The colonial
power sometimes used Christianity to dominate the people.
Missionaries changed much of my forefathers' culture, and
imposed the culture of their own foreign church on our
forms of worship.

But I am thankful that the gospel came to my people. I do not resent the fact that today my own country still has foreign missionaries working in it; their presence reminds me that the gospel is universal. Among my friends are missionaries from Japan, Australia, Switzerland, and other countries helping to evangelize and disciple my own Canadian people.

I want to acknowledge my indebtedness to Byang Kato for the part he played in the development of my own attitudes. This is true of numerous other black and white colleagues, as we prayed and struggled in thought over the relationship of the church and mission.

I also thank Igbaja Seminary for the assignment that encouraged me to put down on paper the experience which God has given SIM and ECWA. Since giving the lectures, I have updated them and added supportive material to produce this volume. Grateful acknowledgement is due the authors and publishers whose work I have quoted on several pages.

The greatest impression made on me by these studies is that Christ, as Head of His Body, directs His people in missionary outreach. As we allow His Holy Spirit to empower our lives, we can turn human tensions into dynamic relations that will fulfill His will.

W. Harold Fuller
July 1, 1980

NOTES: INTRODUCTION

1. W.E. Mulwa, Bishop of the Africa Inland Church, in an address to A.I.M. missionaries in Kenya, Nairobi, Dec. 1978.

2. Vergil Gerber. In a manuscript critique to the author Jan. 18, 1978, Gerber states: "Serious consideration of the subject is long overdue. While we attempted to come to grips with it at Green Lake '71, really the whole matter was left hanging in midair, and I think you have now brought it down to comprehensible terms...."

3. Orlando Costas, *The Church and Its Mission* (Tyndale House, Wheaton, 1977), p. 154.

4. For definitions of terms used most frequently in this book, see appendix A.

5. Cicero, quoted in George Macauley Trevelyan's *History of England* (London: Longmans, Green, 1926), also Cicero's letter to Atticus, Oct. 1, 54 B.C.

Part One

Dynamics In Retrospect

1

The Historical Perspective

At the front of a Nigerian church is the photograph of a
white man. The pastor and the thousand adherents who
stream into the church on Sunday mornings put the photograph there to honor the missionary they look upon as their
spiritual "Father." Before the town had a road, post
office, school, or dispensary, the missionary came to live
among them. His first home was the grass-roofed entrance
hut of a compound. He learned their language, treated
their sick, taught their children, and led some of their
people to trust in Christ as Savior. But he would never
have wanted his portrait displayed in the church.

Today the town is on a main highway; it boasts a large
hospital, a midwifery training school, and a secondary
school, all started by the mission. The two schools have
frequently taken top place academically.

But although the people consider the missionary as their
"Father of Enlightenment," some look upon his photograph
with mixed feelings. They honor him, yet resent the policy
he represented 40 years ago. Those who look up at his
photo today did not know him personally, but their parents
told them that he and other missionaries tried to hold back
the progress of the people -- tried to stop them learning
English and wearing Western suits. The feeling became so
strong that a group of pastors revolted and left the missionary's work to join other denominations.

How could a missionary who left his country and lived in such difficult circumstances to bring the light of the gospel, want to hold back the people? Why has the deep misunderstanding of those days not been entirely overcome, even though for the past 25 years the town has been a center of high-standard education? How have such misunderstandings affected church-mission relations right up to today?

The missionary died not understanding why he was both loved and resented. In fact, he likely did not realize he was resented. And to this day, the people don't understand what motivated him and influenced his policies. But they like to keep his portrait at the front of the church.

Interestingly, it was in this town that Nigerians responded to the pioneer missionary's challenge, and they too became missionaries, going to a neighboring country. Moreover, they also ran into misunderstandings with the nationals they served. Resentment arose, and some of the Nigerian missionaries had to leave their mission field.

Of even greater interest to us today, the problems faced by the pioneer white man and later the Nigerian missionaries are problems which churches and missions have run into all over the world -- ever since the apostle Paul's day. They are tensions which missionaries from Africa, Asia, Latin America, Europe -- anywhere -- will face in the future.

Can we identify the tensions?

Can we discover their real causes?

Can we avoid them in the future?

Can we turn them into a dynamic force to complete the task of missions?

To begin with, let us go back to Paul's day and see what kinds of tensions he faced. Then let us take a quick look at missionary-church tensions through the intervening years. Perhaps we can come up with some patterns that will enable us to place today's tensions in perspective. To do so, we shall need to get a brief overview of the development of missions. This should help us see how certain policies and images of missionary work developed and have come to affect current church-mission relations.

APOSTOLIC PERIOD

Before the crucifixion, Jesus sent His disciples out to witness, but there was not the same sense of mission (special assignment or calling) which motivated them after the resurrection. This awareness of being "sent" followed Jesus' declaration recorded in John 20:21: "As my Father hath sent me, even so send I you"; the Great Commission recorded in Matthew 28:19,20; and Jesus' parting declaration recorded in Acts 1:8. The sense of mission, under the power of the Holy Spirit, transformed the disciples from a fearful, divided group seeking their own interests, into aggressive witnesses who declared to everybody that which they had seen and heard about Jesus Christ.

While history and tradition tell us much about the apostles, we are not certain how many churches were founded by them. God used them to organize and instruct groups of believers which sprang up along the trade routes of the Roman Empire. These early Christians were largely anonymous; nearly all seemed to be active witnesses. Strong church centers soon grew up in places such as Antioch, Rome, and Alexandria.

Since we wish to examine tensions between church and mission, let us look at those which became apparent right from the first days of the New Testament church.

1. Tension between the sending church and the missionaries

Cross-cultural outreach. In Acts 11:1,2,20-22, we gain the impression that the church leaders in Jerusalem were not happy about how Peter took the gospel to foreigners -- the gentiles. Later on, Paul's missionary work among gentiles raised questions in the Jewish church; there were misunderstandings which he tried to clear up (see Acts 21: 20,21; Gal. 2:1-10).

2. Tension within the mission

Cultural ritual matters. The early church leaders were under pressure to insist that foreign (gentile) Christians should observe the cultural and ritual traditions which Jewish Christians observed from their national background (see Acts 15:5-31; Gal. 2). The apostles prayerfully considered the matter, and wisely separated the cultural from the essentials of the gospel.

Missionary problems. Tension between missionaries affected the work as well. Paul and Barnabas disagreed over taking John Mark with them (see Acts 15:39). Paul faced unfaithfulness among fellow missionaries, illustrated by Demas' forsaking him (see II Tim. 4:10). His work was also affected by self-seeking "apostles" (see II Cor. 10:12).

Methods of missionary support. Paul was despised by some other workers because at times he did not follow their method of missionary support. At times he worked for his own living (see I Cor. 9:6). At other times he received support from other Christians (II Cor. 11:8,9).

3. Tensions within the local churches

Sectarianism among converts. Christians were beginning to follow their favorite missionaries rather than Christ (see I Cor. 1:12).

Discrimination between ethnic groups. Grecian Jews complained that the Hebrews were neglecting their widows (see Acts 6:1). Later Paul had to remind the Christians at Ephesus that Christ had broken down the "partition" between Jew and gentile (see Eph. 2:14-19).

4. Tensions between missionary and local church

Ethnic-sectarian divisions. Although the problem centered around Judaistic cultural controversy, Paul also had to "withstand Peter to the face" because he took sides on an ethnic-sectarian basis (see Gal. 2:11-13). At first Peter was happy to fellowship with the gentile group, but because of his fear of criticism by the Jewish group, separated himself from the gentiles. This also involved a tension between the "old" and the "new."

Christian practice. The missionary experienced frustration when converts did not practice their new faith. Paul had to write strongly about their immaturity, lack of conviction, and failure to condemn sin, regardless of their pagan context which condoned it (see I Cor. 3:1, 2; 5:1-7).

Finance. The missionary had to challenge the young church at Corinth to give faithfully, generously, and joyfully (I Cor. 16:1; II Cor. 9:7). Lack of Christian giving in a young church is often a tension point between a missionary and new believers.

Knowing the people's traditional suspicion about han-
dling finances, Paul sought to avoid this tension. Funds
collected to help the Christians in Jerusalem were sent by
reliable men chosen by the churches themselves (see I Cor.
16:3; II Cor. 8:19-21).

Doctrine. Paul's Epistles contain many references to
doctrinal error which had arisen, and the missionary had to
write to the young churches to correct them through the
instruction of the Holy Spirit (see Gal. 3:1; 4:17; Phil.
3:2; Col. 2:18-23; II Cor. 11:4; Gal. 1:6). These doctrinal errors often became a point of tension between the missionary and the new believers, as well as between churches.

Traits. Although Paul does not specify a problem, he
warns Titus of national traits arising from temperament and
culture, which affected the work and required special attention (see Titus 1:12, 13).

Anyone familiar with tensions between churches and
missions today will recognize similarities in these New
Testament era tensions. Did the church remember these
lessons in intervening centuries? Let us take a very
cursory look to find out.

ROMAN AND MEDIEVAL PERIOD

Roman World

From the second century to the fifth century, we note
characteristics of Christianity developing which affected
the future of the church and its missionary outreach.

There was rapid but uneven expansion of the Christian
faith, centered mainly in Rome, Asia Minor, and Roman gar-
risons of North Africa. Stephen Neill estimates that out
of a population of perhaps 50 million people in the Roman
Empire at that time, possibly 10 percent were Christian by
the end of the third century. Among the reasons for this
rapid spread listed by Neill is that of burning conviction
among the early Christians. He quotes Eusebius of Caesarea
(c. A.D. 260-340), who shows something of the early missionary vision:

At that time [about the beginning of the second
century] many Christians felt their souls in-
spired by the Holy Word with a passionate desire for perfection. Their first action in

obedience to the instructions of the Savior
was to sell their goods and to distribute them
to the poor. Then leaving their homes, *they
set out to fulfill the work of an evangelist,*
making it their ambition to preach the Word of
the faith to those who as yet had heard nothing
of it, and to commit to them the books of the
divine Gospels. They were content simply *to
lay the foundations of the faith among these
foreign peoples:* they then appointed other
pastors, and committed to them the responsibility for building up those whom they had
merely brought to the faith. Then they passed
on to other countries and nations with the
grace and help of God.[1]

However, there were factors which slowed down the missionary expansion of the church. Christian communities in
North Africa tended to become close-knit fellowships centered around bishops, rather than reaching out to the people around them. The Christians were mainly Romanized
elements of the population, and the churches cared for them
while neglecting concern for the general population of
Berbers and others. Jews, of which there were many in the
Roman centers, were regarded as enemies rather than a
mission field.

Early persecution of Christians served to strengthen
Christian conviction, and conversions multiplied among the
Romanized elements. The official recognition of Christianity by Emperor Constantine in A.D. 313 finally brought the
official persecution to an end. However, the church was
not prepared to move out in missionary endeavor, having
been weakened by the Donatist controversy, which centered
mainly around attitude to Christians who had failed under
persecution. The Donatist arguments weakened the church
for centuries, contributing to the eventual takeover by
Islam in North Africa.

Another weakening factor was the occupation of North
Africa by the Vandals from Europe (A.D. 429-533). They were
Arian in doctrine, and indiscriminately destroyed the
Trinitarian churches, both Augustinian and Donatist.[2]

However, during this period the church expanded through
missionary work into Mesopotamia, India, Ethiopia, Armenia,
and parts of Europe, including Ireland and France.

Medieval period

During the period from A.D. 500 to approximately 1500, called by K.S. Latourette "the Thousand Years of Uncertainty," the church faced two major struggles which would indelibly affect the development of the church and its missionary outreach -- and as a result, church-mission relations.

Struggle with Islam. Muhammad's flight from Mecca to Medina in A.D. 622 as self-proclaimed prophet of the living God, signaled the rise of the major post-Christian religion, Islam. It became more than either a religion or a state; it became a complete divine system governing every aspect of life, as Judaism had been.

Ten years later, although Muhammad was dead, his followers were able to unite the Arab tribes under a new monotheistic message that spread rapidly across North Africa and into Europe, until it was checked at the Battle of Tours in France in 732. It also spread eastward until the great Eastern capital of Constantinople fell in 1453 and the East Roman Empire ceased to exist. One possible explanation for the lack of Christian resistance in the East is the fact that Eastern Christians welcomed rulers who were opposed to the imperialism under which they had been living.

Of significance to the churches in Africa today is the fact that the vast Muslim areas of North Africa were once spheres of Christian influence. To some Christians they may now seem beyond evangelization, but before Muhammad's birth there were a thousand bishoprics in North Africa. Very few remained by A.D. 750. Two "Christian" kingdoms in Northern Sudan had fallen to Islam by the first of the 16th century. [3]

What took place was an Islamic evangelization of Christians, aided by political and societal pressure. Sometimes Christians were tolerated because their skills were needed by Muslims. However, the Muslim attitude was one of superiority, making the Christians feel inferior and putting pressure upon them to become Muslims. The Christians failed to try to convert their new Muslim masters.

Struggle with barbarians. These were "the hordes of Europe." They were animists -- pagans, polygamists, savages. Missionaries moved northward from Rome to reach them with the gospel. The conflict was between the eternal God and the local pagan gods. Missionaries destroyed pagan shrines, not out of hostility or lack of respect for local customs, but as a test of the pagan deities. Neill calls it "an act akin to the trial by ordeal."

For instance, the Germans were convinced that anyone who defiled the sanctuary of Thor would be destroyed by the gods. The missionary Boniface (724) chopped down the sacred oak of Thor at Geismar, without anything happening to him. The Germans were convinced that Boniface's God was supreme.

Here we see in early European Christian history the type of confrontation, or power encounter, between Christianity and European paganism which later took place in Africa, and which has been condemned as destruction of culture.

The early missionaries often used what we today would call the "team ministry" concept of utilizing professional missionaries and also men who assisted in self-support and community development. They probably started out with a mission station concept -- a place where they could farm, carry on occupations, and have contact with the people around them. However, instead of becoming centers for outreach, their monasteries became closed-in fortresses in many instances.

When Charlemagne was crowned as Emperor by Pope Leo III on Christmas day 800, the Holy Roman Empire came into being and lasted until around 1800. In the early years Christian expansion accompanied armed force, with periods of resurging paganism and martyrdom for Christians, between surges of forced conversion. The Teutonic Knights mixed politics and religion. One of their treaties with a conquered pagan tribe of Europe reads as follows:

> All who were not baptized must receive the
> rite within a month, that those who declined to
> comply should be banished from the company of
> Christians, and any who relapsed into paganism
> should be reduced to slavery, that paganism
> was to cease, that such Christian practices as
> monogamy were to be adopted, that churches

were to be built, the Neophytes must attend
church on Sundays and feast days, that provision must be made for the support of the
clergy, that the converts must observe the
Lenten fast, make their confessions to a
priest at least once a year, and partake of
the Communion at Easter.[4]

Missionary policy took little notice of local customs
or desires. The church litany was conducted in Latin,
although missionaries and monks in the north of Europe
tended to use local languages in their general work. Policies were dictated from Rome, producing local tensions
between church and mission.

For instance, in the seventh century in Britain, the
Celtic Christians had their own ideas as to the date on
which Easter should be observed and the manner in which
the ritual shaving of monks' heads ("tonsure") should be
carried out. The matter had to be referred back to Rome,
where the Pope made the decision. This was part of the
pattern of uniformity which Rome exercised throughout its
churches for over a thousand years.[5]

Christianity also spread eastward as far as China
through the work of Nestorian missionaries in the seventh
century. However, 300 years later, by A.D. 1000, traveling
monks could find no trace of Christians in the Chinese
Empire.[6]

The tragic Crusades. As Western Europe became united
politically and religiously, its attention turned to the
Muslim threat. Islam was pressing in on Europe and also
expanding eastward, threatening the eastern bulwark of
Christendom and occupying the Holy Land. Crusaders responded to Constantinople's appeals and sought to free
Jerusalem from the Muslim unbelievers, but for the Pope
there probably was a second motive -- diverting the knights
from the constant internecine wars in Europe. For two
centuries, from 1099 to 1291, the tragedy of the Crusades
continued -- "a long act of intolerance in the name of
God."[7] They left behind a trail of religious and political
bitterness, and weakness in the face of Islam's eastward
advance.

There were Christian voices raised against the religious
militarism of the Crusades. "Roger Bacon maintained that
the Crusades were an expensive and futile folly. Thomas

Aquinas held that even the infidel had certain natural
rights which must be respected. Almost the first Christian,
however, to attempt to act on these more liberal principles
was Francis of Assisi."[8] We shall hear more of the
latter's methods later on.

Abortive attempts in Asia and Africa. News of the
Christian faith moved with travelers to the Far East,
bringing contact with the Mongols and other Chinese groups
in the 13th century. The explorer Marco Polo recounts that
the Mongol ruler Kubla Khan requested the Pope to send 100
men of learning, devoted to the Christian faith, who would
be able to prove "to the learned of his dominions, by just
and fair argument, that the faith professed by Christians
is superior to and founded on more evident truth than any
other." That was in 1266. Twenty years passed before anything was done, and then only a single man was sent.[9] The
church failed to respond effectively and promptly to a missionary open door -- unlike Paul, who responded to the
Macedonian vision.

There were also contacts with India and with Africa. In
1444 explorers made the first recorded contacts with people
of tropical Africa. The first known Portuguese mission to
the Congo (now Zaire) set out in 1490. In 1518 the son of
an African king and queen was made Bishop of Utica, and in
1521 he returned to West Africa as its first "Vicar Apostolic." However, 100 years later there was hardly a trace of
this work left. In spite of the missionary efforts made
during the 15th century, by the end of the century Christianity still had not regained lost territory in Asia and
Africa or made significant progress in new territory.
Except in Europe, missionary activity had not brought into
being stable and enduring churches. Neill attributes this
lack to the following:[10]

1. Great distances and difficulty in travel;

2. Islam's control of land and sea routes;

3. No printing presses available to spread the Word
in vernaculars, even when Scriptures were translated;

4. Latin missionaries were slow to produce an
indigenous priesthood;

5. Christianity lacked dynamic conviction producing
holiness and witness.

Forerunner of new missionary spirit and methods

However, between the 13th and 15th centuries, we see signs of new attitudes to missionary work arising -- or the rediscovery of apostolic New Testament methods. A few men set forth principles which would influence later developments.

Ramon Lull, from the Spanish Island of Majorca in the 13th century, became the first known missionary to develop a theory of missions, and was one of the greatest missionaries in history. His three main tenets were (a) thoroughly learn the local language; (b) develop instructive literature concerning the Christian faith; (c) carry on a courageous witness among the people even to the point of death. Lull once wrote: "Missionaries will convert the world by preaching but also through the shedding of tears and blood and with great labor, and through a bitter death." He died of injuries received while preaching to Muslims in North Africa in 1315.

Francis of Assisi. Whereas for five centuries the missionary enterprise had been based in the monastery, Francis moved out of the monastery and traveled with the Fifth Crusade to Egypt, setting a new pattern for outreach. Two orders of Friars arose: the Franciscans and the Dominicans. Around 1300 the Dominicans formed "the Company of Brethren Dwelling in Foreign Parts among the Heathen for the Sake of Christ."

AGE OF DISCOVERY

The sixteenth Century (from 1501 to 1600) was to Europe "the Age of Discovery," when men set forth to explore distant horizons. This resulted in the discovery of the New World of the Americas, as well as the South Pacific. Missionaries accompanied these explorers with two great purposes: to reach unknown nations with the gospel; and to make contact with Christian churches which they believed existed in other lands, especially in the Far East.

It was during this time (1493) that the Pope took upon himself to divide the trade and evangelism of the world into two main spheres, with a line drawn on a map from the North Pole to the South through the Atlantic Ocean west of the Azores -- everything west belonging to Spain, everything east belonging to Portugal! In 1494 the line was moved westward, putting Brazil in the Portuguese zone.

The Jesuits

Another development in the missionary outreach of the
Roman Catholics was the founding of the Jesuit Order by
Ignatius Loyola in 1534. One of his companions was Francis
Xavier (1506-52), who worked in India and eventually as far
east as Japan. An interesting transition in his thinking
which affected the attitude of missions is noted between
his reports of India and of Japan. In India he had followed the thinking of medieval missionaries that everything
in non-Christian life and systems should be abolished
before Christianity could be built up. In the civilization
of Japan he came to realize that everything was not worth-
less, but that the gospel could transform and build on
many of the better elements of Japanese society.

There were political reactions and persecutions in the
midst of the outreach of this period, and missionaries
were accused of being seditious even in those days as
governments misunderstood their motives. Serious weaknesses also showed up as Roman Catholic missionaries tended
to sprinkle (baptize) entire communities into the Christian
faith without personal conversion. Another weakness which
was especially apparent in Latin America was the lack of
any serious attempt to indigenize the leadership. One
Spanish official wrote to the King of Spain in 1525: "If
out of these Indians one priest can be produced, he could
be of more use, and bring more Indians to the faith, than
50 European priests."

It was during this period that the Protestant Reformation took place in Europe, and it laid the foundation for
new developments in Protestant missions, as we shall see
later on.

Changing European attitudes

Roman Catholic work. With the beginning of the 17th
century, European attitudes were radically changing.
Europeans thought of their civilization as the superior one
in the world. This feeling was abetted by the industrial
revolution, technological development, expanding world
trade, and colonial dominions, accompanied by Darwin's
theory of evolution, which presumed that the white man must
be the latest and best human link!

As missionaries accompanied the spread of European influence around the world, they now seriously had to face

the challenge of other established religious systems such
as Islam, Hinduism, and Buddhism. They seldom followed the
principles of Lull, and often did not give the careful instruction and pastoral care needed to bring about true
conversion and establish lasting churches.

Roman Catholic missionary work showed grave weaknesses
in Africa, where there was little instruction and nationals
were baptized on the same basis as children: they could
not comprehend the Christian faith but wished to become
Christians. Among the Portuguese missionaries, the impression was given that to accept baptism also meant accepting
the sovereignty of Portugal. In fact, Roman Catholic missionaries were considered agents of the colonial government
during Portugal's 300 years of expansion. The government
and the Vatican signed "a concordat and missionary agreement."[11]

In South America the Jesuits maintained complete control
of Christians, discouraging initiative and independence
among them. The Roman church insisted on people everywhere
accepting its own local rules, such as celibacy of the
clergy and use of Latin for liturgy. The Bible was not
given to the people in their own language at the earliest
opportunity, as has been the principle among Protestant
missions. Also, we must recognize that much of the Roman
Catholic missionary work was based on nominal rather than
spiritual conversion.

Protestant beginnings. The Reformation period consumed
the energies of evangelicals in Europe as they fought for
their very existence. They were even reproached by the
Roman Catholics for not reaching out in missionary work.
Some Protestant groups took refuge behind a hyper-
Calvinistic emphasis, stating it was not necessary or
obligatory to reach the non-Christian world. One leader,
Johann Gerhard, stated that the command of Christ to preach
the gospel to all the world ceased with the apostles --
they had made the offer of salvation to all nations, and
there was no need for a repeated offer!

There were a few Protestants who stood out against these
isolationist views, and particularly in North America gave
heroic missionary service to reach the people. Among these
were the Presbyterian John Elliot, and David Brainerd.

Protestant missionary work really received its major
impetus from the Pietist Movement, which developed within

the Protestant churches in the 17th century.   As the Word of
God got into the hands of the people following the
Reformation, many began to see the need for personal
conversion, holiness of living, and responsibility for
witnessing to others. The Danish Pietist missionaries
Bartholomew Ziegenbalg and Henry Plutschau became the first
non-Roman Catholic missionaries to reach India from Europe,
and they set forth five principles of Pietist missionary
work which have since been followed by evangelicals:

1. Christians must be instructed to read.

2. The Word of God must be available to them in their
own language.

3. Missionaries must have accurate knowledge of the
local people in order to preach the gospel effectively.

4. The aim must be definite, personal conversion.

5. As early as possible an Indian church with its own
Indian pastors must be formed.

One of the most active and effective Pietist groups to
send out missionaries all over the world were the Moravians,
who date the beginning of their missionary work August 21,
1732. They were simple and dedicated people who went to
some of the most difficult places on earth to demonstrate
the power of the gospel in daily life. (See chapter 4 for
further comment on Pietist missionary work.)

Missions and colonial governments. Contrary to the
popular concept of some who oppose missionary work, these
Protestant missionaries venturing forth to a foreign land
did not go as the agents of colonialism to subjugate the
people. (Even critics of continuing missionary work note
that "the fundamental motive of the missionary awakening
was love and compassion.")[12] It is true that colonial
governments were impressed with the way in which missionaries could live peaceably among people who otherwise were
antagonistic to foreigners. However, the hostility of
colonial government officials and colonial merchants was
most evident. The East India Company opposed missionary
effort because it feared the Christian faith might upset
the people, provoke resentment against foreigners and therefore the development of commerce, and weaken its control of
the country. In Africa slave traders -- black and white --
were unhappy with missionaries.

In the South Pacific, the work of missionaries seeking
to help the people was in stark contrast to that of traders and government officials. One told missionary John G.
Paton, "Sweep these creatures away, and let white men
occupy the soil." A British government official in India
was reprimanded for even attending the baptism of six converts of the CMS (Church Missionary Society -- Anglican) at
Amritsar in 1859. In West Africa, Islam penetrated the
black animist kingdoms most actively from 1770 onward.
When the British and French occupied the territories a
century later, they did not want to complicate their administration through the introduction of Christianity.

In Northern Nigeria, the British government tried to
restrict missionary work and prevent missionaries entering
certain areas -- in spite of the fact that some Muslim
rulers would have gladly welcomed a missionary, not on the
basis of his faith, but because he was an expatriate. In
1900 the Northern Administrator, Sir Percy Cirouard, wrote
Lord Lugard: "Personally I should like to see the missions
withdraw entirely from the Northern States."[13]

Because of the attitude of the British government, R.V.
Bingham, then General Director of SIM, and his fellow
missionaries determined to preach the gospel in the far
north even if it meant "expulsion or imprisonment," to
draw the attention of the world to the fact that Britain
was suppressing religious liberty! SIM and other missions
joined in a delegation to present their case to the British
Foreign Office in London.[14]

Britain's Queen Victoria, a professing believer herself,
was not hostile to missions, but made it clear that she did
not wish her colonial governments to force Christianity
upon anyone. In accepting responsibility for administering
India, Queen Victoria signed the following proclamation:

> Firmly relying Ourselves on the truth of Chris-
> tianity, and acknowledging with gratitude the
> solace of religion, We disclaim alike the right
> and desire to impose Our convictions on any of
> our subjects. We declare to be Our royal will
> and pleasure that none be in any wise favored,
> none molested or disquieted by reason of reli-
> gious faith or observance, but that all shall
> enjoy the equal and impartial protection of
> the law. . . . And it is Our further will that,
> so far as may be, Our subjects, of whatever

race or creed, be freely and impartially admitted to offices in Our service, the duties of
which they may be qualified by their education,
ability, and integrity, duly to discharge.[15]

THE MODERN MISSIONARY ERA (19th-20th CENTURIES)

The beginning of the 19th century saw further profound
changes in the world which influenced the growth of missions. In Europe there was a psychological change to an
attitude of colonization and interest in overseas dominions.
On all continents the result of scientific and economic advance was felt. Exploration continued. Islam appeared to
be receding. The evangelical revivals in Britain and
America stimulated spiritual concern for others. Christian
leaders took up the battle against the slave trade until it
was finally abolished.

"It is indisputable that the conscience of Europe was
roused to a pitch of concerted and determined action to put
down the African slave trade, largely because of pressure
from the missionary lobby at home and because missionaries
alone in the early 19th century were in a position to offer
eye witness accounts of the slave trade."[16]

Protestant developments

Until now the major Protestant churches had seemed un-
willing to attempt much missionary work. The influence of
Pietism had waned, and for almost 300 years Protestants had
practically no mission agencies. The English Baptist,
William Carey (1761-1834), was one of a few evangelicals
who felt a burden for taking the gospel to others. When
Carey proposed to a group of Baptist pastors that missionaries be sent to India, one of them, in the spirit of hyper-
Calvinism of the day, declared that the heathen did not need
their help -- when God was ready to convert them, He would
do so by himself. However, Carey and his family sailed for
India in 1793, marking a new impetus among English-speaking
people in overseas missionary work. In a 32-year period,
12 societies were formed.

Carey put into effect the earlier Protestant principles
we have noticed: (1) widespread preaching of the gospel;
(2) aiming for personal conversion; (3) distribution of the
Bible in local languages; (4) study of the culture of the
people, and (5) establishment of an indigenous church with
national leadership as soon as possible.

It was during this period that the missionary methods
with which we are now so familiar developed. The early
missionaries were primarily preachers, but these were soon
joined by teachers, doctors, agriculturists, and technolog-
ically trained missionaries who could train printers, arti-
sans, and others. Most of the first missionaries were
married. It was only in the middle of the 19th century
that both Protestant and Roman Catholic missions began to
send single women.

From the middle of the 19th and into the 20th century, a
number of nondenominational mission societies arose. In
some cases this was because of the personal concern of individuals who could not find backing from their denominations. In other cases it arose from evangelical convictions which were not shared by the mission societies of
some denominations. Neill states:

> The missions connected with the great historic
> churches have remained stationary; or, if they
> have grown, cannot show growth comparable in
> its rapidity to [the nondenominational] mis-
> sionary society. As an example we may mention
> the Sudan Interior Mission, founded in 1893 as
> a venture of faith by the Canadian, Rowland V.
> Bingham. . . . It professes a simple biblical
> theology, holds to an extreme Free Church type
> of policy, and in recent years has committed
> itself to a more definite Baptist point of
> view. . . .Today, with 1300 missionaries, it
> is probably the largest single Protestant mis-
> sionary organization in the world, and has
> spread its operation -- evangelistic, medical,
> and literacy -- across the very heart of
> Africa.[17]

As a case study, we shall later examine some of the
church-mission tensions which SIM has experienced, and how
she and the church have sought to solve them.

Early African churches

Since our case study involves Africa, we could well give
a whole chapter to the history of mission and church in the
continent, but space will permit only a brief summary.

The first known missionary work in Africa was by an
African -- resulting from the conversion of "the Ethiopian

eunuch" (Acts 8:27), who was from a city north of present-
day Khartoum in Sudan. Two Christian kingdoms eventually
arose in the area, as a result of the work of missionaries
sent by Empress Theodora of Byzantium (Turkey). We have referred to the early spread of Christianity in the Roman en-
claves of North Africa, where at one time there were over
1000 bishops; and early church thinking in Europe was influenced by the writing of Augustine, a North African,
whose mother was a member of the Tuareg tribe.[18]

Underlining the fact that Christianity is not "the white
man's religion," S.O. Odunaike, President of the Association of Evangelicals of Africa and Madagascar, stated:

> One fact of history not often reckoned with is
> that although Britain is the mother of modern mis-
> sionary effort in the field of Christianity,
> Africa knew Christianity before Britain. We know
> that Jerusalem is the cradle of Christianity.
> The proximity of Jerusalem to Africa is very
> pertinent. Alexandria in Egypt was the home of
> Clement (born about A.D. 155) and of Origen (A.D.
> 188-255), the greatest scholar of the church in
> the eastern part of the Roman Empire. The Cath-
> olic Church has endorsed three great creeds, viz:
> the Apostles' Creed, Nicene Creed, and Athanasian
> Creed. The great debate of St. Athanasius in-
> spired the Nicene Creed. So Athanasius had to do
> with two of the three great creeds of the Chris-
> tian religion. And the home of Athanasius was
> Egypt. All this time Britain was still a pagan
> country, and it was not until the 5th century
> that Christianity was introduced to Britain.
> This was 300 years after the death of Africa's
> Origen, 150 years after Athanasius, and 100
> years after the birth of Africa's St. Augustine.
> Thus Christianity came to Africa before it
> reached Britain.[19]

Today Africa has two large independent and indigenous
churches whose history predates Islam: the Coptic Church,
based in Egypt; and the Ethiopian Orthodox Church. The
latter came into being through lay witness, when two Syrian
Christian young men, shipwrecked on the coast of Ethiopia
in the third century, were taken into the royal household.
Through their influence the king and his family became
Christians and made Christianity the official religion.

David Livingstone (1813-1873) set out for Africa in 1840. "I place no value on anything I have or may possess, except in relation to the kingdom of Christ," he wrote. His travels, along with the work of his father-in-law, Robert Moffat, helped open up Southern and East Africa to the gospel in face of great opposition from Arab slave traders.

Early believers in Uganda and other East African countries underwent fierce persecution. After ordering the Anglican bishop James Hannington to be speared to death, King Mwanga (Uganda) turned on the young Christians, enraged that they would not submit to the homosexual immorality he had learned from Arab merchants. Outside the capital city, Kampala, there stands a cross in memory of the African martyrs -- 32 of whom were burned in a great pyre on one day in June 1886. The subsequent history of the church in Uganda and Ruanda, with continuing revival in this century, is well known.

Moorhouse points out that pioneer missionaries often had to stand by "helplessly" as they observed massacres and violent customs.[20] Later, as they received the backing of the colonial power, at times they called on the government to overcome these practices. Some tribes rebelled -- such as the Kikuyu in their opposition to missionary banning of female circumcision. The rise of the Mau Mau movement has been partly attributed to that. It is interesting to note that since independence, the Kenyan government has itself banned the injurious custom.

Some missionaries and pastors also kept an eye on abuses by settlers. "Church leaders in East Africa protested against the exploitation of blacks by the settlers, and a Bishop Weston published *The Serfs of Great Britain*."[21]

In West Africa, much of the early Protestant missionary work followed the beginnings made in Sierra Leone, a colony developed by the British for freed slaves. The CMS founded Fourah Bay College there in 1827, and the first student enrolled was Samuel Ajayi Crowther, who later became Nigeria's first black bishop. Christian freed slaves finding their way back to Nigeria from Sierra Leone called for missionaries, and the Anglicans and Methodists responded. The Basel Mission opened work in Ghana (then Gold Coast), introducing both the gospel and cocoa.[22]

Expatriate missionaries quickly succumbed to malaria and other tropical illness (the CMS lost 50 in 20 years in Sierra Leone alone). Among the outstanding national missionaries were Crowther (who with the Anglican Henry Townsend founded a work in Abeokuta, Nigeria, in 1844) and the Methodist Thomas Birch Freeman. Freed slaves from Jamaica accompanied the Presbyterian missionary Hope Waddell to open a mission in Calabar, eastern Nigeria, in 1846.

Indigenous movements

Possibly the most renowned early indigenous evangelistic work was that of the Prophet Harris. William Wade Harris was a Liberian Episcopalian (Anglican), who traveled into neighboring Ivory Coast and from 1913 to 1915 evangelized the small coastal animistic tribes. His message was simple: faith in one God, the abandoning of fetishes, and reliance upon the Word of God. It is estimated he baptized 120,000 people. The French administration eventually banned him from the country, possibly fearing any foreigner (although African) with such a large following. But Harris told his converts to wait for Bible teachers to arrive. Then years later Methodist missionaries did so, and many of Harris's followers became Methodists. However, there is still today a "Harris Church" (Eglise Harriste), with over 100,000 adherents.

What David Barrett calls "the phenomenon of independency" has marked the growth of Christianity in Africa. Different terms have been used to describe these churches: spiritual, native, schismatic, separatist. Barrett estimates that these churches now include over 7 million adherents, and by the end of this century may well "have become comparable in size, power, and prestige to the entire Protestant and Catholic communities on the continent."[23] John Dean estimates that 500 "Christian" sects have emerged in the last 15 years in Nigeria alone.[24]

The causes of these movements are of particular interest to our study of church-mission tensions, and we shall examine them further in Part Two under Tension Points (chapter 7).

In passing, we need to recognize the influence which nationalism has had on the church and the mission -- and tensions between them. National awareness frequently arose from the education which missions brought, and sometimes

resulted in a backlash against the foreign missionary.
Examination of this factor will also be handled under
Tension Points.

In concluding our very brief overview of Africa, we
should note Barrett's prediction that by the end of the
century, in Africa south of the Sahara the majority religion
will be Christianity.[25] That prediction is based on research in church growth rates. However, what such figures
really represent will depend on the virility of the gospel
in the life of the church of Jesus Christ. The figures
include every type of church and sect, many without a
scriptural conversion experience in their doctrine.

In spite of the problems which the communicators of the
gospel may have had, the widespread establishment of
Christianity in most of sub-Sahara has been phenomenal. We
must remember that this has taken place chiefly in the past
200 years in spite of language barriers, physical problems
of travel, illness and death, and spiritual opposition of
other religions. Perhaps we should call it supernatural,
not phenomenal. The Spirit of God has done this in spite
of human error.

SUMMARY OF HISTORICAL DYNAMICS

From our very cursory historical perspective we have
observed typical tensions caused by culture and structure.
We can also detect definite phases in the attitude of the
church in its missionary outreach -- phases which affected
its manner of work, and which linger on to form the historical background for some mission-church tensions today. We
can classify them as follows:

1. Apostolic period

The missionary had a *servant attitude*, as had his
Savior (Phil. 2:7) who sent him forth (John 20:21). In the
face of criticism, opposition, and persecution, he was
gentle, not pompous (I Thess. 2:6). He had to win his way,
not fight for it. Paul called himself a slave not only of
Christ but of the believers (II Cor. 4:5), and suggested
that an apostle was the "offscouring of all things"
(I Cor. 4:9-13).

2. Medieval period

   The missionary often had the attitude of the *militant
victor*. This was the era of political-religious wars.
Christianity had state backing, the sword and the cross
went to battle together in the face of militant animism and
Islam. Therefore many missionaries developed an aggressive
and often pompous image.

3. Colonial period

   As there was colonial expansion in government, trade,
and culture, the missionary was often looked upon as part
of a *superior society*. The missionary found himself in a
respected status. While a few missionaries reveled in this
status, most shunned the aura of superiority and sought
only to be humble servants of Christ. "Nationals were well
aware of the distinction between colonial government and
missionary," states A. (Tony) T. de B. Wilmot, who has
served in government and industry in Africa for 40 years.
"It is only in retrospect that some have chosen to identify
the two as one."[26]

4. Current period

   The missionary theoretically has returned full circle to
the original position -- the *servant attitude*. Unfortunately not every missionary has moved into this period, but
the fact remains -- today he has no special status as an
expatriate; he along with all other foreigners has been
pushed off the pedestal. The true missionary has no
alliance with any government force -- even appearing to
have would compromise his message. He is simply a human
being. True, he is carrying a divine message; but he
carries it as a servant of Christ, not a colonial emissary.

   Today a missionary is in the fortunate position of being
divested of superior racial status and political backing,
so that his message stands on its own merits. Unfortunately
while this is the real situation, there are those who link
the colonial era with the missionary and distort his image
and his message.

   Although I have divided this historical survey into
these four periods, I would refrain from generalizing to
the extent of putting all missionaries into any one group
in any one period. In each period there have been true
"servants." Conversely, in the apostolic period, marked by

a servant attitude, there were those whom Paul described as "pompous."

I have actually described the *image* which the missionary in general has had during each period -- how the people of the world have seen him, not necessarily how he has always acted. It must be remembered that the public's memory may not distinguish between missionaries who were agents of the political-religious "concordat" days and missionaries who were violently *opposed* by colonial regimes. "Imperialist" types tend to loom larger in the public's memory than the self-effacing types who sacrificed all they had to identify with oppressed peoples. Yet the resultant image produces reactions which affect all expatriate missionaries.

As the modern missionary era opened, the image and practices of missions through the previous centuries provided the backdrop for church-mission tensions which developed. Let us see how churches and missions, councils and individuals, sought to overcome these tensions. We shall also see new theological trends emerging, introducing additional tensions.

STUDY QUESTIONS: CHAPTER 1

1. List the main tensions which arose between the early church, the missionaries, and their converts. Discuss why these arose.

2. During the Roman and Medieval Period, what factors hindered the spread of the gospel?

3. Describe the missionary spirit which Ramon Lull and Francis of Assisi demonstrated, and how it would affect the spread of the gospel.

4. What image of missions developed during the Age of Discovery and Colonial Period? What were the major factors in formation of this image?

5. How did William Carey's work mark a new beginning in missions? What principles did he rediscover?

6. How does the present status of missionaries relate to the missionary attitudes of the apostle Paul?

NOTES: CHAPTER 1

1.   Stephen Neill, *History of Christian Missions*
     (Baltimore: Penguin Books, 1964), p.39. Italics – WHF.

2.   Michael Smith, *The Church under Siege* (Downers Grove,
     IL: InterVarsity Press, 1976), for a full treatment
     of this.

3.   W. Harold Fuller, *Run While the Sun Is Hot* (Chicago:
     Moody Press, 1968), p. 139.

4.   K.S. Latourette, *History of the Expansion of
     Christianity*, Vol. II (Grand Rapids: Zondervan,
     1938), pp. 205-206.

5.   Stephen Neill, *History of Christian Missions*, p. 71.

6.   *Ibid*, pp. 94-97.

7.   S. Runciman, *A History of the Crusades*, Vol. III,
     p. 480.

8.   Stephen Neill, *A History of Christian Missions*, p. 116.

9.   *Ibid*, p. 126.

10. *Ibid*, pp. 132-133.

11. Elliott Kendall, *The End of an Era* (London: SPCK,
     1978), p. 22.

12. *Ibid*, p. 41.

13. E.A. Ayandele, *The Missionary Impact on Modern
     Nigeria* (London: Longmans, Green and Co., 1966),
     pp. 146-152.

14. Rowland Bingham, *Seven Sevens of Years and a Jubilee*
     (Toronto: Evangelical Publishers, 1943), pp. 87,88.

15. Stephen Neill, op. cit. p. 323

16. Geoffrey Moorhouse, *The Missionaries* (New York:
     J.B. Lippincott, 1973), p. 329.

17. Stephen Neill, *History of Christian Missions*, p. 459.

18. Byang H. Kato, *African Cultural Revolution and the Christian Faith* (Jos: Challenge, 1975), p. 38.

19. S.O. Odunaike, "He Gave Every One a Pound," message given at the Second World Black and African Festival of Arts and Culture, Feb., 1977, Lagos, Nigeria.

20. Geoffrey Moorhouse, *The Missionaries*, p. 61.

21. *Ibid*, p. 330.

22. In answer to allegations that missionary work led to exploitation and poverty, it is interesting to note that cocoa trees provided livelihood for farmers who had been barely subsisting, and also formed the base of the economy of Ghana, which became the world's largest cocoa producer. Later mismanagement of this resource and exploitation of the farmers was not the result of missionary work, but arose under a Marxist regime! -- WHF

23. D.B. Barrett, *Schism and Renewal in Africa*, An Analysis of Six Thousand Contemporary Religious Movements (Nairobi: Oxford University Press, 1968), p. 278.

24. John Dean, Scripture Union Africa Secretary, in conversation with the author, Nov., 1977.

25. David B. Barrett, in *Time* magazine, Jan. 21, 1980, p. 44.

26. A.T. de B. Wilmot in a letter to the author, Jan. 20, 1977.

2

Forming Patterns

What patterns of mission-church relations developed from this historical background? On what principles were they based? What main issues have come into focus?

Latourette called the period 1800-1914 "The Great Century of Missions." As the work of missions increased and national churches were formed, foreign missionaries and national pastors had to face searching questions concerning the development of the work and the relationship of church and mission.

What should be the form of the organization? Many missionaries went out simply to preach the gospel, but found themselves falling back on the structures which they knew in their own lands, and the national churches therefore often became a copy of those structures. Missionaries had to ask themselves, "What is a mission?" and "What is a church?" What should a foreign missionary do after a large number of ordained national colleagues had been raised up? There were different views.

Henry Venn, Secretary of the Anglican Church Missionary Society (CMS), put forward one theory in 1854: *The aim of the mission is to call into existence self-governing, self-supporting, self-propagating churches. Once this is accomplished, the mission should die out and the missionaries should go on to other unreached regions, leaving the church to function by itself.*[1]

A.R. Tucker of Uganda (1890-1908) had an opposite view: *The church is a brotherhood in which both national and foreigner should continue working together on a basis of genuine equality.*[2]

There was a third view, as we have seen, held by medieval and to some extent colonial era missionaries: *The foreign mission represented the "Mother Church" and should continue to have control over the national "daughter" church.* This view steadily decreased as national churches not only showed their ability to take responsibility, but also rightly expected to.

A fourth view stated: *The mission has a calling from God to continue its ministry as a separate organization even after the indigenous church is formed. The indigenous church is responsible for its affairs, and the mission is responsible for its own affairs. One does not dominate the other.* This view arose from the concept that the foreign mission should not dominate or "mother" the indigenous church, but also that it had a special calling from God to continue its work.

To help us review patterns of mission-church relations let us look at several examples.

1. CMS, Nigeria. Henry Venn, Secretary of the CMS, was an evangelical who approached the problem of church-mission relations from the standpoint of a major denomination, the Anglicans, of which the CMS was a missionary arm. When CMS missionaries went to another land, they automatically found themselves within an Anglican church diocese. It might have been many times the size of England but with only a handful of members, most of them expatriate government officers. Yet it had a bishop, and was a church entity.

With this background, it was logical that there should be no place for the mission society in the diocese once national churches had been formed. Those churches were immediately part of the worldwide Anglican communion. Once the church was able to support itself and its activities, he felt the mission should move out.

Venn enunciated basic principles which have been used by missions all over the world. He defined the three signs of church maturity as self-support, self-government, self-extension. (A Congregational missionary, Rufus Anderson, developed the same "three-self" formula in his own thinking, without knowing of Venn's theory.)

   Venn was well intentioned, convinced that young churches
should be dependent upon the operation of the Spirit and
not upon a mission society. However, there developed an
unfortunate division of responsibilities: the missionary
society was seen as the organization that should move on in
missionary witness, whereas the local church was given the
role of caring for administration of its parish. This
division of role was not intended by Venn, but it resulted
in the stagnation of some indigenous churches.

   Beyerhaus and Lefever state that Venn's great contribution after a long period of patriarchal and individualistic
mission work by other missionaries was to point the way to
a church-related mission, although he left unsolved the
problems of relation of the foreign missionary to the
mission outreach of the national church.[3]

   The unintended separation of role between church and
mission brought disaster in several countries. In Sierra
Leone in 1860, a "native pastorate" was established and
missionaries were completely withdrawn from participating
in the work of the pastorate. Stephen Neill, an Anglican
bishop who was totally against any colonial domination of
the church by the mission, nevertheless states that this
"inflicted on the church a paralysis from which a whole
century has not availed to deliver it."[4]

   A similar arrangement was made in Tirunelveli in South
India in 1880. In Neill's view this would "have proved
equally disastrous had not a new generation of missionaries
succeeded in putting the clock back by taking over again the
control and direction of the church which had not yet
attained the growth and maturity without which 'independence' is only a synonym for disintegration and decay."[5]

   The Anglican Mission on the Niger provides another
example of wrong *timing* in applying Venn's principles.
Samuel Ajayi Crowther, freed from a slave ship by the
British Navy, was trained at the CMS Teacher Training
College in Freetown, and in 1841 accompanied a British
government expedition to explore the Niger River. His abilities in communicating with the people were recognized, and
he was given theological training in England. He returned
to Nigeria with the CMS as its first African minister.

Venn noticed the tensions between English missionaries
and African ministers, and felt the solution was to have an
African bishop in charge. In frustration he wrote:

> Missionary operations are essentially abnormal.
> The European minister is an exotic amidst
> native congregations, and all attempts to
> regulate the relations between him and native
> clergymen have hitherto failed. The true
> remedy may be found in a native bishop.[6]

Venn personally pled with Samuel Crowther to agree to be
consecrated bishop, and he was, on June 29, 1864. The
principle was good, but unfortunately it was not based on
Venn's three-self principles. Crowther's consecration as
bishop was the plan of the CMS in London, and not of any
parish in Africa. He was sent back to be bishop of
"Western Africa beyond the limits of our dominions" without
any church which was self-supporting, self-governing, and
self-propagating.

Bishop Crowther did a magnificent work under very
adverse circumstances, having to use African Sierra
Leoneans, some of whom felt superior to the local people.
The Mission on the Niger under an African bishop was fully
dependent on foreign (Sierra Leonean and English) missionaries and overseas support. It was not truly indigenous,
and although congregations were formed, the work in general
degenerated and gave a bad name to the principle of hasty
indigenization.

The problem originally arose from the desire of Europeans in London to develop the work rapidly, but unfortunately the results were criticized on racial grounds by
younger English missionaries, and by nationals, producing
great hurt and bitterness for Crowther and his African
colleagues.[7] Bishop Crowther was succeeded not by an
African but by a series of expatriates, from his death in
1891 until 1951. Venn's attempt to overcome church-mission
tensions through appointing national leadership before
there was a viable indigenous base proved abortive, and
actually increased tensions for three-quarters of a century.

Before leaving Venn's views, we should mention Roland
Allen, whose books, *Missionary Methods: St. Paul's or Ours?*
and *The Spontaneous Expansion of the Church*[8] have been
studied by most missiologists. Also an Anglican, Allen's
views were similar to Venn's. He saw the stifling effects

of missionary domination and resulting tensions during his years of work in India, and his recommendations on the indigenous church were ahead of his day. He rightly stressed that the indwelling Christ is immediately effective in the young churches. However, Beyerhaus and Lefever warn that an extreme application of this concept can cause a mission to withdraw before the new believers are properly confronted with the Word of God.[9]

2. *Korean Presbyterian Church.* This work was started by an American Presbyterian missionary, John L. Nevius, who first visited Korea in 1890. He had published a book, *The Planting and Development of Missionary Churches,* which built on the "three-self" principles of Venn and Anderson. He developed the work with the following principles, now referred to as "The Nevius Method":

a. Missionary personal evangelism through wide itineration.

b. Self-propagation, with every believer a teacher of someone and a learner from someone else better equipped than himself.

c. Self-government, with every group under its own chosen but unpaid leaders; circuits under their own paid helpers who will later give place to pastors; circuit meetings training the people for later district, provincial, and national leadership.

d. Self-support, with all places of worship provided by the believers, each group as soon as founded beginning to pay toward the circuit helper's salary; even schools to receive only a partial subsidy, and no pastors of single congregations to be provided for by foreign funds.

e. Systematic Bible study for every believer under his group leader and circuit helper; and for every leader and helper in the Bible classes conducted by the missionaries.

f. Strict discipline, enforced by biblical sanctions.

g. Cooperation and union with other bodies, or
    at least territorial division.

h. Non-interference in private lawsuits or any
    such matters.

i. General helpfulness on the part of the mis-
    sionaries, where possible, in the economic
    problems of the people.[10]

One of the greatest emphases of the Presbyterian missionaries in Korea was adequate Bible teaching not only to
church leaders but to all members. As a result of using
the old Korean script known to most people, most Christians
were literate and able to read the Bible for themselves.
Every church developed Bible classes and many self-
supporting Bible institutes were conducted, in which
members could spend from one to two months each cold season,
taking a course over a period of five to six years. The
church thus had a whole army of Bible-taught lay members
who could assist the work.

Giving was taught as a result of Bible study, so that by
1927 every baptized member gave *15%* of his annual income to
the church, and adherents gave 5%. In seven years the
church income rose by 75%, as a result of Bible teaching in
Christian stewardship.

The question of church-mission relations was solved when
a Church-Mission Conference was formed in 1954, involving
all Korean members and missionaries. This Conference had
responsibility for the work formerly done by the mission,
although the mission continued to be the legal owner of
mission property.

The missionaries continued to have an active part in the
Korean church, all ordained missionaries being voting
members at the invitation of the Korean church. It has been
stated that "the Korean church has found a way of utilizing
its foreign missionary associates to the full without sacrificing its own autonomy." Their help is welcomed as
teachers, advisers, and initiators of new projects.

Witness has been another emphasis of the Korean Christians with the slogan, "Each Christian teaches another
person." The church has sent missionaries to China, Thailand, and Taiwan, and periodically proclaims a "Forward

Movement Year" to remind members of their missionary
calling.

Revival has also been a mark of the Korean work, with
personal confession of sin in prayer meetings and spontaneous witnessing involving visitation of every home in most
communities.

3. *The China Inland Mission.*[11] James Hudson Taylor was
an Englishman who first went to China in 1853, age only 21,
and spent seven years learning Chinese while working with
the Chinese Evangelization Society. At the end of that
time he was led to resign from that society and to depend
on God for his material needs by faith, and also to identify
himself more closely with the people -- one way being to
adopt Chinese dress. In 1865 he started the China Inland
Mission, which became one of the largest missions in
history, and which set forth principles followed by a
number of evangelical missions. Among these principles
were the following:

a. Interdenominational. The mission was conservative in
theology and would accept missionaries from any denomination if they signed the doctrinal declaration and evi-
denced spiritual life according to scriptural practice.

b. While other missions had accepted chiefly professionally trained people, the CIM was open to membership of missionaries who did not have specialist training. This gave
a greater scope for people who had missionary vision and
personal ability but were not accepted by other societies
looking for professional qualifications. Some of these
with little formal education became self-taught scholars
through their experience.

c. The authority and direction of the mission would be in
China and not in England. This principle was meant to
overcome the remote control of missionary work experienced
by other missions and resented by local Christians.

d. Missionaries would wear Chinese dress and identify
themselves with the people as much as possible.

e. Evangelism was the primary task of the mission. Church
development and education were also undertaken, but never
in such a way that the primary aim would be set aside. The
indigenous church and the mission developed side by side
until the Communist takeover in 1949, around which time

foreign missionaries had to leave. The event caused the
CIM to completely reassess its method of work and to change
its name to Overseas Missionary Fellowship.

The OMF reiterated the principles of Hudson Taylor,
opened its membership to nationals of any country, provided
they were serving in another land and were supported by
their own churches. When the OMF missionaries returned
after World War II to work in other parts of the Far
East and Pacific, they returned as servants of the church
rather than leaders of it. However, they were still
engaged in pioneering missionary work in such places as
unevangelized islands of the Philippines.

4. *The Christian and Missionary Alliance.* Louis L.
King, President of the C&MA, tells of his own personal
experience in India.[12] The mission started work at
Gujarat in 1893. At the turn of the century a devastating
famine broke out and missionaries gave aid to overcome the
great problems. They opened orphanages, churches, schools,
industrial training programs, and farms. Nearly all church
members were literate with a number of professional and
business people.

In spite of all the mission had done for the church and
its members, the church-mission relations were not harmo-
nious. In 1932 signs appeared on the walls of mission
compounds: "Missionary Go Home!" Anti-mission leaflets
prepared by Christians were distributed in the community.

That same year the church was officially organized with
a Presbyterian form of government. All missionaries were
made members of the church and were eligible for any
office.

When King arrived in India in 1947, there had been no
church growth for the past 27 years. The number of pastors
had decreased. There were no converts from non-Christian
faiths. Missionaries still held the responsibilities they
had held from the beginning, and their presence was not
appreciated. Pastors and congregations made more and more
demands for money from abroad each year. Pastors were paid
from overseas and had the attitude toward their church
members, "I get my salary paid whether I serve you or not
and whether you like me or not." So the church members
responded, "What is the use of worrying about the work?
The pastor gets paid whether we like him or not."

King studied the situation and came to the following conclusions:

a. Although he was a member of the church, he should decline any church office at any level in order to make way for Indian Christians.

b. With well-educated church members available, well-taught in the Word, he should refrain from entering into the church's problems, but depend upon the Holy Spirit to work in national Christians as He does in missionaries.

c. The church must look to its Head, Christ, for all its answers, and not to the mission or missionary.

d. The missionary's authority should be spiritual, emanating solely from preaching and teaching the Word of God in the power of the Holy Spirit.

e. The missionary must set a diligent example in witnessing and in establishing churches.

f. Although he would be acting differently from his missionary colleagues, he must not allow this to be the cause of contention among the missionaries. He needed to put his views to work in order to make them convincing.

King was later given administrative responsibilities with the C&MA work in the Pacific Islands. He put his principles to work through holding conferences with missionaries and church leaders. Through study of the Scriptures together, both mission and church came to see the need for the church to be self-supporting, self-governing, and self-propagating. Relations slowly improved, so that today there is generally good rapport between church and mission.

Except in Zaire, where the government forced all missions into fusion, C&MA and their national churches follow the principle of parallel existence, with the church fully autonomous and the mission also autonomous. They work in close harmony through joint councils, but do not dominate each other. R.P. Chavan, Moderator of the General Assembly of the C&MA of India, and a national, states, "The emerging church can better develop if it stands organizationally separate from the mission which brought it into being."[13]

5. *"The Brazil Plan."* During the late 1800s, the
U.S. Presbyterian Mission work in Brazil fully merged with
its national churches. However, both pastors and missionaries felt frustrated in this relationship -- the pastors
feeling dominated from within and the missionaries feeling
restricted in reaching out as they saw a need. After
mutual study and agreement, the mission and church separated again in 1917. The mission then evangelized in the
interior of Brazil, handing newly planted churches over to
the Brazilian church denomination. "Partnership in obedience, as they worked out in the Brazil Plan, has been a
sound principle," states William Read,[14] and growth
statistics seem to support the statement.

6. *CLAME.* The Latin America Mission is a North
America-based para-church service agency. That is, its
purpose is to provide services to help churches, and out of
these services much evangelism and some church growth have
developed. In this respect it differs from the usual
mission, which has the primary goal of planting churches,
and operates services such as medical, education, and media
as means to reaching that goal.

With its different approach, LAM did not have a strong
central church structure, but rather strong central
departments. Therefore, when turning over its work to
national leadership in 1971, LAM set up the Community of
Latin American Evangelical Ministries (CLAME in Spanish).
National churches had already been autonomous for 15 to 20
years. A General Assembly is the meeting point for at
least 13 autonomous organizations which are responsible for
such ministries as publications, the seminary, student
ministries, evangelism. The LAM now is also one of the
autonomous organizations, with its main sphere of operation
in North America.

LAM reports that tensions in some areas of work were
reduced (although Costas states that the transition
initially increased tensions, especially among missionary
personnel),[15] and emergence of new Latin-American leadership. Negative results initially included internal bitter
"politicking," and a tendency for the autonomous entities
to work independently even in the same areas, causing over-
lap and duplication. Several of the organizations did not
adequately understand the cultural needs of new missionaries whose orientation therefore suffered. The LAM itself
wondered who should "assume a new initiative in the
evangelization of a Latin America wide open to the gospel

message," without violating the autonomy of other members of CLAME. The image of LAM as a strongly evangelical mission was threatened because the seminary, as a separate autonomous member without any church control, invited professors of diverse doctrinal background to join the faculty, thus changing its theological emphasis.[16]

7. CEVAA. The Evangelical Community for Apostolic Action (CEVAA in French) has grown out of the work of the Paris Mission. Formed in 1971, the Community embraces 13 churches in Europe and 10 in Africa and the Pacific, relating to each other in a collegial way.

8. Burundi: Free Methodists. This North American denomination developed mission work in Africa, Asia, and Latin America. In Burundi, East Africa, the mission at first considered fully merging with the church, but felt that this could be as frustrating for the missionary as the former relationship (nationals serving under missionaries) had been for the Burundi church. The mission opted for a partnership concept -- the mission continuing responsibility for the recruitment and care of its personnel, and the church being responsible for the work in Africa. Agreement on policies, personnel assignment, budget, and property is handled by a joint "negotiating body" with equal representation of church and mission. The model was based on Peters' "Pattern of Mutuality and Equality" presented at Green Lake '71,[17] and was designed to avoid two potential tension points in working together: interference in church matters by missionaries, and loss of morale among missionaries in cross-cultural problems. The original constitution (1961) guaranteed missionary representation on the church administration board, but this guarantee was dropped in favor of a liaison committee to handle matters affecting care of missionaries.[18]

9. Mutuality and Equality. George Peters has developed a pattern of Mutuality and Equality, or Partnership in Obedience, as a balance between the two extremes of fusion (complete merger of the church and mission) and dichotomy (complete separation of the two). Church and mission work together through a "negotiating body," on which they have equal representation. (See appendix B.)[19]

10. Indigenous responsibility. This pattern develops from a partnership relation between church and mission. During partnership, the national church gains experience and capability, until it is able to take over responsibil-

ity for the work in its own church area. Assuming responsibility is a follow-through of the indigenous church
principle.

When the church takes responsibility, the mission no
longer directs the work, but continues working with the
church as needed. Missionaries work under the leadership
of the church but are cared for by their sending organization. A liaison officer of the mission acts as consultant to the church leadership and a link between the church
and the international structure of the mission. The church
has full jurisdiction over its work, but if mission
personnel face insurmountable problems in working through
the church, the liaison officer has responsibility to find
solutions with the church leaders. Projects needing the
international mission's participation are mutually nego-
tiated between the church leaders and liaison officer --
neither one being able to commit the other without mutual
agreement. At this level such matters as evangelization of
unreached areas can be mutually planned for.

This structure recognizes both the responsibility of the
mature church to lead the work, and the goals of the missionary mandate. The two are brought together in an
international partnership, with the church fully indigenous
in its responsibilities. Missions such as Africa Inland
Mission, Africa Evangelical Fellowship, and Sudan Interior
Mission have followed this pattern with their related
churches in Kenya, Zambia, and Nigeria respectively.
(See appendix C, "Redefining the term Indigenous.")

POSSIBLE PATTERNS

Here is a summary of several patterns which both
churches and missions have tried, in an effort to prevent
or overcome problems.

1. Don't have a church! (This actually happened in Japan
in the "non-church movement" Mukyokai.) The Japanese
leader, Kanzo Uchimura (1861-1931) stated: "The truly
Christian temple has God's earth for a floor, and His sky
for the ceiling; its altar is the heart of the believers;
its law is God's Word, and His Holy Spirit is its only
pastor."[20] He was so afraid that Christians would pay
attention only to the externals of church life instead of
the internal spiritual matters, that if a group of believers showed signs of forming an organized church he would
disband it.[21]

2. Nationalize leadership before there is a church. This seems to have happened in the early stages of the Mission on the Niger.

3. Make your mission a church or your church a mission. The Christian and Missionary Alliance and the United Missionary Church are two instances where mission-centered Christians have made their missionary organization an actual church denomination which sends out its own missionaries.

4. The mission and church exist separately, in complete dichotomy. There are still a number of examples of this type of relationship.

5. The mission and church retain separate identities, but work together in what George Peters calls "partnership of mutuality and equality."[22] The Association of Evangelical Churches of West Africa (ECWA) and SIM operated successfully in this type of relationship for many years.

6. Indigenize the leadership of the work in the country, with the national church taking responsibility, and continuing in an international partnership with the mission. SIM and a number of other interdenominational missions have entered into this further stage in relationships.

7. The national church organize its own mission. This is true of ECWA, which has its Evangelical Missionary Society.

8. The church expand spontaneously without a mission organization. Peter Wagner tells how a church in South America multiplied from a struggling group of 30 members to become seven churches with 1500 members in a period of six weeks.[23] However, in developing cross-cultural missions, a special missionary department or board would seem necessary to care for the extra work involved.

9. Fuse the mission with the church and pretend that you don't have missionaries. A number of denominational missions have done this, calling missionaries "church visitors, fraternal workers, and people sharing in mission." Further semantic games are played by changing "sending churches" to "responding churches" and "receiving churches" to "inviting churches."

10. Declare a moratorium. We have referred to this in chapter five. While there is a time for voluntary,

strategic withdrawal, the concept of an imposed moratorium
is not scriptural. The demand may come from resentment of
missionary domination, which needs to be solved by mature
mutual discussion and prayer.

These few examples, by no means exhaustive of different
patterns of church-mission relations, are given as background for further discussion on solving tensions. In each
case, as the national church developed maturity, the basic
question was how to relate the young church to the founding
mission. In some cases the solution was imposed, either by
the mission or the church, or by external circumstances.
In other cases a relationship was worked out by the church
and mission together, meeting their mutual needs and en-
suring continued effective functioning of the work. Patterns vary from "fusion" to "dichotomy," from "community"
to "parallelism."

Venn learned by experience that "principles which may
apply to one mission may often be inapplicable to a different field, as well as different stages of advancement in
the same field." He wrote to Anderson that he had learned
to follow divine guidance instead of his own set formulas.[24]

The most important thing in any relationship is not the
organizational structure but the attitude of the parties to
one another. The most ideal structure can be ineffective
if there is lack of mutual respect, trust, and cooperation.

We shall later discuss basic factors in strengthening
the maturity of the church and at the same time preserving
the mandate of the mission.

While missions have been thinking through their patterns
of relationship, some major changes have been taking place
in the theological world which affect the whole question of
mission. We shall examine these in the next chapter.

STUDY QUESTIONS: CHAPTER 2

1. What were Henry Venn's main principles for missionary
    work? What unintended dichotomy sometimes resulted?

2. List the main points of "The Nevius Method."

3. What was J. Hudson Taylor's concept of the main task
    of missions? Give his other principles and discuss how
    these gave new impetus to missionary work.

4. Discuss the advantages and disadvantages of the various patterns of mission-church relations cited.

5. What pattern fits your own organization (or one with which you are familiar)?

NOTES: CHAPTER 2

1. Stephen Neill, *History of Christian Missions*, (Baltimore: Penguin Books, 1964), pp. 259, 260.

2. *Ibid*, p. 260.

3. Beyerhaus & Lefever, *The Responsible Church and the Foreign Mission* (Grand Rapids: Eerdmans, 1964), p.30. Used by permission.

4. Stephen Neill, *op. cit.*, p. 260.

5. *Ibid*, p. 260.

6. *Ibid*, pp. 66, 67.

7. J.F.A. Ajayi, *Christian Missions in Nigeria* (London: Longmans, Green and Co., 1965), pp. 250-255.

8. Roland Allen, *Missionary Methods: St. Paul's or Ours*, and *The Spontaneous Expansion of the Church* (London: World Dominion Press, reprints 1960).

9. Beyerhaus & Lefever, *op. cit.*, pp. 26-30.

10. *Ibid*, pp. 91, 92.

11. For an up-to-date history of the China Inland Mission and its successor, the Overseas Missionary Fellowship, see Leslie Lyle, *A Passion for the Impossible* (Seven Oaks, Kent, England: OMF Books, 1976).

12. Louis L. King, "Mission-Church Relations" in *Missions in Creative Tension* (South Pasadena, CA: William Carey Library, 1971), p. 179.

13. R.P. Chavan, *The Church's Worldwide Mission*, Ed. H. Lindsell (Waco, TX: Word Books, 1966).

14. William R. Read, *New Patterns of Church Growth in Brazil* (Grand Rapids: Eerdmans, 1965).

15. Orlando Costas, *The Church and Its Mission* (Wheaton, IL: Tyndale House, 1974), p. 157.

16. W. Dayton Roberts, report in *Emerging Models of Christian Mission*, Overseas Ministries Study Center, 1976. Also verified in a personal interview with Juan Isais, CLAME Director for Mexico, Oct. 27, 1977. See also *Latin-American Evangelist* (Bogota, NJ: LAM) Nov.-Dec. issue 1974; and *Evangelical Missions Quarterly* (Wheaton: Evangelical Missions Information Service) April 1975 (entire issue).

17. Vergil Gerber, *Missions in Creative Tension: The Green Lake Compendium* (South Pasadena, CA: William Carey Library, 1971), p. 229.

18. Gerald E. Bates, *Processes of Conflict Resolution*, unpublished dissertation, Michigan State University, 1975.

19. Vergil Gerber, *Missions in Creative Tension*, p. 229.

20. Stephen Neill, *History of Christian Missions*, p. 329.

21. *Ibid*, p. 330.

22. George W. Peters, "Mission-Church Relations Overseas" in *Missions in Creative Tension* (South Pasadena, CA: William Carey Library, 1971), p. 208.

23. C. Peter Wagner, *Look Out! The Pentecostals Are Coming* (Carol Stream, IL: Creation House, 1973), pp. 53-63.

24. Beyerhaus & Lefever, *The Responsible Church and the Foreign Mission*, p. 71.

3

Dynamics Of Debate

Near the beginning of this century, in 1910, more than 1200 representatives of mission societies from all over the world met in Edinburgh, Scotland, for a World Missionary Conference. The chairman, John Raleigh Mott, had earlier coined the slogan: "The evangelization of the world in this generation."

Recently in Tanzania, a group of Third World theologians spoke critically of "the view that Christianity was superior to other religions, which had to be replaced by 'the truth.'"[1]

More recently in Ivory Coast an evangelical spokesman stated that "the command to proclaim the good news to everyone 'til all have heard' is a pressing duty."[2]

These statements reveal tensions which have grown between liberal and evangelical viewpoints over the concept of mission. A lot has happened in missionary thinking since Edinburgh. A brief study of international missionary and church councils over the past century shows how the debate developed.[3] The debate involved the uniqueness of the gospel and the need for personal salvation, and therefore the existence of a missionary emphasis and how it should relate to the church.

The first missionary councils

As missionary societies increased and national churches
developed in the 19th century, the need was felt for
sharing information, mapping of common strategy, and discussion of mutual problems. Inter-mission conferences
were held on almost all continents. William Carey proposed
an international conference in 1810, and in 1888 the German
historian of missions, Gustav Warneck, proposed an international missionary conference to be held every 10 years.
Such conferences were indeed held in Liverpool in 1860,
London in 1888, and New York in 1900.

However, it was the World Missionary Conference held in
Edinburgh, Scotland, in 1910 which became known as the First
World Missionary Conference, in that it was the most representative -- although only 18 delegates were actually
from the younger churches.

The Edinburgh conference stressed that each generation
of Christians bears responsibility for evangelizing its
contemporaries. The expansion of missionary work, publication of the Bible in many languages, and planting of
many churches even in lands traditionally hostile to the
gospel seemed to justify the hope that the Church of Jesus
Christ could indeed evangelize its world in its own generation.

The topic was Evangelism but Edinburgh's ecumenical
inclusivism revealed theological trends which would affect
the whole question of evangelism in the future. Because
of the wide range of background, it was decided not to discuss "questions of doctrine or church policy with regard
to which the churches or societies taking part differ among
themselves."[4]

Writing in 1910 and subsequent years, Rowland Bingham,
first General Director of SIM, commended the vision of
the conference but pointed out a number of inherent weaknesses and warned about dangerous trends.[5]

Edinburgh was followed by the formation of the International Missionary Council in 1921, for the purpose of
planning common strategy in communicating the gospel
around the world.

Changing world views

By the time of the second great World Missionary Conference, held at Jerusalem in 1928, the coming trends were
more evident. In 1910, most of the leaders had been
confident of the uniqueness of the gospel and Jesus Christ
as the only Savior of the world, of the necessity of reaching unevangelized people with the gospel that they might be
saved, and the obligations of the Great Commission.

In the intervening 18 years, liberal theological views
and universalism increasingly spread from German thinkers
to other countries of Europe and to North America. Liberal
theologians were not sure that Jesus Christ was the unique
Savior. They increasingly called for "sharing" between
various world religions, which were becoming more aggressive. At Jerusalem, the IMC secretary personally circulated a book, *Reality*, which questioned the deity of Jesus.
An Egyptian church leader, Marcus Daoud, complained to the
conference chairman, and the secretary had to make a public
statement dissociating the conference from the distribution
of the book.[6]

At the same time, there were political changes following
World War I and a new sense of national awareness. Third
World delegates reflected national feelings when they met
in Jerusalem in 1928. The missionary enterprises encoun-
tered the church at Jerusalem; delegates from missions and
churches were on a 50-50 basis.

From then on, the question of church-mission relations
became a topic that could not be ignored.

At the third World Missionary Conference, held at Madras,
India, in 1938, the theme had shifted entirely from
Edinburgh's "evangelization" to "the church." "According
to Tambaram, missionary activity is not simply the task of
a small number of people who have been seized by the idea;
it is the task of the church as a whole. Indeed, missionary activity may be said to be the outward sign of the
church's being, that sign through which it is recognized as
being genuinely a church . . . . Mission means also church;
and a church means also mission."[7]

This identification of missionary work as the responsibility of the church was commendable. There was a
definite attempt to bring delegates back to "biblical
realism -- back to fundamentals, to such a radically

religious conception of life as is revealed to us in the
Bible."[8]

The conference convenors did not intend any joining of
forces with non-Christian religions to bring about a better
world. However, there had been new theological trends
afoot even at the earlier Jerusalem Conference. The
National Christian Council of Japan had submitted a proposal that the spiritual world of the great religions of the
East might well take the place of the Old Testament. The
question was asked, "Is not Christ the fulfillment of
Indian religion, the Crown of Hinduism?"[9] At Tambaram,
universalist theology was redefining the church and its
missionary task in different terms from that understood at
Edinburgh.

Religio-historical relativism was beginning to find
expression. The Tambaram delegates did not take for
granted the right of Christian missionaries to evangelize
in the non-Christian world. "The problems of the origin,
the nature, the order, the commission of the church had become the central point of theological discussion, just
about the same time as that at which the epoch of theological reflection began in the missionary world."[10]

The emphasis of Madras (Tambaram) was more for an in-
tense desire for the unity of the churches rather than for
evangelism. Madras reflected the theological ambivalence
of the older churches of the West, and the lack of theological instruction of the younger churches of the developing
world -- a lack which the younger churches pointed out,
commissioning the IMC to develop theological training in
the younger churches.[11]

The next International Missionary Council meeting was
held at Whitby, Ontario, Canada, in July 1947, following
World War II. Its emphasis was evangelism under the slogan
"Partnership in Obedience," showing the awareness of the
need for churches and missions to work together. However,
it also proposed that a missionary should not go to another
land unless invited by the national church.[12]

The next year, 1948, the World Council of Churches held
its first Assembly in Amsterdam, and the ecumenical church
movement, as we now know it, was officially launched. Following the WCC's Assembly, the IMC was assigned the task
of studying the missionary obligation of the church at a
conference in Willingen in 1952.

The theological debate

In preparation for Willingen a Dutch scholar in the
Theology of Mission, J.C. Hoekendijk, prepared a paper on
"The Church and Missionary Thinking."[13]   Among other things
Hoekendijk stated:

> In history a keen ecclesiological interest has,
> almost without exception, been a sign of spir-
> itual decadence; ecclesiology has been a sub-
> ject of major concern only in the second gen-
> eration; in the first generation, in periods of
> revival, reformation, or missionary advance,
> our interest was absorbed by Christology,
> thought-patterns were determined by eschatology,
> life became a doxology; and the Church was
> spoken of in an unaccented and to some extent
> rather naive way, as being something that
> "thank God a child of seven knows what it is"
> (Luther).

Hoekendijk stated that the church-centered orientation
of missionary work leads to a narrowing of its scope: "Its
whole horizon [is] completely filled by the church. The
missionary now hardly leaves the ecclesiastical sphere....
He tries to define his whole surrounding world in ecclesiological categories....The world has almost ceased to be
the world and is now conceived of as a sort of ecclesiastical training ground. The kingdom is either confined within
the bounds of the church or else it has become something
like an eschatological lightning on the far horizon.

"Church-centric missionary thinking is bound to go
astray, because it revolves around an illegitimate center."
He pointed out that Christ himself and not the church is
the true center of gravity for missionary thinking.

In discussing these concepts, the Willingen conference
recognized that "the missionary enterprise cannot and
should not go back to its former situation of existing
independently alongside the church; for the sake of mission
and church alike, that road is barred to it, but it must
always be on guard to insure that this closer fellowship
with the church does not involve a narrowing of its
horizon, or a bringing into captivity of its ideas or of
its activities. To put it in other words; the missionary
enterprise can regard itself as an activity of the church,
only on condition that the nature of the church itself is

defined in terms of the missionary enterprise."[14]

In reporting on Willingen, W. Andersen commented: "A
new formulation of the basis of the missionary enterprise
must take its start not from the doctrine of the church
but from the doctrine of the person of Christ....To accept
the cross as the only possible starting point for a
theology of missions is to escape the danger of seeking a
speculative basis without theology.... Thus from the cross
are derived both the possibility of missionary witness and
its necessity . . . 'and this gospel of the kingdom will be
preached throughout the whole world as a testimony to all
nations; and then the end will come' (Matt. 24:14)."[15]

Andersen, a German Lutheran, points out that the conflict of theological viewpoint between the church and the
mission arises from doctrinal emphasis. The Anglicans
stress the ontological character of the church, its nature
as the body of Christ being an extension of the incarnation
of Jesus Christ. Andersen points out the weakness in this:

> The incarnation is regarded as a saving event
> par excellence; an event which is of course
> confirmed by the cross, but over against which
> the cross contributes nothing new and abso-
> lutely distinctive.

> The cross and resurrection give impetus to the
> missionary mandate. Only after the resurrec-
> tion of Jesus Christ and the sending of the
> Holy Spirit does God himself give the sign for
> the beginning of the world mission of the
> church. . . . The source of the missionary
> enterprise is God and His triune nature.

> It is the responsibility of the missionary
> enterprise to say to the church in love, but
> also in terms that admit no doubt of their
> meaning. "We live in a misunderstanding of
> the situation that is fraught with deadly
> danger, if we do not realize ourselves to be
> that company of men among whom Jesus Christ
> is active according to His word and work, if
> we do not believe and recognize ourselves to
> be instruments of the active word of Jesus
> Christ, and act accordingly. A church with-
> out missionary activity can indeed for a
> period retain its form as a stiff and life-

less corpse, but the process of putrefaction
will in time inevitably set in."[16]

Another theological factor giving rise to church-mission
tensions was pointed out by Norman Goodall in his evaluation of the Willingen Conference -- the relations between
missions and eschatology. If the kingdom of God has
already come, "the purpose of the missionary enterprise is
not the winning of the world for Christ; on the contrary,
since all power in heaven and earth has already been given
to Him, He sends messengers forth to make His already
existing kingdom known to all the world. If this point of
view is accepted, no place is left for futurist eschatology."

Goodall continued: "For the other group it is this
futurist element that has the deepest significance....
Church and kingdom of God must be clearly distinguished
from one another. The church is the pilgrim people of God,
always striving forward toward the coming kingdom.... In
the cross the reconciliation of the world has indeed been
perfectly accomplished; but the full redemption of the
creation is yet awaited; the question of domination is not
yet solved.

"The missionary enterprise is an eschatological entity
.... It is the sign both of the kingdom that has come and
of the kingdom that is yet to come."[17]

Willingen was not able to state a definite Theology of
Mission, but stressed the importance of theological study
of the problem. The report concludes:

> The experience of the church in its pilgrim-
> age has once and again, and most conspicu-
> ously in recent times, been strikingly the
> same; that a theology which allowed its
> problems to be posed and its tasks to be
> imprisoned within the dominant intellectual
> tendencies or views of the world and of
> existence, failed to speak a decisive word
> to contemporaries or to provide them with
> the help that they need. Conversely, that
> theology which was engaged in a dialogue with
> the revealed Word of God, and recognized that
> it was called to bear witness to the "effec-
> tive Word," was enabled to speak a word of

power directly to the intellectual situation of the time.18

Willingen took place after the effects of World War II
had begun to sink in to Christians' thinking. The wind of
independence was blowing around the globe. Mission and
church leaders were rightly becoming concerned about the
expatriate leadership in Third World countries. Some went
further and questioned the continued existence of separate
mission organizations because of the "foreignness" being
imposed on the churches by some of them.19

Stifling mission

In 1957 the International Missionary Council met in
Accra, Ghana, where a proposal was put forward to merge IMC
with the WCC. Great opposition was expressed by several
members, who withdrew from the IMC when it was officially
integrated with the WCC in 1961 at New Delhi. While again
it would seem commendable if the church were acknowledging
its responsibility for missionary work through this integration, the merger in fact smothered the healthy self-
criticism and theological study which marked the Willingen
Conference.

At the Fourth Assembly of the World Council of Churches
held in Uppsala, Sweden (1968), Anglican John Stott publicly decried the increasing lack of the churches' missionary
concern for the unevangelized: "The World Council con-
fesses that Jesus is Lord. The Lord sends His church to
preach the good news and make disciples. I do not see this
Assembly weeping similar tears."20

Since 1961 the ecumenical movement has been church-
centric. Delegates to the WCC's Conference on "Salvation
Today" held at Bangkok in January 1973 were representatives
of churches, not missions. Since it was supposed to be an
ecumenical missionary gathering, the Bangkok conference
neatly redefined the term "salvation" itself, and therefore
changed the significance of mission.

Peter Beyerhaus describes the results: "Here, under a
seemingly biblical cover, the concept of salvation has been
so broadened and deprived of its Christian distinctiveness
that any liberating experience can be called 'salvation.'
Accordingly, any participation in liberating efforts would
be called 'mission.'"21 Even apostasy was cited as a
relevant form of "Salvation Today."22

Byang Kato states: "The birth pangs of the illegitimate baby of the World Council of Churches, salvation without the inherent authoritative Bible, finally arrived at Bangkok!"[23] It was logical that several delegates at Bangkok called for all missionary work to cease -- a moratorium of foreign missions.

At an African consultation on religious liberty set up by the WCC after their Central Committee meeting in Enugu, Nigeria, in 1965, a Nigerian church leader, A. Adegbola, redefined evangelism: "So, evangelism, as the task of the church, is not to be interpreted in the narrow sense of 'saving souls,' but in the wider and more practical sense of serving the world which God so loved that He gave His only begotten Son to serve."[24]

The call for moratorium which went forth at Bangkok was again taken up at the meeting of the All Africa Conference of Churches in Lusaka, Zambia, in 1974. John Gatu, Presbyterian minister and President of the Central Committee of the AACC, called for the complete withdrawal of all mission personnel and resources for at least 5 years. (We shall examine "moratorium" in chapter 5.)

The logical sequence of de-emphasizing missionary work and redefining evangelism and salvation was carried further at the WCC Assembly in Nairobi in 1975. Kato reported, "I attended a session on 'spirituality' and found people searching for union with nature and other aspects of the universe. Not a single reference was made to the Scriptures while I was in this group." One participant told Kato that he wondered if he were in a meeting of the United Nations or of church people. "Over 300 million people in Africa are without Christ. The Assembly left Africa with the impression that concern for the salvation of these people was not a priority."[25]

Vermaat quotes an Asian contributor to the Nairobi Assembly as forecasting that dialogue will give rise to a completely new theology which will not emphasize the uniqueness of the teachings of any one religion. At a WCC consultation in Sri Lanka (1967), a session was led by a Buddhist monk, an Anglican priest, and a Hindu swami.

Vermaat points out the effect that Asian thinking has had on the WCC's concept of dialogue in place of proclamation. "Eastern religions are strongly inclusivistically orientated and certainly do not reject the Christian

religion. Instead they try to absorb the Christian
teaching into their own broad religious system. Missions
to these countries have always found a completely different
atmosphere and response in contrast to countries where for
example the aggressive and intolerant Islam was in control.
The result is that in the East there is a much stronger
tendency towards relativism and a vagueness of definition
with regard to Christian affirmations. Asiatic missionaries and theologians have therefore always been inclined
toward adaptation. The idea of Dialogue and Common Worship
has its origin here."[26]

In Africa, liberal theologians have linked the stereo-
typed image of the colonial-era missionary with the evangelical emphasis on the uniqueness of the gospel -- an
emphasis at variance with their own universalism and
syncretism.

"The theology of the Christian churches at this time
[colonial period] not only suited the colonization process
but was also fed by it," stated the Ecumenical Dialogue of
Third World Theologians, Dar es Salaam, 1976. "The sense
of military and commercial superiority of the European
peoples was underpinned with the view that Christianity was
superior to other religions, which had to be replaced by
'the truth.'"[27]

The statement endorsed the theology of liberation and
declared that commitment should be "the first act of
theology." It called for "Christianity to enter into a
dialogue" with traditional religions and cultures, in the
belief that "the Holy Spirit is actively at work among
them."

A follow-up Pan-African Conference of Third World
Theologians at Achimota, Ghana, (1977) was less vitriolic,
but endorsed the view that African theology must be
liberation theology and contextual theology. "The beliefs
and practices of the traditional religions of Africa can
enrich Christian theology and spirituality."[28]

"When we talk about African theology, we should mean
the interpretation of the pre-Christian and pre-Muslim
African people's experience of their God," states Agbeti.[29]

Redefinitions

With familiar words being given new definitions, it is
not always easy to know what is really being said. The
Latin-American liberation theologian, Gustavo Gutiérrez,
for instance, sounds like an evangelical missionary when he
says that the church is a means not an end, a visible sign
that points to what salvation is all about. . .that she has
no meaning in herself except in the measure in which she is
able "to signify the reality in function for which (she)
exists."[30]

However, one has to understand what liberation theologians mean by salvation, evangelism, and the gospel. Their
writings make it clear they refer to a politico-societal
"salvation" essentially, not a personal spiritual regeneration in the biblical sense held by evangelicals. "Salvation" is any liberating action that enables man to create
a new world. Gutiérrez has stated that man "is saved if
he opens himself to God and to others, even if he is not
clearly aware that he is doing so. This is valid for
Christians and non-Christians alike."[31]

Some liberal theologians have gone to the extreme of
defining all religious belief as ideological and historical. The Christian message is seen as the result of a
cultural perspective in history; it is relativistic, not
absolute truth. Therefore, according to this viewpoint,
the Christian missionary cannot go out to declare a
universal message based on faith in absolute truth. He
must go forth not with an apologetic for the truth, but
rather *apologetically* for a relativistic, culturally based
message. He can no longer declare, "Thus saith the Lord,"
but only testify to an insight which he has gained from his
particular cultural viewpoint.

To state the Scripture truths emphatically is now
labeled "biblistic." Scripture itself is being relegated
to the cultural wastebasket by liberal theologians. Even
some evangelicals, eager not to be left behind in modern
trends, on the one hand aver that "Scripture is without
error in all that it affirms," but also add that inspiration applies only to passages which are "spiritual," not
those which are "cultural."

This futile theological exercise affects the mission of
the church. The result is to leave the church and her
messengers with a cultural viewpoint rather than a divine

revelation. According to this liberal view, it would be
"aggression" to declare the gospel to men of other religions, because they also are struggling toward the truth
from their cultural viewpoints. So liberal missionaries
can no longer be sure of their message nor that they should
take it to anyone else![32]

Summary of liberal trends

Although it began with a concern for personal, spiritual salvation for people worldwide, in half a century the
Ecumenical Movement completely reversed its position. Here
is a summary of the stages:

1. The Ecumenical Movement shifted from biblical theology
to a universalist theology, causing it to lose its
conviction that the gospel is unique, and that Jesus
Christ needs to be presented to all mankind as the only way
of salvation.

2. After the founding of the World Council of Churches,
the Ecumenical Movement became strongly church-centered, so
that the right of existence of missionary organizations
separate from church organizations was questioned.

3. The International Missionary Council was merged with
the World Council of Churches on the basis of missions
being the task of the church -- a commendable principle,
but in practice a move which would from then on enable
church-centric leaders to dominate the missionary movement
of the church.

4. Having officially absorbed the missionary movement of
their members, the WCC first considered evangelism to be
proselytization, and discouraged it because some member
bodies (such as the Greek Orthodox Church) were opposed to
evangelism being done in their lands by any other group.

5. The WCC went on to redefine such basic terms as
mission, evangelism, conversion, and salvation, making them
meaningless from a scriptural, spiritual standpoint.

Gerber aptly describes the result of current liberal
theological views on church and mission -- "an institution-
less church minus a church-less Christianity minus a
Christianity-less gospel minus a gospel-less social
involvement. It is a reductionism of the gospel to the
destruction of its very foundations."[33]

The missiological implications of these major theological trends were obvious to evangelicals. They readily responded to the debate.

Evangelicals speak up

Following the Nairobi Assembly of the WCC in 1975, B.J. Nicholls of Yeotmal, India, analyzed the basic crises which the WCC is facing, and which have affected its views on the church's mission:

1. "The WCC faces a crisis in the nature of its authority. Of the three alternatives -- experience, tradition, and Scripture -- Nairobi opted for the first."

2. "The real crisis of faith is in the WCC's changing attitude toward Scripture.... The rejection of the unity of Scripture in favor of a plurality of gospels within the Bible prepared the way for a new hermeneutic that replaces the historical and grammatical hermeneutic of the Reformers."

3. "The WCC is facing a crisis of dogmatics. By focusing on what we might label Pantheism, in which God is in everything and everything is in God -- an interlocking relationship between the Personal and the all -- a new dogmatic theology is emerging which offers a basis for consensus theology, inter-faith dialogue, and a plurality of cultural gospels."[34]

In a commentary on preliminary materials sent out by the WCC before the Commission on World Mission and Evangelism in Bangkok, Donald A. McGavran, Dean Emeritus of the School of World Mission and Institute of Church Growth, Fuller Theological Seminary, noted these redefinitions:[35]

a. "Mission" ceases to be the propagation of the gospel *and becomes* everything God wants done by Christians or non-Christians -- which necessarily limits what God wants done to the field of ethics.

b. "Evangelism" ceases to be proclaiming Jesus Christ by word and deed and persuading men to become His disciples and responsible members of His church, and *becomes* changing the structures of society in the direction of justice, righteousness, and peace.

c. "Conversion" ceases to be turning from idols to serve the God and Father of our Lord Jesus Christ, as revealed in the Bible, and *becomes* turning corporately from faulty social configurations to those which liberate men and incorporate them in the great brotherhood.

d. "Salvation" is apparently going to be put through the same rolling mill and brought out flattened and focused on temporal improvements.

Kato's comment was that "the liberal definition of salvation today has been confused. Instead of taking it from the book of Romans, the ecumenicals have taken it from the book of Exodus."[36] In making this pithy contrast, Kato was not intending to imply that the theme of salvation does not run throughout Scripture.

Because of this theological shift, and the danger of a scriptural fulfillment of the Great Commission being thwarted by liberal power blocs, evangelicals met in 1966 to consider their own position in the light of Scripture and to declare their stand. The Berlin Congress on Evangelism defined evangelism and the Great Commission in scriptural terms. The same year 1000 delegates attending the Congress on the Church's Worldwide Mission held in Wheaton, Illinois, declared their intention "to bring the biblical mission of the church back into focus."

The Declaration rejected the ecumenical view of mission, including syncretism and universalism. It decried too much foreign missionary control in church growth, but also stated "that the proper relationship between churches and missions can only be realized in a cooperative partnership in order to fulfill the mission of the church to evangelize the world in this generation; and that the mission society exists to evangelize, to multiply churches, and to strengthen the existing churches. Therefore we recognize continuing distinction between the church established on the field and the missionary agency."[37]

An evangelical theological viewpoint was given by a group of German theologians and scholars meeting in Frankfurt, March 1970. This was called the "Frankfurt Declaration on the Fundamental Crisis in Christian Mission." The scholarly Declaration refuted point by point the liberal redefinitions of the missionary task made by the ecumenical movement in New Delhi (1961), Mexico City (1963), and Uppsala (1968). (See appendix D.)

When Beyerhaus, one of the signatories of the Frankfurt Declaration, sought to bring the Declaration to the attention of the delegates at Bangkok (1973), he was told that it was an issue which should be discussed in Germany -- that he should not bring "Western concepts" into the Conference.[38] Yet the ecumenical leadership overlooked the fact that it was essentially liberal theology from Germany which had helped to bring about the universalist attitudes at Bangkok. They tried to silence a biblical viewpoint by an ethnic insinuation.

It was not thought incongruous when another *German* delegate criticized the report of a *Thai* pastor (who told about people being saved from sin through gospel preaching in his country) as being "a slap in the face" to the Conference idea of dialogue![39]

It is ironical to note that at Uppsala in 1968 the WCC had adopted the following recommendation:

> The member churches of the World Council, which have already experienced something of the correction and edification which is made possible by our common membership in the Council, need also the contribution of the evangelical churches.... In view of the fact that there is in the membership of several member churches a considerable body of those who would accept the name "conservative-evangelical" whose theological convictions, spiritual experience, and missionary zeal might well find more vital expression in the life of the World Council of Churches, this Assembly hopes that these. . .will seek ways by which this witness may be more adequately represented in the life of the Council."[40]

After this and other open invitations to evangelicals to play a more active part in the WCC, at Bangkok the WCC seemed intent on shutting them up when they did speak!

A major evangelical conference on missions took place in Green Lake, Wisconsin, in October 1971, under the title "Missions in Creative Tension." The two opposing forms of church-mission relations were studied: fusion and dichotomy. The consensus of Green Lake was that a modified version of each -- meeting half way -- was the most practical, resulting in joint action and "mutuality."[41]

The International Congress on World Evangelization in
Lausanne, Switzerland, in 1974 emphasized missionary work
throughout the world. More nations (a total of 150) were
represented than in the UN's membership at the time.
Nearly half of the 2430 official participants were nationals from "Third World" nations. The purpose of the
Lausanne Congress was to face the task to be done on earth
-- to evangelize 2.7 billion of the world's population.
The theme was "Let the Whole Earth Hear His Voice."[42]

A paper by Ralph D. Winter, "The Highest Priority:
Cross-Cultural Evangelism," demonstrated that 87% of the
world's population will not be reached without cross-
cultural "missionary" evangelism. It was reported that
Third World churches now have 200 mission boards of their
own sending out 3400 missionaries to other lands or cultures.

Through practical sharing of experiences and study of
the Scriptures, delegates were encouraged to believe that
Christ's Commission could be fulfilled in their generation,
through the power of the Holy Spirit and obedience of the
church.

At the close of the Congress, delegates endorsed "The
Lausanne Covenant" which had been worked on by a cross-
section of evangelicals from around the world. Concerning
church-mission relations, the Covenant declared:

> In the church's mission of sacrificial service,
> evangelism is primary. World evangelization
> requires a whole church to take the whole gos-
> pel to the whole world; the church is at the
> very center of God's cosmic purpose and is His
> appointed means of spreading the gospel. The
> church is a community of God's people rather
> than an institution, and must not be identi-
> fied with any particular culture, social or
> political system, or human ideology.... We
> rejoice that a new missionary era has dawned.
> The dominant role of Western missions is fast
> disappearing. God is raising up from the
> younger churches a great new resource for
> world evangelization.... Thus a growing part-
> nership of churches will develop and the

universal character of Christ's church will
be more clearly exhibited.

The rising evangelical leadership in Africa, Latin
America, and Asia is increasingly entering the theological
debate -- which so affects the whole concept of their own
missionary outreach. The young churches accepted the Bible
as God's Word, but as liberal theologians have made their
syncretistic and universalistic pronouncements, evangelicals have had to give "a reason of the hope" that is in
them.[43]

From examining liberal theology, evangelicals have
observed that much of it is the reasoning of unregenerate
minds -- men who have approached theology from man's view
rather than God's. While recognizing that theological
expression in Africa, Asia, and South America must divest
itself of European or Western contextualization, Third
World evangelicals desire most of all *biblical* theology,
applied to meet the needs of their context.

"We believe we should both de-Westernize, and where we
have been guilty of syncretistic tendencies, de-indigenize
our theological teaching in the light of biblical, historical, and cultural research," declared members of the Second
Asia Evangelical Consultation, Singapore, 1971.[44]

After discussing liberation theology and dynamic-
equivalence theology, African theologian Tokunboh Adeyemo
writes: "Contrary to aforementioned brands, this writer
proposes biblical theology in an African setting.... It
presupposes the infallibility and authenticity of the Word
of God, which is its primary source."[45]

"African Christianity cannot be the translation of
Western Christianity into African thought-forms, nor will
it be the Christianizing of traditional beliefs and
practices," states Kwame Bediako of Ghana.[46]

"No matter how much we develop our traditional African
religions, they fall far too short of the truth," states
Nathaniel Olutimayin, Principal of the ECWA Theological
Seminary, Igbaja, Nigeria.[47]

"There is a basic offensiveness to the human heart about
Christianity," stated Kola Ejiwunmi, Nigerian Fellowship of
Evangelical Students. "To say with Peter that 'salvation
is found in no one else; for there is no other name under

heaven given to men by which we must be saved,' is to articulate this offense. Yet if we are to remain truly Christian, we would have to state this humbly, graciously, patiently, and also clearly, firmly and unashamedly. This is not denying the God-consciousness in all other cultures and religions.... as in Acts 17:27-28 and Romans 1:19-23."[48]

Kato told undergraduates at the University of Nairobi: "It is not black theology we need, but the application of Christian theology to the black situation. It is not a black Jesus or black God, but obedience to the omnipotent God of the Bible.... In our effort to express Christianity in the context of the African, the Bible must remain the absolute source. It is God's Word addressing Africans and everyone else within their cultural background."[49]

Addressing the Third General Assembly of the Association of Evangelicals of Africa and Madagascar, Bouake, Ivory Coast (1977), S.O. Odunaike, AEAM President, declared: "You do not require a doctorate in theology to know that a professor has lost his bearing when he starts to question the lostness of man or the necessity for missions."

Odunaike listed among AEAM's theological distinctives the following:

> The authority of the Holy Scriptures, their inerrancy, supremacy, and finality in all matters pertaining to faith and practice.

> The uniqueness of the Lord Jesus Christ as Redeemer, Savior, Lord.

> The necessity of repentance, the new birth, and personal salvation.

> The command to proclaim the good news to everyone 'til all have heard is a pressing duty. All forms of syncretism, universalism, and neo-universalism are anathema.

"The AEAM was established in response to the heartbeat of millions of evangelicals in Africa who hold to these truths," Odunaike stated.[50]

It is not within the scope of this book to discuss theological issues in depth. However, this summary will serve to give the theological background for our further study of tensions which affect church and mission.[51]

STUDY QUESTIONS: CHAPTER 3

1. What was the emphasis of the first missionary councils?

2. What theological trends began to affect thinking about missionary evangelization? Discuss how the effect began to show itself.

3. How did theological trends increase the gap between church and mission as institutions? What tensions arose between churches and missions because of theological concepts? How would you define a church-centric position?

4. What steps led to the virtual stifling of missions in the World Council of Churches?

5. What reply do evangelicals give to the liberal interpretations of mission and salvation? What further answers would you give to liberal arguments?

NOTES: CHAPTER 3

1. Ecumenical Dialogue of Third World Theologians, Dar es Salaam, Tanzania, Aug. 5-12, 1976.

2. AEAM General Assembly, Bouake, Ivory Coast, July 28, 1977.

3. For a complete study, see Arthur Johnston's *The Battle for World Evangelism* (Wheaton, IL: Tyndale House, 1978).

4. William Richie Hogg, *Ecumenical Foundations* (New York: Harper and Brothers, 1952), p. 109.

5. Rowland Bingham, *The Missionary Witness* (Toronto: R.V. Bingham, Publisher) May 3, 1910, p.66; Aug. 1910, p. 127 and subsequent writings.

6. Told to the author by Rev. Marcus Daoud of the Coptic
    Church, in Heliopolis, Egypt, June 4, 1979. Daoud is
    an evangelical scholar who has been helping revise
    the Arabic New Testament.

7. Hartenstein, *Das Wunder der Kirche*, p. 194.

8. Kraemer, *The Christian Message in a Non-Christian
    World* (New York: International Missionary Council,
    1938), p. 31.

9. W. Andersen, *Towards a Theology of Missions* (London:
    SCM Press, 1955), p. 25.

10. *Ibid*, p. 29.

11. Tambaram Series, Vol. IV, pp. 211-212.

12. Beyerhaus & Lefever, *The Responsible Church & The
    Foreign Mission*, p. 173.

13. J.C. Hoekendijk, *The International Review of Missions*,
    July, 1952, pp. 324-336.

14. W. Andersen, *Towards a Theology of Missions* (London:
    SCM Press, 1955), p. 38.

15. *Ibid*, pp. 41-43.

16. *Ibid*, pp. 49-55.

17. *Ibid*, p. 56.

18. *Ibid*, p. 61.

19. Willingen Report, *The Missionary Obligation of the
    Church*, pp. 14, 19.

20. Norman Goodall, *The Uppsala Report 1968* (Geneva:
    WCC, 1968), p. 26.

21. Beyerhaus, *Theology of Salvation*, p. 17.

22. Ralph D. Winter, (Ed.), *The Evangelical Response to
    Bangkok* (South Pasadena: William Carey Library,
    1973), p. 112.

23. Byang H. Kato, *Theological Pitfalls in Africa* (Kisumu, Kenya: Evangel Publishing House, 1975), p. 146.

24. A Consultation Digest, WCC, 1965, p. 19.

25. Kato, *Theological News*, AEAM January, 1976, p. 1.

26. J.A.E. Vermaat, "The W.C.C.'s Programme of Dialogue," in *Beginning op Berrijding in de Oecumene* (Hilversum, Holland: Evangelisher Omroed, 1975).

27. Ecumenical Dialogue of Third World Theologians, Dar es Salaam, Tanzania, August 5-12, 1976, from a typescript statement.

28. Pan-African Conference of Third World Theologians, Achimota, Ghana, Dec. 17-23, typescript news communique.

29. J.K. Agbeti, *Presence*, Vol. V, No. 3, 1972, p. 6.

30. Orlando E. Costas, *The Church and Its Mission*, pp. 237-238.

31. Gustavo Gutiérrez, *Theology of Liberation* (Maryknoll, New York: Orbis Books, 1972), p. 151.

32. For more on this view, see Dehainart, "Cultural Relativism," *Occasional Bulletin*, Missionary Research Library, New York, July-August 1976. This includes reference to Karl Mainheim's "Sociology of Knowledge."

33. Vergil Gerber, "Report on the Consultation on Latin America," Elburn, IL. in *Latin America Pulse* (Wheaton, IL: EMIS, Oct. 1970).

34. Lausanne Committee on World Evangelization Bulletin 1976.

35. Ralph D. Winter, *The Evangelical Response to Bangkok*, p. 31.

36. *U.E. Action*, Summer, 1975. p. 18.

37. Harold Lindsell, *The Church's Worldwide Mission* (Waco, Texas: Word Books, 1966), p. 230.

38. Winter, *The Evangelical Response To Bangkok*, p. 79.

39. *Ibid*, p. 64.

40. Orlando Costas, *The Church and Its Mission*,
    pp. 187, 188.

41. Vergil Gerber, (Ed.),*Missions in Creative Tension*
    (South Pasadena: William Carey Library, 1971).

42. *Let the Earth Hear His Voice*, World Wide Publications,
    Minneapolis, 1975.

43. I Peter 3:15.

44. Second Asia Evangelical Theological Consultation,
    Singapore, June 8-12, 1971 -- an "Open Letter"
    issued by the Consultation.

45. Tokunboh Adeyemo, *Perception* (Nairobi: AEAM,
    Jan. 1978), p. 4.

46. Kwame Bediako, quoted in Africa Christian Press
    Newsletter, Accra, Ghana, Nov. 1977).

47. Nathaniel Olutimayin, mimeographed report on PACLA,
    Jan. 15, 1977.

48. Kola Ejiwunmi, "Syncretism" in *Facing the New
    Challenges*, PACLA papers (Kisumu, Kenya: Evangel
    Publishing House, 1978), p. 219.

49. Byang H. Kato, "Black Theology and African Theology,"
    a lecture delivered at the University of Nairobi,
    published in *Perception,* AEAM, October 1976.

50. S.O. Odunaike, Keynote address to AEAM General
    Assembly, Bouake, Ivory Coast, July 28, 1977.

51. David Barrett, Nairobi, Kenya, relates theological
    liberalism to declining evangelism on the part of the
    West, but notes a different response in other lands.
    Barrett says that the percentage of Christians in the
    world steadily rose from 18% in 1800 to 23% in 1850 to
    28% in 1900. But in the 20th century this rate of
    increase fell off sharply. "In fact, soon after
    Edinburgh itself, the momentum slowed down, the sense
    of a world mission faltered, and Western interest in

world evangelization fell sharply off. . . . The goal
of world evangelization long espoused by the Western
churches has receded from their grasp. As a result,
some Western theologians have attempted to come to
terms with this defeat by developing a theology of
secularization in which evangelism and conversion
assume a lesser role than hitherto. Whilst this
theology may be valid for the West in the waning
decades of the fourth recession in Christian history,
a different theology more related to evangelization is
emerging in lands where the fifth pulsation is
gathering momentum." David Barrett, "AD 2000: 350
Million Christians in Africa" IRM lix (1970) pp. 51-52.

Part Two

Dynamics Of Relations

4

Where Is The Center?

"The national assistants represent the limbs, but the missionary must be the living heart which drives warm blood
through all the limbs."   --Indonesia, c. 1865[1]

"Churches have become 'societies' with vested interest,
content to communicate within a restricted milieu."
                                           --West Africa, c. 1956[2]

The above quotations are not only widely separated in time
and space, but also in the situations they reflect. In the
last chapter we saw the developing struggle between two
main views; today we are faced with problems because of the
tension between those same two diverse views.

They arise from a distorted theological question: Which
is central in God's cosmic plan for this age -- "the
church" or "the mission"?

As we shall see later, the question should never arise.
But because of a polarization of church and mission in the
thinking of many, the question is there. For some people,
"the church" has come to mean the visible institution of
the Christian community *in contrast* to "the mission" as a
society for witness and outreach. There has been a separation of the priestly function (thought of as "the
church") from the prophetic function (thought of as "the
mission"). God can use both a church denomination and a
mission society, but the polarization of the two, the
complete dichotomy of the two, the rivalry of a church

versus a mission -- these raise a seeming tension: which
is central to God's plan for this age?

    Since the purpose of this volume is to examine the
dynamics of church-mission relations, at this stage we
shall simply recognize that the dichotomy exists and shall
examine why it exists, because we believe this is basic to
understanding the resultant tensions.

    Although in the last analysis the tensions are felt
between a local church denomination and a mission society,
in people's minds there are also tensions between the
abstract concepts of "church" and "mission." Let's look at
them.

CHURCH-CENTRIC

    A church-centric position sees everything from the view-
point of a church denomination. Some people may feel they
are scripturally justified in this. Jesus gave emphasis to
the building of His church, in response to Peter's statement of faith (Matt. 16:18). It is a divinely ordered
body of which the Head is Christ himself (Eph. 1:22,23),
who loved it and gave himself for it (Eph. 5:25). The
church is typified as the bride waiting to be united with
her bridegroom, Christ himself (Rev. 21:9). The missionary Paul called himself a servant of the church
(Col. 1:24-29).

    Although these Scriptures refer primarily to the uni-
versal church, that body is supposed to be represented by
the local church, which is also recognized in Scripture as
having specific roles and responsibilities. In this view,
mission is an adjunct or activity of the church.

Values of a church-centric view

    There certainly is great value in a church-centered out-
look in carrying out the work of the gospel in this age:

1. It recognizes the visible body of Christ, and does not
seek to by-pass the local church in missionary work.

2. It builds up the body by directing the use of spiritual
gifts into it (Eph. 4).

3. It relates the results of missionary work to an organized body which can then assume responsibility for discipling.

4. It makes missionaries and converts responsible to the visible institution (the local church) which represents Christ's body on earth.

5. It does not dichotomize evangelism and pastoral care.

6. It can reduce foreign-national tensions by emphasizing the authority role of the church, and keeping mission activity from being in competition with it.

Dangers of a church-centric view

There are also inherent dangers in a one-sided church-centered viewpoint:

1. The local church can become an end in itself, so that there is pride in its existence rather than a vision of the role which it has to play. In referring to the church, Scripture emphasizes the Head (Colossians). Where Scripture discusses the body (Ephesians), it stresses the body's function and its relation to the Head -- not its self-importance (Eph. 4:15-16). Nowhere does Scripture teach ecclesiastical narcissism.

2. The church may become monopolistic as an institution. It may feel threatened by any so-called para-church agency, forgetting that these agencies are part of the overall church. A strongly church-centric group of Baptists in America in the early 19th century opposed mission societies and Sunday schools because -- among other reasons -- "(a) No authority can be found in the New Testament for missionary societies or Sunday schools. Such societies are man-made and contrary to Scripture: (b) missionary associations usurp the authority of Christ over His church. He alone can call men to preach, and He alone can assign fields of labor."[3]

What those church leaders overlooked was the fact that the Bible is also silent about church denominations, yet God has been pleased to use them as He has Sunday schools and mission societies.

3. A church-centric position is usually accompanied by a
strong church union attitude, which can overshadow evangelism. All Christians should be concerned about sectarianism and unnecessary divisions. Some see disunity as an
obstacle to witness. However, if the goal of organizational
union is put ahead of witness, it may be self-defeating.
Union may demand compromise that hinders witness. Lack of
church union can be used as an excuse for not witnessing.

John Mbiti rightly urges the church in Africa to the
task of missions. "Any Christianity which does not carry
out its missionary task is like a big clock which has no
hands.... True mission-mindedness is one where the church
is making an aggressive expansion.... From the very beginning of its history the church was mission-oriented, and if
any branch of the church loses that orientation it also
risks the extinction of its own life."[4]

However, after this challenging start, Mbiti attributes
ineffective witness to the lack of church unity. "Division
retards growth.... Church divisions are against the proper
execution of mission in our continent, and until we wipe
them out or greatly reduce them we shall be fighting a
losing battle.... Church division is a relic of imported
Christendom and this import is costing us a high rate of
customs duty.... Ecumenism is the central force in mission,
for until we reach Christian unity our plans and execution
of mission will be half-hearted...."[5]

Unscriptural division is to be deplored. However,
evangelicals have overcome the problem of multiplicity not
by church union, but by forming nonconciliar fellowships,
or associations, which give them a common voice and
strengthen one another's hands. These are not organizational unions, which tend to produce compromise, but are
loose associations allowing for diversity in unity, based
on the cardinal doctrines of Scripture. Outstanding
examples of these are the Evangelical Fellowship of India,
and the Association of Evangelicals of Africa and
Madagascar. Both are strongly mission-minded. In Nigeria
and several other countries, the New Life for All evangelism program has shown how believers in a cross section of
like-minded churches can be mobilized in effective, united
witness, without any thought of organizational union.

Historically, church union has never increased missionary work, but rather has been accompanied by a decrease.
The World Council of Churches (with a strong church-centric

view), represents only 6% of the world's missionary task force.[6] Certainly declarations made by WCC assemblies and committees have shown increasing preoccupation with preserving the status quo of member bodies rather than concern for meeting spiritual need through aggressive evangelism.

"One wonders," writes Orlando Costas of Latin America, "whether the WCC has not been guilty at times of quenching the energies of sodalities and thus concentrating so much on preserving the unity of its member churches (which in some cases simply means keeping happy the ecclesiastical 'hierarchy') than in fulfilling the Great Commission."[7]

It is noteworthy that Neill, discussing the effect of denominational differences on mission work, concedes that "less harm was caused by Christian divisions than might have been expected. Hinduism and Islam are both religions of innumerable -- and sometimes mutually excommunicating -- sects. They did not expect of Christianity a unity which they did not possess themselves. To the simple tribesman in New Guinea it did not seem out of the way that the Dutch tribesman should do things rather differently from the German tribesman."[8]

While mainline Christianity spends much energy trying to achieve organizational unity because "division retards growth," the 6000 or more schismatic churches in Africa outstrip the major denominations in booming expansion, regardless of their divisions. Also, the nonschismatic churches with the fastest growth rate and most missionary activity are the conservative evangelical groups which are not part of the ecumenical movement and are not pressing for church union. The central force of missions for them is not ecumenism but a personal witness of Jesus Christ as Savior and Lord. They believe that undue emphasis on organized union is a distortion of scriptural oneness, and can reduce effective witness through compromise. At the same time, they work together in the unity of the Spirit with those who are "all one in Christ Jesus."

4. Missionary outreach can be stifled by the church's internal self-interest. In a survey commissioned by the Anglicans and Methodists in West Africa, J. Spencer Trimingham reported that Islam was spreading more rapidly than Christianity because the older churches had settled down to care for their own parishes without reaching out to the unevangelized around them.

Today the orthodox churches are largely concerned with their internal life, with the
priestly and not the prophetic and missionary
aspects of the Christian message. Consequently
they are displaying symptoms of arrest, in
danger of becoming static bodies, irrelevant at
any vital level to the society in which they
are placed. Few of the leaders realize that
they have more to do than organize themselves,
but must express their Christian attitude in
all spheres of their national and social
life.[9]

Winter expressed the issue succinctly: "If the future
of the world is not more important than the future of the
church, then the church has no future."[10]

Self-interest may keep the church from endorsing the
sense of call of a member to go out as a missionary. The
church may not want to lose a gifted member who can help
the local work. Or it may not want to see funds diverted
to the missionary's support. Or it simply might have no
interest or vision.

Elliott Kendall[11] feels that the church's endorsement of
a missionary's sense of call should always be obtained.
This is ideal, but not always practical. William Carey
would never have gone to India if he had waited for his
Baptist church's endorsement (chapter 1). The SIM founders
in vain asked their churches for endorsement. Church-
centric self-interest stifles missionary concern.

5. A church-centered view can be essentially a holistic
view, which has its advantages and its disadvantages. If
the church is God's central purpose, and if in order to
fulfill God's purpose it should be organizationally one,
then there is no need for separate mission organizations
within or outside it. This can give rise to the concept
that "all is mission" -- with the danger that "nothing is
mission" because it is no one's special concern. A holistic view would be in keeping with oriental thought
patterns.

6. A logical conclusion in an extreme church-centric
outlook is to give evangelism the nasty name of proselytizing and to call for a ban on it. If all churches are
one, then they have no need of evangelistic efforts from
one another -- that would be "fishing in someone else's

pond." If "all is mission" then there is no need for specific evangelism. "Presence" replaces "proclamation." Also, if you are not feeding your own sheep, you don't want someone else to feed them -- the sheep might leave you. If church union is a paramount desire, evangelism by one church among members of another church becomes a great embarrassment: this readily leads to a call for moratorium on missionary work.

7. If the church is central, the feeling may arise that there can be no place for continuing mission representation. The presence of a mission may be seen as an obstacle between the "national church" and the "foreign church" in its response to the church's requests; all communication must be direct between church and church. Such a situation may reveal lack of maturity, openness, and mutual trust. It also shows misunderstanding of the true role of a mission agency.

The demand of some national churches for the complete disappearance of the mission, to the point of the church having direct contact with the home denomination instead of its mission board, may have arisen partly from the fact that many missions did not have on-the-spot authority to act. They were controlled from a "Mission Board" to which they had to refer all recommendations, and in fact a lot of management decisions. This was reflected in a paper by S.C. Leung, Chairman of the Kwangtung Divisional Council of the Church of Christ in China, published in 1925 and presented at the World Missionary Conference in Jerusalem in 1928 (italics mine -- WHF):-

> It seems to me that the time has now come when missions and missionaries might well consider the question of reorganizing themselves on a different basis, so that the missions and the Chinese church will hereafter not appear as two parallel organizations, and that all activity initiated, maintained, and financed by the mission should be expressed only through the Chinese church. This means a recognition of the Chinese church as a chief center of responsibility, the transfer of the responsibility now attached to the mission to the Chinese church, the willingness of missions to function only through the Chinese church, and the willingness of the individual missionaries to function as officers of the church,

and no longer as mere representatives of the
mission boards, *who are entirely beyond the
control of the Chinese church....* That such
things as determination of policies of work;
allocation of Chinese workers as well as missionaries to various fields; the appropriation
of funds from Chinese sources, as well as from
mission boards; *the official presentation of
appeals to the mission board for help;* and the
holding of property in trust, be placed under
the complete control of the Chinese church
through the highest church council. I think
that they (the missionaries) ought to be treated equally as the Chinese workers. They
could be elected to the highest office or the
highest church council, just as any Chinese
worker might be elected without distinction.[12]

If the mission leadership in a country does not have
authority of its own, but has to refer back to the unseen
and remote mission board, the churches may see the local
mission organization as an obstacle in their communication
with the all-powerful overseas mission board or denomination. As recently as 1976, legal documents transferring
property from a certain mission to a church in Nigeria had
to be sent overseas for signatures.

Hudson Taylor (China Inland Mission) sought to avoid
remote control feeling by placing the center of authority
in China, not England. OMF (successor of CIM) now has its
headquarters in Singapore.

In the case of SIM, the Director and Council in each
country have had full power to act within the country on
behalf of the mission, within overall policies laid down
by the General Council and controlled by the General
Director. In such mission structure, the relationship between church and mission has been somewhat different, and
the churches do not see local mission representation as an
obstacle to communication; they feel it can aid communication.

8. Undue emphasis on the central position of the church
may be associated with the concept of salvation through
the church. Gunter Linnenbrink writes of "the church-
centered mission who do not see the need of personal conversion, and who restrict the kingdom of God to the
church."[13]

The Pietist movement, referred to in chapter 1, was in part a reaction to the church-centric attitudes of their day. Pietists reacted against the sterile theological debates of the church which produced no practical change of behavior -- no piety of life. They opposed wholesale "conversion" by declaration of a priest, missionary, or government emissary, which brought communities into the church but left people far from the kingdom of God.

The Pietists worked for the spiritual renewal of the church, which resulted in "a church within a church" -- a movement of spiritually regenerated people within the body of nominal Christianity. Their concern about the spiritual state of others led to the formation of mission societies. Today some may fault the Pietists for their individualism, but we can understand this as a reaction to the lifeless church-centricism of their day.

9. Diaconal activity can easily dominate the church-centered group, because service needs in this world are so great. The goal of evangelism tends to be pushed aside increasingly, unless it is kept constantly in focus.

10. The responsibility for individual witness can be lost in the emphasis on the primacy of the corporate church. For their own good, individuals should work in concert with the church -- the community of the King; the community can give backing to them. However, if the individual's responsibility before God to witness is forgotten, the person can cast his personal burden of evangelism on the corporate church and feel absolved of responsibility. Also, if the church feels it should control individual witness, and if its own light grows dim, there is no continuing individual witness.

An interesting characteristic of mission societies belonging to churches with liberal trends is that their missionaries usually have comprised the more evangelical elements, because these were concerned for the salvation of unevangelized people. When these missionary societies have phased out, the younger national churches have developed closer ties with the "parent" church denomination, and have therefore been more influenced by its liberal theology. This partly explains the transition taking place in Africa, where work which has been evangelical in its beginnings is now in danger of being taken over by liberal theology.

11. Some denominational missions are more inclined to a church-centric viewpoint than interdenominational missions. This is because the denominational missions already represent distinct denominations, and usually go to another culture or land with the express purpose of planting their own church in that land. The term "missionary" can tend to take on merely a cultural definition (being simply a Christian worker of a particular denomination serving in a different culture), rather than a theological definition of a "sent one." While rightly relating a missionary to being responsible to a church, if care is not taken, it can rob him of a biblical sense of mission or task in fulfilling the Great Commission. However, there are denominational missions which have remained true to the scriptural imperatives of the Great Commission. They are not church-centric in the sense of giving primacy to the church as an institution at the cost of their missionary vision.

MISSION-CENTRIC

Those who are mission centered see everything from the viewpoint of a mission organization and its activities. Certainly Christ commanded His disciples (Matt. 28:19,20): "Go ye therefore and teach all nations"; He also prophesied (Matt. 24:14): "This gospel of the kingdom shall be preached in all the world for a witness unto all nations, and then shall the end come." The latter Scripture would seem to imply cross-cultural missions as the only way the prophecy could be carried out, since it was given to Jews who would need to pass it on to people of other cultures. Mission organizations can therefore help fulfill this prophecy.

A.T. Pierson declared that Christ's Commission given to His disciples in Acts 1:8 ("Ye shall be witnesses unto me . . . unto the uttermost part of the earth") is "the *whole* task of the *whole* church for the *whole* age."

Certain of Paul's writing could be used to emphasize a mission rather than a church viewpoint: "Christ sent me not to baptize, but to preach the gospel" (I Cor. 1:17). "God was in Christ, reconciling the world unto himself, not imputing their trespasses unto them; and hath committed unto us the word of reconciliation. Now then we are ambassadors for Christ, as though God did beseech you by us: we pray you in Christ's stead, be ye reconciled to God" (II Cor. 5:19,20). We have already cited references to Paul's telling his converts to evangelize those who had not heard the gospel.

In this view, the ministry of mission is central in God's purpose, with believers being gathered into local assemblies or churches, as a result, to form the glorified bride of the Lamb. The local church is an adjunct of the mission.

Values of a mission-centric view

The following values arise from a mission-centric viewpoint:

1. The emphasis is on obedience to Christ's Commission.

2. A Christian has a high sense of calling and motivation.

3. The Christian witness is not diverted from his main goal by what he would consider to be the institutionalized church.

4. This view concentrates on seed planting, with the church watering or developing it. A Congregational missionary to China, A.H. Jowett Murray, stated this viewpoint in 1919: "Our task as missionaries is not to establish an institution, but to teach a way of life -- not merely individual life, but corporate life in Christ. Such a church has no material basis. What is sown is a living seed. We believe it will grow because we believe in the gift of the indwelling Spirit. The outward form and organization will be the outcome of inward spiritual need, and is not introduced merely because there is such and such an ecclesiastical system in the West...."[14]

5. This viewpoint develops evangelism into missions: church planting resulting from evangelism. John H. Bavinck makes an interesting distinction between *evangelization*, which can be among those who have become spiritually cold, although they may be "churched" (the "no more" spiritually alive) and *missions* among those who have not received the gospel (the "not yet").[15]

6. Where a church is inactive in fulfilling the Great Commission, a mission society can take action. This may not be the ideal pattern, but it has proved to be necessary through history, as pointed out by Ralph D. Winter in his intriguing article, "Churches Need Missions Because

Modalities Need Sodalities."[16] Winter questions the
analogy "that the church is the central and basic structure,
whereas the mission is somehow secondary or perhaps merely
temporary aid in establishing churches, [and that] the
scaffolding must come down when the building is done."

Winter forcefully demonstrates from history that
"modalities [in which he would include churches] are
characteristically impotent apart from careful maintenance
of consensus," and that it has taken special groups or
fellowships or societies ("sodalities") to undertake
specific tasks such as cross-cultural evangelism. Winter
strongly urges that the younger churches develop mission
"sodalities," or special societies for carrying out missionary tasks.

We have already referred to Trimingham's report on *The
Christian Church and Islam in West Africa*. Although
written basically from an Anglican church-centric background, Trimingham was so appalled by the lack of missionary outreach among the established churches that he
recommended: "The work of missions is not done until the
whole people have made their decision; and therefore the
separateness of the mission and its message within the
church should continue."[17]

The Revelation of Jesus Christ to John (chapters 1-3)
gives a striking illustration of the fact that though most
of the churches of Asia had failed in their witness, the
Holy Spirit was not silenced, but himself warned them of
their state and its consequences.

7. A mission-centric viewpoint makes the question of
church union for the purpose of witness irrelevant, because
believers, regardless of denomination, can mobilize their
efforts to evangelize on a common doctrinal basis of
fundamentals of salvation. The Federation of Mission
Societies in India is one example. We have already cited
New Life for All.[18] Such evangelism avoids the danger of
being organizationally tied in (church union) with churches
which are not committed to the preaching of the gospel of
salvation through faith in Jesus Christ.

8. This viewpoint sets an example for the national church
to be missionary minded.

9. A mission-centric view encourages Christians to set up their own church organization, distinct from the mission. Although this can produce misunderstanding, it encourages the church to be self-reliant, not dependent on the mission for its basic functions and administration. In the early stages of church growth, this can be a healthy form of dichotomy, in that it can prevent missionary domination of the church's autonomy. (It also has its dangers, as seen below.)

Dangers of a mission-centric view

There are also dangers in this viewpoint:

1. A harmful romanticism may accompany a mission-centric view. A missionary is simply a Christian taking the message of salvation to others across cultural or sub-cultural boundaries. No special merit is won by witnessing in a foreign land. Any missionary going to another land should demonstrate his sense of responsibility and his spiritual gifts by witnessing through his own church in his own land first. Otherwise his foreign pilgrimage could be an attempt to escape the mundane in favor of what is supposed to be exotic and exciting.

2. The mission-centric viewpoint may attract the more individualistic person. "Many missionaries presumably become members of an interdenominational mission because they prefer the freedom of working outside rigid denominational structures," stated one young missionary.[19]

Individuality is valuable in pioneering and some other aspects of missionary work, but it causes problems if it results in extremes such as careerism, search for adventure, maverick projects, and empire building. Pride and arrogance may follow. Many a rugged individualist, while accomplishing great results himself, has not realized the example of a leader which he was setting before the emerging church leadership. "The medium is the message."

"When missionaries were here, they were everything," Christians in one church district told their denomination's leader. "They left and a national pastor took over; now he is everything."

The same syndrome can be found in some para-church organizations. The leader of one confessed to the "arrogance toward the church" shown by his own and other bodies, at a recent consultation.[20]

3. The mission-centric emphasis on evangelism is commendable, in the face of so much current neglect of man's basic spiritual need. However, unless this is followed up with in-depth teaching -- discipling -- the work can quickly die out. An illustration is seen among the Golas of Liberia, where 72 people were baptized after initial evangelism. Ten years later only five were continuing in the faith because of lack of discipling.[21] In Chad there were phenomenal results from evangelism in the early 1970s but the churches did not have the capacity to instruct the new converts before an idolatrous "authenticity" campaign swept many away.

C. René Padilla says that church growth statistics can be deceptive, and that we need to ask what is growing -- "baptized heathenism"?

Perhaps the most urgent need in relation to rapid church growth is for a new stress on Christian discipleship as placing the totality of life under the Lordship of Jesus Christ.[22]

Samuel Escobar, another Latin-American leader, sees the same problem:

> The danger of evangelicalism is that it will present a saving work of Christ without the consequent ethical demand, that it will present a Savior who delivers from the bondage of spiritual slavery but not a model of the life that the Christian should live in the world. A spirituality without discipleship in the daily social, economic, and political aspects of life is religiosity and not Christianity.[23]

James Engel calls the problem "Great Commissionitis."

> This is when evangelism is defined as the sum and substance of both individual and corporate Christian life. Evangelism, of course, is central, but it does not lie at the core of spirituality. The unfortunate outcome is that other phases of church life centering on the

maturity and vitality of the believer become
downgraded and secondary to outreach. The
inevitable result is a starved laity who, in
the final analysis, are unable to witness to
a good news that they are not experiencing...
the health of the church must be taken
seriously or the cause of world evangelization is futile.[24]

In a debate between good friends, Peter
Wagner and the author [Engel] have taken
strongly opposed positions on this issue.
Wagner argues, quoting Donald McGavran, that
it is a grave missiological error to confuse
the issues of evangelism and discipleship and
treat them together in a strategy of outreach.
The author, on the other hand, contends that
it is a grave missiological error *not* to do
so, for the reasons already cited. Not only
does it do offense to Scripture, but it causes
an imbalance in church outreach.[25]

Part of our problem in evangelistic superficiality may
arise from a difference between a Caucasian "bounded set"
outlook and a non-Caucasian "centered set" outlook. In
Western church growth thinking, once a person has made his
decision, he is within the "bounds" of the church -- he can
be counted as a statistic. In much of the rest of the
world, a decision may not mean stepping across a line so
much as changing direction toward a different "center."
Much instruction may be needed before the "center set"
convert has really come into a saving experience of
regeneration.[26] Therefore statistics of Third World
conversions reported by Western missions may be misleading.

A secular historian, Geoffrey Moorhouse, notes this
factor:

K.A. Busia, a distinguished sociologist as
well as politician, has recently remarked of
his own people that "it is commonplace to
describe Christianity in Ashanti and the Gold
Coast generally as a thin veneer. The description is not inaccurate or superficial if
it means that the people have not taken over
the concept of the universe and of the nature
of man in which Christianity finds its fullest
meaning. "[27]

4. A theological shallowness may accompany a mission-
centric view, unless purposely safeguarded against.
Orlando Costas warns: "The crisis of contemporary evangelization is not methodological but theological. Lacking
sound theological foundation, the methods can't help but
produce shallow results. When the base is weak, the
results are also weak, whether or not the best methods have
been used in the process."[28]

Byang Kato clearly pinpointed this weakness in a paper
on theological education in Africa, given at the General
Assembly of the Association of Evangelicals of Africa and
Madagascar (AEAM) in Limuru in 1973. He pointed out that
the development of evangelical churches has suffered and is
now endangered because many missionaries did not have
sufficient theological training and did not realize the
importance of such (apart from rudimentary Bible knowledge)
for national pastors.

5. A mission-centric view may also be a supra-church view,
through overemphasizing the mystical nature of the church
and by-passing the local church. National pastors and
members can't understand why such missionaries seem to
prefer to work outside of and separate from the local
church.

"I know missionaries who don't want to join the local
church," says Aaron Gamedze of Swaziland. "They keep at
arm's length. Our members don't like this -- they interpret
it as a form of apartheid. It can cause additional problems -- such as when an independent missionary supports a
pastor. The pastor then does not feel responsible to the
local church. If the missionary joined the church, his
support money would be seen as part of the church, and the
problem would be overcome."[29]

Norvald Yri sees a tension over mandate which may partly
explain a supra-church outlook.

> The distinctions of the evangelicals are the
> essentiality of personal conversion and the
> "new birth," the call to holiness of life,
> and the mandate for evangelism and world mis-
> sion. And because evangelicals have invariably
> encountered an entrenched Protestant clerical
> hostility in carrying out this mandate, they
> have tended to devote their energies to para-

church and cooperative activities beyond the
reach of the Protestant clergy.[30]

6. Because of a strong belief in the centrality of the
mission concept, missionaries may continue to dominate the
work. At first they had to lead, because there were no
instructed believers. But if they continue long in this
position, telling the young churches what to do or doing it
for them, the churches will remain weak. The missionaries
will paternalistically look upon the churches as "our
churches." Guang calls this the "forever" instead of "mean-
time" attitude to mission work.[31] The para-church "arm"
dominates the church "body."[32]

Some Chadians saw this as a factor in the way many
churches in Chad crumbled under the "authenticity" persecution. Previously, certain missionaries had kept such
direct control of church affairs that pastors and members
had not developed personal convictions, but had followed
what the missionary told them to do. When the missionary's
authority was removed by the government's "authenticity"
campaign, many Christians did what the government told them
to do, and sacrificed to the spirits. They had not learned
the inner authority of the Word of God.[33]

When missionaries were expelled from Southern Sudan in
1964, I asked them what they wished they had done to prepare
for leaving. "Looking back," some said, "we wish we had
turned over responsibility to the believers much sooner, so
they could have learned by experience."

Some missionaries feel that the church should concentrate
on the "spiritual" work and not get involved in operational
functions which the mission has been caring for. This may
result from a concern over the opposite extreme -- in which
churches have lost sight of the spiritual by becoming
totally immersed in the operational. However, saving the
church from this by continued missionary leadership does
not help the church realize the true weight of responsibility, nor does it force the church to utilize the gifts and
ministries ("administration, helps") within it.

A mission may not understand the national church's desire
to take on leadership responsibilities in all spheres of the
work. Instead of recognizing this as a sign of maturity, a
mission may see it as a threat to keep the mission from
fulfilling God's central purpose for it.

7. A mission-centric viewpoint can dichotomize the church
and mission, dividing them into two distinct organizations
which operate unilaterally. "Like oil and water, they can
never mix," wrote one mission executive.

How separately or how closely they work, depends upon
their functional relationship structure. Extreme dichotomy
causes duplication of work, robs the church of the
opportunity of learning responsibility or even how to
conduct the ministries operated by the mission. Since
church and mission operate in two separate worlds, deep
misunderstanding and suspicion of each other arise. This
can only lead to bitterness and in some cases to call for
moratorium or the complete expulsion of the mission.
Dichotomy fits the Western mind set, which tends to
categorize and compartmentalize life. The non-Western
holistic mind set finds it difficult to accept.

A certain amount of dichotomy in the early stages of
church growth can help the church avoid depending on the
mission for its basic functions. However, the relation
needs to change in later stages before dichotomy produces
overlapping redundancy. If carried to its logical conclusion, there could be complete duplication of departments in
both mission and church. Not only is this wasteful in manpower and finance, but great tension can arise between, for
example, the church medical department and the mission
medical department, where there may be differences of
conditions of service and procedures. What happens when
staff members transfer from one to the other?

The tendency to dichotomize can also show up between the
missionary and his home base -- he or his mission agency
can tend to operate entirely unilaterally from the sending
churches. This produces an unhealthy lack of sense of
responsibility between missionary and sending church.

8. A strange result of an extreme mission-centric view is
a reaction against the church which is the offspring of the
mission. Rather than entering into the life of the local
church to work for spiritual growth, some missionaries
stand outside and criticize. They seem almost to resent
their spiritual offspring. If they showed this attitude to
their physical children, they would have enormous family
problems.

The leader of one Third World church expressed his concern over what he felt was a sarcastic attitude on the part of some missionaries toward African Christians. He also noted that whereas "the pioneer missionaries lived and worked among their African brothers and sisters who were primitive," today's missionaries do not seem to fellowship as closely -- although African standard of living is much higher than in the pioneer days. "Instead, they choose to apply for membership in other denominations."[34]

A member of another mission reflected his attitude to the church when he accused the church of seeking "concessions" from the mission, and said, "Accomodation has almost become a virtue." To him the church-mission relations were more in the form of a management-versus-labor struggle, rather than a mission and church together planning what would ensure the effective development of God's work.[35]

The missionary Paul was highly concerned about church problems, such as among the Corinthians. However, he did not despise or disown them for their carnality and immaturity. Rather, he was moved with concern as a father for his children.

Because of his belief in the Spirit's working, Paul was able to have confidence and proper pride in them (II Cor. 7:4), and to forecast their mutual "glorying" in each other (II Cor. 1:14). He was careful not to dominate their faith (II Cor. 1:24), but was ready to sacrifice himself for them (II Cor. 7:3). With this bond of *love* established, he could also fulfill the fatherly role of *chastening* them for their carnality and *instructing* them in righteousness.

9. Parallel to this syndrome is an amazing tendency not to utilize the potential of the national church for missionary outreach. This results in the anomaly of a mission-centric agency ending up with a church without a missionary vision.

Winter expresses surprise that Protestant missions have merely planted churches and have not stimulated national churches to set up mission agencies of their own.[36]

Part of the reason is lack of teaching. Western missionaries at a Chinese missions conference admitted: "We failed to incorporate in our witness, in our teaching, and in our church planting, the unchanging biblical mandate of world missions."[37]

A missionary told a group in Scotland that he normally filed away his missionary messages at the end of furlough, but from now on was going to preach them in his missionary work in Java.[38]

Another reason is related to the dichotomous concept of the church and mission already described. If the missionary thinks of the local church as an institutionalized parish, then he will feel that working with the church amounts to "church development" -- helping the church become a bigger institution in the community. This gives rise to such misleading statements as "95% of the missionary force is in church development."

If the missionary sees the church as Christ's body reaching out in witness, the missionary will consider his time well spent in working with it. "Church development" then means helping the church to develop a greater capability to be a striking force for missions. That means developing a sound base administratively, economically, and theologically. The missionary who shuns this as non-missionary work forgets that he and his colleagues would not be able to be missionaries if their sending churches had not developed just such a base. If the goals are kept in sight at all times, working with the church and its own mission agency may end up in a much greater missionary impact than the missionary could have made by himself in a lifetime.

"One measure of the ethnocentrism of American evangelicals is the uncritical assumption that the evangelization of the world in this or any generation rests primarily on American, or at least Western, shoulders," writes Warren Webster.[39]

A report on Latin American church growth showed that "there is not necessarily correlation between the number of missionaries and church growth.... There may be no more important contribution that missions can make to church growth than the discovery, training, and stimulation of national leadership....

"Wherever the church has been considered irrelevant to the purposes of Christian mission, little or no growth has been experienced."[40]

10. Interdenominational missions, more than denominational missions, are inclined to a mission-centered viewpoint which by-passes the church and tends to work separately. This is because:

(a) they do not represent a denomination in the first place;

(b) their missionaries may have come out of spiritually cold churches which have not had a mission vision; therefore the missionaries seek an interdenominational agency which is formed specially for the purpose of missionary work;

(c) the missionaries may be reacting against a church-centric sectarianism which they have seen in their own lands and wish to avoid;

(d) the members of an interdenominational mission may have received their call through a para-church organization such as Inter-Varsity, Campus Crusade, Scripture Union (all of which are doing a commendable work).

THE REAL ISSUE

The liberal-evangelical controversy over the Ecumenical Movement cannot be divorced from our study of church-mission tensions. It is a major tension itself, raising the basic question of the right to evangelize cross-culturally as well as what such evangelism really means. Unfortunately the real issues in the controversy are lost to view, because the theological liberals tend to be more church-centric, and the theological conservatives (evangelicals) tend to be mission-centric. So on the surface the issue appears to be between holistic and dichotomous viewpoints on church-mission relations -- or, by association, between fraternal and colonial attitudes. Actually the issue is far deeper; it is a theological one.

The problem is made even more complex by the popular view of the history of missions. Missionaries who were not theologically liberal carried with them the gospel of a unique Savior. This was the Bible message that there is no other name given under heaven whereby men can be saved. During the medieval and colonial eras, these missionaries came from a social context which considered itself culturally superior -- even if all missionaries did not consider themselves superior. The scriptural uniqueness of the gospel and the supposed Western superiority were

unfortunately linked together in some people's minds,
although in fact there was no inter-relation -- the unique
gospel does not accept any race or culture as superior, but
places all men equal before God. The apostle Peter had to
learn this lesson early in his missionary work (Acts 10:15,
34, 35).

However, the biblical concept of the uniqueness of the
gospel of Christ as the only way of salvation has become
identified with Western imperialism, so there is a tendency
to reject both together: (1) by liberals who don't accept
the need of personal redemption through Christ, and (2) by
the Third World citizen who has rejected Western imperialism.

Ian M. Hay, General Director of SIM, points up the
tendency for a pendulum swing in church-mission attitudes,
and pleads for balance. Citing the indigenous principles
of Roland Allen,[41] Hay points out:

> There is danger of overemphasis which results
> in misjudgment and misunderstanding between
> missionaries and local churches. Misunder-
> standing the full meaning of indigenous church
> principles has caused missionaries and missions
> to establish such a separation between mission
> and church that isolation results and scriptur-
> al fellowship is lacking ... a gulf arises
> between missionaries and the church, and
> ultimately between the mission organization and
> the church.... The pendulum swings too far.
> Instead of domination there is isolation.
> Instead of over influencing the church, there
> is fear of speaking out at all.

> The result is that missionaries feel they have
> no part in the church, and then they become
> critical of obvious weaknesses within the
> church. In turn the church is critical of
> the missionaries for their lack of understand-
> ing and concern. The result is division,
> heartache, disillusion. Neither Roland Allen
> nor St. Paul wanted this to happen. Allen says
> the churches "were no longer dependent upon the
> Apostle, but they were not independent of him."[42]

The above describes a dichotomous relationship. Referring to the opposite extreme, fusion, Hay continues:

> *Christianity Today* in an editorial [43]
> "Whither Ecumenical Mission?" clearly
> emphasized two distinct dangers in the
> attitudes of the liberal fringe regarding
> missions. They are:
>
> 1. The danger of dominating the church through
> influential personnel and the practical power
> that money represents....
>
> 2. The other danger is that of spoiling or
> pampering the church, fostering within it a
> suppliant attitude, a disposition to lean upon
> help from abroad instead of growing through
> struggle into self-reliance and maturity.[44]

SUMMARY

I hope that this examination of the two viewpoints --
church- and mission-centric -- has not seemed like an
exercise in semantics, nor that I have defeated the purpose
by seeming to generalize.

I recognize that there are worthy motives and convictions
underlying these two views, and both views have their value.
As with most positions in life, however, there can be a fine
line between help and harm, asset and liability. A good
beginning can be distorted into a bad result. Whatever our
orbit, we can develop a "superstar syndrome" in our work.

The main purpose of this study is to help us understand
why there are tensions between perfectly good people over
these views, and where the views may lead if not scripturally reconciled in Christ himself. (We shall discuss this
further in chapter 6.)

These basic attitudes (church-centric or mission-
centric) affect the whole makeup of a mission. People of
either viewpoint will be attracted to that mission which
gives scope for their views. Today the younger churches
may ask, "Why bother us with these discussions now?" However, their own future attitude to the question of church
and mission will be affected by these same basic principles.
In fact, their own missionary outreach will develop around
one or the other attitude.

Actually, there should be no polarization into church-centric or mission-centric extremes. Missionary outreach and church edification should be kept in proper tension and balance at all times -- each feeding into as well as resulting from the other. They are inseparable in a healthy Christian community. (See appendix W for a diagram by Ian M. Hay: Attitude Grid -- Church/Mission Centricity.)

In the next chapter we shall look at ways of maintaining this balance.

STUDY QUESTIONS: CHAPTER 4

1. Define a church-centric position. Discuss its values and dangers.

2. Define a mission-centric position. Discuss its values and its dangers.

3. How do you see a dichotomy between these two extremes will affect the relation of a mission and church? What is the basic solution?

4. What dichotomy do you observe in your own personal attitudes, as well as in your organization (church or mission)?

NOTES: CHAPTER 4

1. Beyerhaus and Lefever, *The Responsible Church and the Foreign Mission* (Grand Rapids: Eerdmans, 1964), p. 78. (Quoting one missionary's view at the time).

2. J. Spencer Trimingham, *The Christian Church and Islam in West Africa* (London: SCM Press, 1956), p. 38. (Results of a survey).

3. Lars P. Qualben, *A History of the Christian Church* (New York: Thomas Nelson, 1942), p. 558.

4. John Mbiti, *The Crisis of Missions in Africa* (Kampala: Uganda Church Press, 1971).

5. *Ibid*, pp. 4, 5.

6. *Ibid*, pp. 4, 5.

7. Orlando Costas, *The Church and Its Mission* (Wheaton, IL: Tyndale House, 1974), p. 173.

8. Stephen Neill, *History of Christian Missions*, p. 460.

9. J. Spencer Trimingham, *The Christian Church and Islam in West Africa*, IMC Research Pamphlet No. 3. (London: SCM Press, 1956), p. 34.

10. Ralph Winter, unpublished comment given at Evangelical Futures Conference, Dec. 10-14, 1978.

11. Elliott Kendall, *The End of an Era* (London: SPCK, 1978), p. 11.

12. Jerusalem Meeting Report, Vol. III, 1928, pp. 12, 13.

13. Arthur Johnston, *The Battle for World Evangelism* (Wheaton, IL: Tyndale House, 1978), p. 311.

14. A.H. Jowett Murray, "The Upbuilding of the Church," *The Chinese Recorder*, March 1919, pp. 153-154.

15. J.H. Bavinck, *An Introduction to the Science of Missions* (Translated by David H. Freeman) (Grand Rapids: Baker Book House, 1960), p. 76.

16. *Evangelical Missions Quarterly*, Summer 1971, p. 193.

17. J. Spencer Trimingham, *op. cit.*

18. Eileen Lageer, *New Life for All* (London: Oliphants, 1969).

19. Jon Didrickson, "The Case for Mission Autonomy," an unpublished paper, SIM, Lagos, 1968.

20. As reported to the author by another participant, Ted Ward, March 24, 1979.

21. Lee Unruh, SIM, Monrovia, Liberia, report September 25, 1978. This case study is documented in the SIM film, "Assignment: Gola!", SIM, Scarborough, Ontario, Canada, 1979.

22. C. René Padilla, "The Fullness of Mission," *Occasional Bulletin*, Jan. 1979.

23. Samuel Escobar, "Evangelism and Man's Search for Freedom, Justice and Fulfillment," in *Let the Earth Hear His Voice*, Ed. J. Douglas (Minneapolis: World Wide Publications, 1975), p. 310.

24. James F. Engel, *Contemporary Christian Communication* (New York: Thomas Nelson, 1979), p. 27.

25. *Ibid.*

26. For a discussion of bounded sets and centered sets, see Hiebert, Paul G., "Evangelicals and Contextualized Theology," *Second Consultation on Theology and Mission* (Grand Rapids: Baker Book House, 1979).

27. Geoffrey Moorhouse, *The Missionaries*, p. 328.

28. Orlando E. Costas, *The Church and Its Mission*, p. 78.

29. Aaron Gamedze, Chief of Protocol, Swaziland, in a personal interview with the author, August 1977.

30. Norvald Yri, *Quest for Authority* (Nairobi, Kenya: Evangel Publishing House, 1978), p. 20.

31. Enrique Guang, *Latin America Pulse*, October 1976.

32. Engel, *op. cit.* p. 28.

33. From the author's interviews with Chadian church leaders and other refugees during the Chad persecution 1973-74.

34. The mission concerned explained that at the time a number of missionaries living in a large cosmopolitan center, not having the vernacular language used in the churches, attended an international English service, which happened to be sponsored by another denomination. Communication between mission and church helped to clear up the misunderstanding.

35. Source on file.

36. Ralph D. Winter, *The Two Structures of God's Redemptive Mission* (South Pasadena, CA: William Carey Library, 1974), p. 134.

37. *The Challenger* (Chinese Christian Mission, May 1978).

38. Missionary News Service, Wheaton, IL. August 1, 1978, p. 1.

39. Warren W. Webster, "The True Goal of Missions," *Christianity Today,* Dec. 22, 1972.

40. Vergil Gerber, report on Consultation on Latin America, Elburn, IL., Sept. 1970.

41. Roland Allen, *Missionary Methods: St. Paul's or Ours?* (London: World Dominion Press, 1912).

42. *Ibid.*

43. "Whither Ecumenical Mission?" *Christianity Today,* Aug. 1957.

44. I. Hay, "Balanced Perspectives," IFMA, 1965.

5

The Sea Of Difference

Give us a full-rounded chance. The sea of difference
between you and us should be no more.
                              --James Aggrey, Gold Coast, 1921

So pleaded James E.K. Aggrey to mission leaders at the
formation of the International Missionary Council in 1921.
Tension was increasing between the colonial era missions
and the rising church leadership in Ghana (then Gold Coast).
Something of the latter's frustrations can be discerned in
Aggrey's plea:

> Give us a full-rounded chance. The sea of
> difference between you and us should be no more...
> our failure to bring any contribution to the
> kingdom of God shall be no more. White folks
> may bring your gold, your great banks, and
> your big buildings, your sanitation and other
> marvelous achievements to the manger, but
> that will not be enough. Let the Chinese and
> the Japanese and the Indians bring their
> frankincense of ceremony, but that will not be
> enough. We black people must step in with our
> myrrh of childlike faith.... If you take our
> childlikeness, our love for God, our belief in
> humanity, our belief in God, and our love for
> you, whether you hate us or not, then the gifts
> will be complete. God grant that you who have
> heard this plea from Africa will trust us, will
> come and educate us, and will give us a chance

to make that contribution to the world, which
is in the design of God.[1]

A Nigerian, James Johnson, revealed similar frustrations
in a letter to a friend in England (Johnson became an
Anglican bishop and preached the Annual Sermon of the CMS
in London in 1900):

> You in England cannot fancy how some of those
> who come here inflated with the idea that they
> are the "dominant race," do treat with some-
> thing like contempt the natives of the country.
> The truth is that they regard us this day in
> pretty much the same light as our forefathers
> were, who were rescued from the iron pangs of
> slavery by the philanthropists of a former
> generation. We are not oversensitive, but at
> the same time we are not unduly pachydermatous
> . . . but does anyone think we have no feelings
> at all, or no rights which are to be respected?
> . . . Having educated us, you will not allow us
> to think and speak like men.[2]

THE MORATORIUM CALL

Similar feelings have been expressed in different ways
and different places through the years as a result of
church-mission tensions. Frustration hit the headlines,
however, when John Gatu, General Secretary of the Presbyterian Church of East Africa, announced in February 1971:
"The answer to our present problems can only be solved if
all missionaries can be withdrawn in order to allow a
period of not less than five years for each side to rethink
and formulate what is going to be their future relationship."[3]

Later that year, speaking in Milwaukee, Gatu added: "I
will go further and say that missionaries should be withdrawn, period. The reason is that we must allow God the
Holy Spirit to direct our next move without giving Him a
timetable."[4]

This proposal came to be called "moratorium" -- "any
authorized delay or stopping of some specified activity."[5]
It was discussed at Bangkok in 1973, and officially adopted
at a meeting of the All Africa Conference of Churches (AACC)
in Lusaka, Zambia, May 1974 -- however, without prior
consultation with member churches. Some of the member

bodies later called the proposal ill-prepared.

At the International Congress on World Evangelization in Lausanne, July 1974, African delegates tackled Gatu on the subject. "After a lengthy battle of words, Gatu explained that the matter had not been discussed by the churches in Africa," reported Kato.[6]

Gatu then reinterpreted the concept: "The African churches are too dependent on the West. But one is misunderstanding the proposal if he thinks that it seeks to stop the flow of personnel and money to Africa as soon as possible."[7]

The AACC reversed its own proposal by approving an appeal to be sent to Western churches in January 1975, for funds to meet a financial crisis in the AACC. Gatu's declaration had first been made to churches in America in the context of decrying Western or Northern domination, and the Lusaka proposal implied that it would be a good thing if moratorium caused "missionary-sending agencies to crumble"; but now an AACC pamphlet explained that moratorium "is a summons to churches in Africa, not to churches in rich countries."[8]

General Secretary John Kamau of the Christian Council of Kenya opposed the moratorium concept at a meeting of East Africa church council leaders in Arusha, Tanzania, early in 1976. It was "too vague, irrelevant, and empty of context," he said. "It has no positive goal. What the church in Africa wants is development toward self-reliance."[9]

The Pan-African Conference on Third World Theologians held at Achimota, Ghana, December 1977 shed further light on what has happened to the moratorium idea: "There is a gap between the rhetoric of church officials, administrators, and theologians, with the reality in the villages. We observe that this has made the African masses passive, so that the problems of limited funds to run these institutions, and the confused concept of stewardship, make it impossible to realize the call for self-reliance and moratorium."[10]

Examining moratorium

Even if the concept of moratorium has itself suffered a moratorium, we must not lightly brush aside this call, whether it comes from frustration or resentment.

"The call for a moratorium and the subsequent controversy has demonstrated that there are serious problems in
missionary work which need urgent attention," states Pius
Wakatama, an evangelical leader. "For many years prophetic
voices have told of the serious problems ahead, but somehow they were not heeded, and business continued as
usual."[11]

The call is understandable where missions continue a
colonial pattern of foreign control, direct or indirect.
The call may arise from the frustrations of a national
church with foreignness within itself, or from resentment
of external foreign influence. It is noteworthy that the
call has come chiefly from churches connected with the
older established denominations (Anglican, Methodist,
Presbyterian), which have a hierarchical system and
European liturgical formulas. Perhaps the greater flexi-
bility of evangelical forms and their emphasis on self-
reliance has avoided some of the frustration.

While the general pattern of evangelical missionary work
has been motivated by a biblical view of the equality of
men before God, we cannot deny that some missionaries and
missions have been so insensitive to the feelings of
national colleagues, that their arrogant and domineering
presence has been greatly resented.

Even where resentment has not been evident, some
missions have used authority and finance unwisely, even if
with the best intentions, so that the younger churches have
not learned to stand on their own feet. In such cases, the
decrease of the missionary presence, or even complete withdrawal of missionaries and financial assistance, may be
necessary to cause the church to recognize its own
responsibility and abilities.

As the Lausanne Covenant states: "A reduction of foreign
missionaries and money in an evangelized country may sometimes be necessary to facilitate the national church's
growth in self-reliance and to release resources for
unevangelized areas."[12] If this is the motivation for
moratorium, it is commendable -- a much healthier attitude
than seeking increasing foreign resources to prop up a
church that is not facing its responsibilities for self-
reliance.

However, there are other reasons in some quarters, which evangelicals cannot support. A prime example is Elliott Kendall's book, *The End of an Era*. Kendall has been a Methodist missionary in China and Africa. He begins with a wrong assumption and ends with a mistaken conclusion. In between those points, however, Kendall does make some very valid statements that evangelicals agree with. One such: "To deny churches overseas their essential responsibility is to reject the missionary nature of the church."[13]

Kendall's basic erroneous *assumption* is that the entire missionary movement of the past 200 years was motivated by the slave trade. His *conclusion* is that the changed conditions today obviate the need for missions.

Missionaries certainly were concerned about the iniquitous slave trade and played their part in abolishing it. However, evangelicals became missionaries for even deeper reasons than humanitarianism. They were concerned for the spiritual needs of men and women, and they went in obedience to their Savior's command to disciple all nations.

The effects of the theological changes in the liberal world can be seen in Kendall's arguments. He accepts the universalist view that salvation is found in all religions, and that all mankind has been redeemed -- the fact only needs to be announced. Salvation, redemption, evangelism all mean something different than they do to evangelicals.

We can therefore easily understand why Kendall can call for the end of proclamation of the gospel by missionaries whose original motivation (the slave trade) no longer exists, and who see no need to preach the gospel in evangelical terms. We should not oppose the withdrawal of *that kind* of missionary, for the spiritual effects of his work would be negative. We can be thankful that Kendall feels that *his* era has come to an end!

Evangelical reply

Evangelicals, however, have largely rejected the moratorium concept. Because of their scriptural basis, they believe in the urgency of the task of world evangelism. They therefore look for other solutions to the mission-church tensions which cause such frustration and resentment. Pius Wakatama has set these forth objectively and candidly in his book *Independence for the Third World Church*.[14]

"We completely resist the idea of moratorium of missionaries in Africa," stated S.O. Odunaike, President of the
AEAM, at the International Congress on World Evangelization
(Lausanne 1974). "How can we talk like this when our own
governments are actively soliciting economic, technical,
and educational aid from overseas? If people are willing
to take the plunge into a river to rescue a drowning
person, I don't see why we need to refer to a committee to
decide whether they should!"[15]

In an address to the Southern German Lutheran Synod,
Byang Kato labeled moratorium as a danger which would
destroy the biblical sense of missions:

> It seems that the advocates of moratorium do
> not take the Great Commission seriously. Their
> attack appears fiercest against those mission-
> aries placing primary emphasis on evangelism
> and church planting. But if finances are
> given for social concerns, and the missionary
> dances to the tune of the advocates of morato-
> rium, then they say there is room for that type
> of mission. Bible-believing Christians, there-
> fore, ready to obey the Great Commission, should
> not pay heed to the call for moratorium. While
> we should make every effort to develop church
> leadership in Africa, we should at the same
> time welcome missionaries, and also send our
> own African missionaries abroad. It is not a
> question of either black or white in missions,
> but both black and white in obedience to the
> Great Commission.[16]

Kato points out that Africans have been used of God to
evangelize in other continents, and people from other
continents, including the Orient, have served in Africa.
"A call for moratorium is merely an emotional appeal without adequate consideration of the ramifications involved.
The church of Christ is one. The unregenerate world is
also one. Moratorium is unbiblical and unnecessary."[17]

Actually, the moratorium call is not a new one. Jewish
leaders at Jerusalem demanded a moratorium on the part of
the disciples. The Jews had failed God's commission to be
a witness to all nations, and had a vested interest in
maintaining the status quo. The Old Testament *ecclesia* had
become an ingrown, self-preserving institution instead of
an outgoing organism.

Jesus Christ had to repudiate the Jewish *ecclesia* and send forth missionary-minded disciples to plant ongoing churches. The new wine of the Messianic kingdom could not be entrusted to the old wineskins of the Judaistic kingdom. The Jewish religious leaders reacted -- they threatened, scourged, imprisoned, and killed the disciples to prevent the message going out. Had they known the word "moratorium," they might have called for one on all missionary work.

The silversmiths at Ephesus demanded that Paul stop preaching. He was damaging their trade, their vested interests. They did not reveal those economic interests, but appealed to the public on an emotional religio-cultural basis.

There will continue to be spokesmen of other religions who raise a great cry against Christian missionary work, while using every possible means to win converts to their own religion. There will be liberal theologians who decry missionary work because of their own theological heresy, and expatriates who take upon themselves all the guilt of colonial missionary attitudes of the past two centuries, and react by abjectly apologizing for even the use of the word "mission."

There will always be people to whom the very idea of someone coming with a message from another culture (whether another sub-culture, clan, tribe, nation, or race) implies that the missionary must think his culture is superior to that of the recipients. There will also be those with vested interests, who want to ban missionary activity because they don't want their own religious kingdom invaded -- they aren't feeding the people, but they don't want anyone else to.

Whereas other eras have seen much physical hardship and persecution for the messengers of the gospel, today's opposition comes more subtly, from unregenerate men and women parading in religious garb, meeting in grand councils to declare what the church may do or not do, what words it may use or not use, and what meaning those words must have, as the church seeks to carry out her Lord's Commission.

In order to overcome the hostility to the image of missions and missionaries, both church and mission have taken to playing games with words. "Missions" was changed to "mission." "Missionaries" became camouflaged under the title "fraternal worker" or "servant of the churches."

One American denomination speaks of its missionary plan as "A Design for the Sharing of People in Mission."[18]

Ecumenicals are talking ESP -- Ecumenical Sharing of Personnel. Evangelicals are talking of a comprehensive para-mission service agency on a worldwide scale, to include missionary assistance from both the "older churches" and "younger churches." "Interdependence" is another concept.

If we have to resort to semantics or other devices in order to achieve better church-mission relations, either the church or the mission must not be mature enough to evaluate the problems of the past, forgive, and forget. Both must still have hangups which will not be overcome by changing words or structure. Unless missionaries and pastors have really changed their outlook, a new label won't avoid the same tensions arising.

It would seem better to study together the historical development of the tensions, how to avoid them, and then to grow in maturity so both church and mission can freely use the word "missionary" in the New Testament sense of "apostle" or "sent one."

When is moratorium valid?

The whole question of moratorium should lead to healthy self-examination for all missions and churches. What are the principles for a missionary withdrawal? When is the job complete? When is the job not complete?[19]

Moratorium is not to be imposed by councils or individuals with vested interests and prejudices, but by the Son of David who opens and closes doors. (See Rev. 3:8.) There are times when He will use force of circumstances to do this, as in Ethiopia in 1936. There were only 48 baptized believers and only one church in the Wolayta tribe when the Italian invaders forced all missionaries out of the country. Five years later, the missionaries returned to find that the number of believers had multiplied to 10,000 in 100 churches, crying out for instruction in the Word.[20]

In Sudan, all missionaries were expelled from the southern provinces in 1964. In 1974 missionaries were invited back, and found there had been a great turning to Christ among the southern people (Juba area), who suffered untold misery during the civil war. As in Ethiopia, the Sudanese Christians called upon missionaries to teach them the Word and train church leaders.

In Korea, the Japanese invaders compelled all churches to resign from overseas organizations in 1938, causing Christians to realize their dependency upon God himself. Later, when they could have fellowship with Christians overseas, they doubly valued their relationships.

Thus there are times when God decides that "moratorium," or strategic withdrawal, is needed to test His people. However, it would be dangerous for man to legislate the circumstances and time; only God knows all the factors, and what will strengthen His church or weaken it. At the same time, both mission and church should always be prepared for such an eventuality, so they will not be caught unawares.

Are there times when a mission should plan on "voluntary selective moratorium," as Wakatama calls it?[21] In considering this, we need to keep several principles in mind:

1. Missions need to examine their policy and attitudes, to make sure there is no cause for resentment and misunderstanding because of their continued presence. This would amount to division in the body of Christ, and lack of harmony and love. Withdrawal should never have to be based on such factors, if they can be avoided by mission and church.

It is unfortunately true that some individuals and missions have not learned from the past, and perpetuate wrong attitudes. Some of these are not only unscriptural and uncultural, but also do not represent effective management or communication concepts. These problems should not be run away from by withdrawal, because their effect will continue to influence the church and its future outreach even if the expatriate missionary is not present. The priority need is to reach mutual understanding in the Holy Spirit.

If tension continues after proper discussion and prayer, perhaps a temporary reduction of expatriates will give opportunity for the church to become more objective in looking at the problems. Missions should be alert to indications of God's direction in this, rather than forcing their presence on a situation with negative results. With-

drawal on this basis should only be as a last resort, however, and with clear guidance from the Spirit. We have
seen Him bring about circumstances which caused a temporary reduction of staff in such situations.

2. Missions need to consider their goals, and whether their
presence is still contributing to those goals. To do this
objectively with the church can be a helpful evaluation
experience for both. Why are expatriates needed? What are
they needed to do -- and why can't nationals accomplish the
same? Is what they are doing really worth the rising cost
of missionary support, or is there a less expensive way to
produce the same results? Is the missionary presence
stifling the church in any way -- demotivating, blocking
national staff development, hindering local financing,
preventing cultural relevance? Along with such evaluation,
mission and church should objectively plan when missionaries should be redeployed. There should be foresight and
cooperative planning -- not panic in a time of crisis or
tension.

This "selective moratorium" has been practiced by
evangelicals. SIM's work in Kuta, Nigeria, is an
illustration. It began in 1919 and developed active
churches. No expatriate missionaries have been assigned
there since 1960, but this did not mean that SIM withdrew
from the country as a whole. There were other tasks to be
done, including training leadership for such places as Kuta,
so that the churches could be effective in their own outreach.

3. Missions must be sensitive to the effect of their
presence on the position of the national church and its
witness. In times of political crisis, is the mission
presence an embarrassment to the church? The mission may
appear to supporters to be very heroic "hanging in there,"
while the church's future may be jeopardized by a foreign
image.

The main point here is simply to ask the church to
state honestly which is better -- to go or stay. The
answer is sometimes surprising.

"When Amin came into power, young people in Uganda
watched to see if missionaries would leave when other
expatriates did," Ugandan Anglican John Sentamu told me.
"There was a therapeutic value when missionaries stayed.
If they had gone and then come back after peace was

restored, the people would have said, 'They don't really care for us -- they only come when there is peace.'"[22]

In Ethiopia, SIM recently asked the church leaders if the Mission were an embarrassment to them, in view of the political situation at the time. Should the missionaries all leave?

"Please don't!" the church replied, "it would be more embarrassing for us to have to explain to our people why the missionaries left us in a time of difficulty."[23]

Summary

The theological shift to universalism, which in liberal thinking removed the necessity for evangelization, coupled with the tensions of cross-cultural communication and the image of the colonial missionary -- all this has led inevitably to the call of moratorium. Evangelicals should be sensitive to the tensions and seek to overcome them. However, in the light of the world's spiritual needs and Christ's commission to witness, they should still reply to any ban on witnessing as did the early disciples, in boldness and humility: "Whether it be right in the sight of God to hearken unto you more than unto God, judge ye. *For we cannot but speak the things which we have seen and heard*" (Acts 4:19,20).

IMPASSE OR BY-PASS?

Moratorium is not the greatest worry of evangelicals. In church-mission relations, their greater concern is a situation which I shall term *impasse*. To avoid impasse, some recommend by-pass.

The organizational structure may change, institutions may close, communication may be difficult, cultural misunderstandings may arise -- but most evangelical missionaries will not be upset by any of these as much as by the failure of the church to continue meeting the objectives of evangelization. In my observation of church-mission discussions, this is the ultimate fear of missionaries.

How valid is this fear? We are increasingly encouraged by reports of Third World missions, and we shall consider them later. First let us examine the problem of churches which have stagnated.

In the Bible we read of religious groups which opposed missionary outreach. Peter was cross-examined for crossing cultural barriers.[24] Paul referred to those who opposed evangelizing the gentiles.[25]

In chapter 1 we referred to the early church in North Africa. Beyerhaus and Lefever cite more recent examples in Korea, Indonesia, and Nigeria. They point out that in the case of the work on the Niger, the Christians "never managed to extend their mission beyond their own quarters and their own people."[26]

Neill states: "Most of the younger churches have extremely little interest in evangelistic work in the cause of the furtherance of the gospel. It might be expected that those who have newly been won to Christ would be eager to share their new discoveries with others. In the first generation it is often so. The experience of many churches shows that with the second generation this impulse has died away, and is not easily recreated."[27]

Trimingham points out the sequence which ends in missionary frustration:

> As local churches have grown and missions have adjusted themselves to the situation by devolution of authority, problems have arisen which have not been solved, for partnership with the local churches has not only saddled them with a Western institution, but has also frustrated the advance into unevangelized areas. Missionaries in partnership with African Christians have to subordinate their aims to those of the churches which, with some exception, are concerned with internal organization and not with evangelism among non-Christians. So absorbed are most missionaries in institutional work that they can do little to arouse the church to the need for wider witness.[28]

> More and more missionaries are disturbed by this situation, tied up as they are in educational and welfare work, and are asking: "We were sent out to preach the gospel; what is our place here if the churches to which we are sent care nothing for evangelism and are

only concerned to use us to maintain institutions for which they have not yet the trained
people?"[29]

The Evangelical Alliance Commission of World Mission
asks:

What if work urgently needs to be done and no
invitation comes? There are bound to be areas
where the local church has become institutionalized and even moribund. Experience in
Britain leads us to believe that this will
happen in other countries; for it is a form of
inverted patronage to assume that churches in
developing countries never face the problems
we face here.

Michael Griffiths has this to say about such a
situation: "Where national churches are in
danger of becoming dull and formal, in the
very nature of the case they do not see their
need. Laodicean churches do not. For one
thing, it implies a loss of face, and flies in
the face of nationalism to suggest that they
need any outside help at all. Yet it is
precisely in this kind of church that missionaries today are having the most effective
outreach."[30]

The Overseas Missionary Fellowship, of which Griffiths
was then General Director, has been able to respond to
requests from such churches for missionary Bible teachers
and cross-cultural evangelists, and has found great
spiritual response. However, some other missions tied into
moribund church situations have not had that liberty.

C. Peter Wagner warns of the "Babylonian Captivity of
the Christian Mission," and cites Bangkok as "a living
example."[31] He feels that the missionary must keep himself
free from serving the institutional church, which could
cause him to lose his missionary mandate of evangelism and
church planting. This would become a "truncated goal."

"The attention of some missionaries has been so drawn
to the fascination of seeing the young church begin to move
forward on its own that this has become their exclusive
interest," Wagner says. His solution: "When missionaries
are out on the growing edge, bringing unbelievers to

Christ, organizing them into congregations, and handing over
the new churches to the denominations, few national leaders
are going to tell *that* kind of missionary to go home."[32]

Ralph Winter's solution to overcome church-mission
tensions and avoid "the syndrome of church development" is
to disengage all missionary-style workers from relationships with national churches, releasing them for direct
evangelism and church planting. This, he points out, does
not mean any lessening need for missions and missionaries.
In doing this, he is not against Christian specialists from
the older churches working directly with their younger
sister churches in the Third World, but would not call them
"missionary-style workers."[33]

Wagner and Winter have a valid point -- that the goal of
missions must not stop with the formation of a national
church, and that missionaries must not lose their goal of
evangelism and discipling. However, we must not become
simplistic in applying those principles:

1. Division of responsibility (arising from Henry Venn's
principles), with the mission doing the evangelistic outreach and the church looking after the converts, is
extremely dangerous; it could kill the church's missionary
motivation. Without diminishing direct missionary evangelism, why not also use missionaries to help equip the church
so it can do the evangelistic outreach as well as the
discipling and church administration?

2. In certain situations, the most effective means of
cross-cultural evangelism may be to equip the young church
to do the job. Missionaries who are building up the church
in this way have not necessarily lost their missionary
vision, but may be seeing it brought to pass more effectively. To think otherwise, is to say that the missionary
must be directly evangelizing cross-culturally (with all
the foreign implications) if he is to be called a true
missionary. This implies that equipping someone else to
carry out such evangelism is not "real missionary work."
That is shortsighted reasoning.

3. Evangelism can become a "truncated missionary goal"
even as discipleship and church development can become
"truncated missionary goals." To bring spiritual babes to
birth and then abandon them amounts to irresponsibility.
The results of dedicated missionary evangelism may be swept
away by persecution, error, or affluence, unless converts

are indoctrinated in the Word of God and motivated to pass on their faith to others.

4. Although many a missionary would like to be out on "the growing edge," in some situations racial antagonism or government policy may make it counter-productive for a foreigner to be seen standing in a marketplace or sitting in a compound "proselytizing." The reaction could defeat the missionary's purpose, whereas training a national to do the job could achieve the goal.

5. J. Robertson McQuilkin makes a helpful distinction:

> Does the answer lie in such either/or solutions?
> Why do we lump all "missionary" activity into a
> single rigid structural relationship? Why do
> we not distinguish the roles of those we send
> overseas? Certainly when *ministry* to the *church*
> is the task, a move toward the servant role is
> long overdue in many places. But when our
> *mission* to the *world* is the task, we must main-
> tain enough structural flexibility to assure
> its completion.[34]

In the event of a church not being ready to evangelize a new area, a simple solution would be for the church and mission mutually to agree that the mission should go ahead and reach those people with the gospel. But it may not be that simple; the church may want the mission to use its resources for projects the church has undertaken, not for some new project. The inevitable accusation will be that the mission really isn't interested in helping the church, but only finds resources for projects it controls. (Mis-sion leaders should remember that in the past they have not always been able to approve the proposals of their own missionaries to start new projects, because of lack of resources.)

Some missiologists recommend that a mission and church sign a formal agreement -- that in the event of the church not being able or willing to undertake an evangelistic project, the mission may move in unilaterally. Such an agreement, they argue, is the only way to guarantee that the mission does not one day face stalemate in its mandate to evangelize and plant churches.[35]

It is true that no earthly power -- church or government
-- has the authority to stop believers from taking the
gospel to others. The early apostles' experience shows us
that. If it is legitimate for believers to preach the
gospel in the face of government opposition, then it must
also be legitimate to do so in the face of church apathy or
hostility. The messengers of the gospel must not commit
themselves to inaction in the face of need. This can lead
to "by-pass" of the church in order to get the job done.

The arguments are valid, and the principle is scriptural.
However, we must consider the practical implications before
by-passing the church.

1. If the church's refusal results from lack of missionary
vision and from selfishness, that is a challenge in itself
to the mission. What went wrong in the process of imparting
the whole Word to the church? Has the mission set its own
priorities in the right place? Has it shown the right
example? Has it sponsored missionary conferences to teach
and challenge the church in missionary outreach? Time and
men and money spent in doing this may well revive the church
as well as bring about a more effective outreach in the long
run, than if the mission "went it alone."

2. If the church's hesitancy is really the result of
shortage of manpower, what can the mission do to train
national missionaries for new areas? That again will
strengthen the work more in the long run than if the
mission by-passes the church.

3. Even if there is a signed agreement that the mission
may enter a new area unilaterally, there could be great
tension and misunderstanding over such action. Although the
mission would be perfectly within its rights, a harmful
dichotomy could result. The mission's resources pouring
into the new venture could be seen as neglect of the
church's priorities, and fellowship in the gospel would
break down.

If an agreement on unilateral outreach is signed, it
should be used only as a last resort, and not as an escape
for maverick missionaries who want "to do their own thing."
Apart from any signed agreements, church and mission need
to keep in such close harmony through prayer and study
together, that they will agree in the Spirit, either to
move into the new area together, or for the mission to
begin a new work on its own.

Causes of impasse

By examining the reasons for impasse between church and mission over outreach, perhaps we can avoid its arising.

Spiritual reasons are the most common. The churches among which Trimingham did his research are known to the author; it is my personal observation that for the most part their ministers were not "born-again" themselves, or else did not have a clear idea how to lead someone to Jesus Christ as Savior. Certainly their membership was largely nominally Christian. In fact, the greatest response to the gospel message in the magazine *African Challenge*[36] came from readers who were members of these churches along the West Coast of Africa. Having little spiritual life, these churches would naturally lack interest in missionary outreach.

Theologically, many of these churches were planted by missionaries with a church-centric view, and an emphasis on church membership rather than personal regeneration. I must quickly add that there were also outstanding evangelicals among them, but their evangelistic emphasis was often outweighed by the overall posture of the churches. As quoted in chapter 4, Costas blames theological shallowness for lack of missionary vision among Latin Americans.

Demotivation by the nature of the missionary work is one reason that Trimingham gives:

> It is primarily the nature of Western missions which has led to the atrophy of the evangelistic impulse, and there is little they can do to remedy the situation. Western missions are too practical and technical, their creative energies are devoted to secondary things, schemes, plans, and methods.[37]

Trimingham felt that this tendency dichotomized faith and daily life for nationals, instead of relating Christianity to every aspect, as traditional religions do. No doubt some of the missionary "machine" gave the wrong impression to nationals, but if spiritual regeneration and motivation had accompanied the "technical" aspects, the results need not have been atrophy. After all, the new Christians would have to learn to cope with the "schemes, plans, and methods" of the changing world around them, introduced by government

and industry. Spiritual life was the great prerequisite
for coping with change.

   Instruction has been a great lack. "Has the evangelistic
impulse which sent out Westerners been handed on?" asks
Trimingham.[38] The answer is no -- in many cases. Met
Castillo, a Filippino theologian, points out that there is
a great lack of missiological education among pastors.
"The missing vitamin in mission strategy," he calls it.[39]
Actually, the percentage of Western/Northern Christians
with missionary vision is very small. Christians need to
be instructed and challenged regarding mission.

   Self-interest may be a reason. A church may feel it has
too many unmet needs itself and can't afford to use money
or personnel to evangelize another community; only faith
and determination will overcome this attitude. Or a church
may have deep resentment about another ethnic group which
has been at enmity with the church's ethnic group. Only
the love of Christ can bridge that chasm.

   ECWA General Secretary Simon Ibrahim pointed out another
possible self-interest. "I've noticed that each tribe
wants to hang on to its missionaries. They say, 'These are
our missionaries.' We should thank God that in the early
days SIM did not stay in one place, but moved out to other
tribes and countries. The founder, R.V. Bingham, told them
they had to do so." [40]

   Because of this natural problem, it is essential that
expatriate missionaries not be stationed by local churches,
but by a central joint church-mission committee which can
objectively see the overall strategy of the work. (The
committee should communicate with the local churches, of
course.) This can also help avoid a "Babylonian captivity
of the Christian mission."

SUMMARY

   We've talked about the "sea of difference" between two
major issues that have arisen from two different sides:
"moratorium" and "by-pass." Although there are exceptions
on both sides, most people holding a moratorium position
tend toward church-centric and liberal theological views.
Most people holding a by-pass position would tend toward a
mission-centric view and evangelical theology.

I can almost hear a number of Christian leaders from Africa, Asia, and Latin America crying out at this stage: "You've spent a lot of time considering negative attitudes -- moratorium and by-pass. Why is either necessary? Isn't there a better way?"

Yes, there is a better way, and some of these Third World leaders have helped to show the way. Let us examine it in the next chapter.

STUDY QUESTIONS: CHAPTER 5

1. What frustrations as well as theological views give rise to a call for "moratorium"? Discuss the lessons we can learn from this -- as missions and as churches.

2. Discuss "by-pass." What problems sometimes cause evangelical missionaries to by-pass the churches?

3. What may be the causes of an "impasse" between a church and a mission society seeking to reach unevangelized people? Discuss how to overcome these causes.

NOTES: CHAPTER 5

1. Edwin W. Smith, *Aggrey in Africa,* p. 188.

2. Geoffrey Moorhouse, *The Missionaries,* p. 306.

3. John Gatu, "Missionary, Go Home," in *The Church Herald* (Grand Rapids, MI, Nov. 5, 1971), p. 4.

4. *Ibid,* p. 21.

5. Webster's New World Dictionary.

6. Byang Kato, *Evangelical Missions Quarterly,* Wheaton, Vol. 10, No. 4, p. 307.

7. J. Verkuyl, *Contemporary Missiology, an Introduction* (Grand Rapids: Eerdmans, 1978), p. 336.

8. *Ibid,* p. 336.

9. Okite Odhiambo, "A Moratorium on Moratorium," *Christianity Today,* Washington, D.C., April 9, 1976.

10. Press release: Pan-African Conference of Third World Theologians, Achimota, Ghana, Dec. 17-23, 1977.

11. Pius Wakatama, *Independence for the Third World Church* (Downers Grove: InterVarsity Press, 1976), p. 105.

12. Lausanne Covenant, Paragraph 9.

13. Elliott Kendall, *The End of an Era* (London: SPCK, 1978), p. 1.

14. Pius Wakatama, *Independence for the Third World Church* (Downers Grove: InterVarsity Press, 1976).

15. S.O. Odunaike, in a panel discussion at Lausanne, as recorded by the author.

16. Byang H. Kato, *Perception* (Nairobi, Kenya: AEAM, April 1975).

17. Byang H. Kato, *Theological Pitfalls in Africa* (Kisumu, Kenya: Evangel Publishing House, 1975), p. 167.

18. *Occasional Bulletin*, Missionary Research Library, Spring, 1976, p. 3.

19. For a helpful examination of these questions, see "Principles for Withdrawal from the Mission Field," a preliminary discussion outlined by Harvey M. Conn, Dec. 3, 1975 IFMA-EFMA.

20. For background on the situations in Ethiopia and Sudan, see the following:
    a. Raymond Davis, *Fire on the Mountains* (Grand Rapids: Zondervan Publishing House, 1966).
    b. Peter Cotterell, *Born at Midnight* (Chicago: Moody Press, 1973).
    c. Malcolm Forsberg, *Dry Season* (Toronto: Sudan Interior Mission, 1964).

21. Wakatama, op. cit., p. 109.

22. John Sentamu, CMS Uganda, in an interview with the author at High Leigh, UK, Nov. 1978.

23. Ian M. Hay, letter to SIM General Council, Dec. 19, 1978.

24. Acts 11: 2,3.

25. 1 Thess. 2:16.

26. Beyerhaus & Lefever, *The Responsible Church and the Foreign Mission,* p. 144.

27. Neill, *History of Christian Missions,* p. 575.

28. J.S. Trimingham, *The Christian Church and Islam in West Africa* (London: SCM, 1956), p. 28.

29. *Ibid,* pp. 34, 35.

30. *One World One Task,* Evangelical Alliance, 1971, p. 133.

31. Ralph D. Winter, *The Evangelical Response to Bangkok* (South Pasadena: William Carey Library, 1973), p. 81.

32. C. Peter Wagner, *Frontiers in Missionary Strategy* (Chicago: Moody Press, 1971), pp. 170, 171.

33. Ralph Winter, *The Evangelical Response to Bangkok,* p. 20.

34. J. Robertson McQuilkin, "The Evangelistic Mission of the Church," in *Church Growth Bulletin,* March 1972, p. 211.

35. Illustration of one such agreement: The Sudan Area Council of SIM, December 1978, passed the following motion, which was discussed by Sudan Interior Mission at its Council meeting of February 21, 1979, and accepted in a letter from the Sudan Interior Church (SIC) Secretary General to the SIM Director, April 29, 1979:

"Believing that God has raised up SIM to spread the gospel of the Lord Jesus Christ wherever He opens the door in Sudan, we confirm that our eyes and hearts will continually be open for areas where there are yet unreached peoples.   When such openings present themselves, it is the desire of SIM that SIC go hand in hand with us in the new advance.   Where SIC is unable to join with us, we will feel constrained to carry out our God-given directive to share the gospel of Christ to all possible peoples, in all possible haste, 'until He comes.'"

36. *African Challenge* was an undenominational Christian
    monthly published by SIM from 1951 to 1970, during
    which time it became Africa's second-largest
    circulation monthly. The author was editor for 12
    years. In 1970 it became *Today's Challenge*, published
    by ECWA Productions Ltd., Jos, Nigeria.

37. Trimingham, *op. cit.*, p. 29.

38. Trimingham, *op. cit.*, p. 25.

39. Met Castillo, *Asia Pulse* (Wheaton, IL: EMIS, May
    1976).

40. Simon Ibrahim, ECWA General Secretary, in message to
    SIM missionaries in Nigeria, March 1977.

6

Relations And Relatives

"Some missiologists state that when a mission turns responsibility for the work over to the national church, its missionary goals will be lost," I told the ECWA executive in one of our church-mission joint consultations. "Evangelism will die out. Concern for reaching the unevangelized will give way to concern for preserving church institutions. What's your opinion?"

"Nonsense!" replied ECWA General Secretary Simon Ibrahim. "If the mission has done its work properly, and has prepared the church to be missionary-minded, the church should continue with the same goals of evangelism."

Missions arising from the vision of Christians in Africa, Asia, and Latin America are increasing in number. According to a survey by James Wong, there were 210 agencies supporting 3000 missionaries in 1973.[1] Some of these are linked with churches resulting from foreign missionary work; several are the work of individual nationals who have become burdened for the spiritual needs of others.

S.O. Odunaike challenged Christians in his message to the Second World Black and African Festival of Arts and Culture:

> It behooves every Christian of every race to
> promote the Christian faith with every ounce
> of his blood and to stand for its defence
> vigorously and strenuously. This is your duty

to your Redeemer. We are not to behave as
if we are merely helping our European and
American brethren to fulfill the task of
evangelization.[2]

At the Nigeria National Congress on Evangelization held
at Ife, August, 1978, 1000 delegates from across the nation
adopted the goal "that everybody in Nigeria may hear the
gospel clearly enough to understand it and sufficiently to
make a decision by the end of 1980."[3] This was a gigantic
goal, considering that a survey for the Nigerian Evangelical Fellowship estimated there were 25 million unevangelized in Nigeria,[4] among the nation's 500 linguistic
groups.[5] Although much of this witness would be done by
local churches evangelizing their communities, the scarcity
or complete absence of churches in some areas would require
cross-cultural missionary communication, delegates realized.
The Ife Congress was an indigenous affair: all speakers
were African, and financing was raised in the country.

The Word of Life Churches in Ethiopia are an example of
missionary-minded churches. Over 100 evangelists are sent
out by the 2500 churches, a number going into other tribes,
especially in the South. A church report tells of 50 men
who dedicated themselves as evangelists at a recent church
conference. The Christians provided their support with
"gifts of money, coffee, cows, goats, and clothes."[6]

The work of the Evangelical Missionary Society in
Nigeria is cited in chapter 10 as part of a case study.
The EMS supports 260 African missionaries, distinct from
the local evangelists supported by their churches.

In 1978, Panya Baba, EMS Secretary, was invited by the
Asia Missions Association (AMA) to speak on the cooperation
of African, Asian, and Latin-American missions. He cited
personnel, training facilities, and resource materials
(publications) as potential areas of cooperation and
exchange.[7]

At the formation of the AMA, Asian mission leaders from
12 countries stated in the Seoul Declaration on Christian
Mission:

> We recognize that we have to turn back from the
> socio-politically oriented Missio Dei and re-
> turn to the Missio Christi, the proclamation of
> His redemptive death and resurrection, as He

enjoined His disciples (Matt. 28:18-20). . .
that we have to turn back from the sociological
dimension of "salvation from sin". . . from
"mission through peoples' organizations," or
liberation movements and return to "mission
through church's ministry."

We recognize that we have to turn back from
the mere dialogue with adherents of other
religions and ideologies and return to mission as proclamation of the biblical gospel
to the lost . . . that we have to turn back
from the modern liberal mission based upon a
"social foundation" and return to the Christian mission based on a "biblical foundation."[8]

Asian leaders from 25 countries who met in Singapore
November 1978 to discuss the topic "Together Obeying Christ
for Asia's Harvest," stated:

About 95% of Asia's 2 billion people remain to
be reached with the gospel. Most of these
people are not in contact with any Christian
witness. We believe that there are many in
this category who would be receptive to the
gospel. While Christ's Great Commission was
given to the whole church, yet because God has
placed us in Asia, we recognize that the
evangelization of Asia is primarily our
responsibility. The millions who have never
heard the gospel even once are our "neighbors,"
our kinsmen, and countrymen.[9]

In Burma, where Western missionaries are not permitted
to work, 300 young unpaid Burmese volunteers began three
years of missionary outreach after celebrating the centen-
nial of the gospel's advent among the Kachins. Although
they are currently confined within Burma by political
restrictions, the Kachin church believes she is entering a
new era of missions which will eventually reach out to
other parts of Asia.[10]

In Brazil, the Third Encounter of Brazilian Cross-
Cultural Missions (October 1978) reported that Brazilian
evangelicals are sending missionaries to 16 countries in
South and North America, Europe, and Africa. Out of 736
total, 250 are serving in non-Portuguese languages.[11]

While these missionary agencies rightly wish to be self-reliant, they do not want to isolate themselves from the rest of the world's missionary efforts.

In "The Devlali Letter," 400 delegates to the All-India Congress on Mission and Evangelization in 1977 endorsed this principle: "Servants of Christ who have come to India from abroad have had a significant role to play. We continue to maintain a partnership with them in the work before us. However, we believe that mission and evangelization in India should truly be the responsibility of the church in India. At the same time, we realize that the Indian church is called also to share in the task of reaching all nations of the world with the gospel."[12]

A Chinese delegate at a study on missions in March 1978 in the Philippines expressed what was believed to be the sentiment of many: "Cooperation between Chinese and Westerners should be well planned on an equal basis, with an attitude of openness, love, and patience. This cooperation should be on all levels and in all areas. The task is too great. We cannot afford the time and effort involved if we think only of 'we Chinese' or 'we Westerners.' We all belong to Christ, and all need to join together to fulfill the Great Commission that Jesus has given to us."[13]

With this kind of missionary vision, it is surprising that some missions from the West/North have not recognized the full potential of Third World missions sooner.

In fact, a strange syndrome can be detected in the attitude of some Western missionaries, almost amounting to rejection of their own spiritual children. This is found chiefly in missionaries with a strongly dichotomous view. Part of it may be ethnocentrism. They take it for granted they can do it better, that the task depends wholly on them.

The *Church Growth Bulletin,* to which we owe much for its stimulating articles and statistics, nevertheless seems to imply this in an article comparing the work of two missions in the Philippines.[14] Mission A has been there 80 years, now has few expatriate missionaries, and 40,000 communicants. Mission B has been there only 30 years, has over 100 expatriate missionaries, and 40,000 communicants. Without giving any further facts, the *Bulletin* suggests that the difference in growth rate is because Mission A turned over its work to a small denomination. That may be true,

but it is a simplistic deduction implying that only massive
foreign presence can ensure rapid church growth. Certainly
in this case there are other factors it would be helpful to
have information on. For instance, we happen to know that
Mission A has a different theological position to Mission B.
Has this hindered not only church growth but also missionary
vision, so that after 80 years the first mission left its
work to a dormant church? What other factors were involved?

Neglect of development of missionary vision in the Third
World church may also arise from a Western/Northern desire
to see instant results. It takes time to develop the
capability of others -- and meanwhile we can't report
phenomenal results from *our* work!

Have some missions kept supporters' enthusiasm high by
reporting results only, or have they helped supporters to
understand the whole picture -- how it takes time, people,
patience, and finance to develop the missionary capabilities
of the national church? Have missionaries understood this,
or do they not consider working with the church to be
"missionary work"? It can be, if the goals are kept in
sight.

> An Indonesian pastor pointed out that nearly
> everything God accomplishes in this world is
> by cooperation. A single grain of rice does
> not grow unless the heavens and the earth work
> together. In the same way, he concluded, the
> present phase of missionary work can truly bear
> fruit only if the old church, with its rich
> theological treasures, works closely with the
> young church. The old church does much more
> than simply offer assistance; its task is
> much greater and more profound: the two work
> together, the old church is itself active in
> the one great communal missionary project.
> The work of the two churches cannot be un-
> raveled. The work of both is so interwoven
> it cannot be separated or distinguished. But
> one thing is certain, the task of the old
> church is still a missionary task, even
> though it is now conducted on a cooperative
> basis.[15]

Perhaps we have a naive attitude to the Third World
church. We may think that because people have come to
Christ through missionary outreach, they should be mission-

ary minded. We may think that because they are nationals,
they will know how to reach other nationals -- even across
sub-cultural borders. We may think that somehow the
struggling church will develop a support base for missions,
without instruction. We forget that Western missionary
work is the result of a great deal of intensive development
of people, support, and structure. Third World missions
need as much motivating and developing.[16]

Scripture and also management principles teach that it
is better to develop others to do the work than to try to
do it all oneself. Christian management principles use the
work to develop people. Evangelicals should develop one
of the greatest resources God has given His church to
fulfill the Great Commission -- Third World missions.

Much of the tension between missionaries and the church
arises from the polarization of church-centric and mission-
centric outlooks (chapter 4). But even more basic is a
misconception about the nature of the church and its task.

Charles Mellis writes helpfully about the church as
"committed communities." He feels the following order of
priority is crucial:
(1) our commitment to Christ is the indispensable
foundation;
(2) a community is formed by our commitment to one
another; and
(3) we express our original (foundational) commitment in
community by way of a shared commitment to a task.[17]

Howard Snyder makes a further distinction. Redeemed
people are the "Community of the King," or the church
proper. All *structures* are para-church (from *para:*
"alongside, beside"). This includes church denominations,
non-denominational structures, and mission agencies.

> Thus the church is a spiritual reality which is
> always cross-culturally valid. But para-church
> structures are not the essence of the church.
> Believers within these structures, in their
> common life as a people and a community, are
> the church. When such para-church structures
> are confused with the church, or seen as part
> of its essence, all kinds of unfortunate mis-
> understandings result, and we bind the church
> to its particular cultural and structural
> expression . . . . Thus the crucial consider-

ation for structure becomes not biblical
legitimacy, but functional relevancy.[18]

Tension between church and mission is reduced if we look
upon both the church denomination (including the local
church) and the mission agency as para-church structures
to enable the people of God, or the community of the King,
to fulfill God's will and glorify Him. They are not rivals;
one is not greater than the other. They are not ends in
themselves, but means to accomplish an end. The end to
which they both work, and for which both are needed, is the
extension of the community of the King, the bride of
Christ.

Peter Wagner[19] lists "Four Major Phases of the Progress
of Missionary Work."

Phase I. The mission goes out to a group of non-
Christians to evangelize and to plant churches.

Phase II. The mission works at church development,
"teaching them to observe all things whatsoever I
have commanded you."

Phase III. The mission becomes a consultant. The
new church is autonomous, caring for its internal
matters.

Phase IV. The church launches a mission. This is
the real goal, but one that has been somewhat
neglected . . . . Not nearly enough missionary
strategy has been planned in terms of Phase IV.
Missions have seemed to be a necessary activity
of the churches in the sending countries, but for
some curious reason not too necessary in the emerging
churches.

Costas feels that mission societies are the result of
the missiological failure of the church.[20] Winter argues
that in any church, a mission society (sodality) is a
necessity to ensure effective outreach.[21]

Costas points out that sodalities (e.g., missions) should
not be fabricated from the outside. "They emerge naturally
and spontaneously as part of concrete historical situations." He adds that a foreign mission should not set up
a national mission.[22]

It could be argued that if church denominations and
mission agencies are both really para-church organizations,
a foreign mission has as much business planting a mission
as it has planting a church! The truth is that both should
come about as the result of the felt need of the people of
God, the members of the kingdom, as they feed upon the Word
of God. In doing so, they recognize their own need for the
structural local church and for a structure to enable them
to reach out to others effectively -- in other words, a
mission agency.

Edward Pentecost describes "the funnel philosophy" of
missions which look upon formation of the indigenous church
as their ultimate goal. He feels that interdenominational
missions, in particular, end up with fragmented local,
autonomous churches which have little sense of community
outreach in evangelism. Pentecost suggests:

> Let's invert the funnel and send the church out
> to evangelize. . . . Let's think of the church
> as the beginning, not the end! Let's think of
> the church as the place to begin to reach out
> to every individual in all the world. Let's
> make the church the dynamic party, not the
> missionary. This philosophy sees the church as
> the initiator and means, the individual as the
> end. Is this not the teaching of Ephesians
> 4:11, 12, "He gave (gifts) for the perfecting
> of the saints, for the work of the ministry"?
> . . . Is our vision centered upon forming new
> local bodies as the end, or is our vision
> centered upon the end of seeing the church
> reach out in widespread and broad evangelism?[23]

The dynamic sequence

While we have been trying to reconcile the relationship
of two para-church structures, the church denomination and
the mission agency, let us remember that they will fall into
place only as we recognize that Christ is the Head. The
earthly structures of His body are subordinate to Him.
There should be no extreme position of the church organization being central or the mission organization being
central. Christ, the Head, is central, and the earthly
organizations are meant to glorify Him and to fulfill His
will. We could thus liken the local church and the mission
to His body visibly in action on this earth -- the ongoing,
outreaching church. (See appendix F.)

The Scriptures center the whole dynamics of church-mission relations around Christ as follows:

1. Christ is Head of the church (Eph. 1:22). Instead of making either the local church or missionary outreach central in our concept of God's instrument for fulfilling His plan for the age, we need to look at the Head, who directs His body to carry out His will through witness.

2. Christ has commissioned His disciples to witness and disciple others (Acts 1:8). His commission has not been abrogated.

3. Christ empowers His body to carry out His mission, or task, in this age (Matt. 28:19, 20). "The vocation of the church as a missionary church belongs to its very essence. . . the church lives only so long as it is engaged in missionary activity."[24]

"There is no participation in Christ without participation in His mission to the world. That by which the church receives its existence is that by which it is also given its world mission . . . . God sends forth the church to carry out His work to the ends of the earth, to all nations, and to the end of time."[25]

"It is of tremendous significance to realize that we are not doing mission work *for* Christ but rather *with* Christ (Matt. 28:20; Mark 16:20)."[26]

4. The Holy Spirit is the agent sent by Christ to empower His body to witness, to the glory of the Father (Acts 1:8; John 14:16).

5. The apostle or missionary has a responsibility to help new believers on to maturity. The concomitant of a responsible church is responsible mission, not abandoning newborn babes. The apostle Paul continued his missionary concern for the churches, "night and day praying exceedingly that we might see your face, and might perfect that which is lacking in your faith" (I Thess. 3:10). Paul felt a father-son relationship (I Cor. 4:14, 16; I Thess. 2:11).

6. God's purpose for this age does not dichotomize church and mission, but is fulfilled in His body, the church, obeying His commission. This is not a question of which comes first, the chicken or the egg -- church or missionary

outreach. The two are inseparable in God's purpose for
this age. It is not a case of "worship" versus "witness."

The structure of church-mission relationships is not the
essential question, but whether the church is responsibly
carrying out its mission. "If the church is to remain a
living body, it is a question of life or death whether or
no it remains in contact with the missionary enterprise."[27]

Paul's letters to the young churches indicate the
continuing flow of God's purpose. A missionary brought the
Word, and believers forming a local church passed it on in
missionary outreach to others, who in turn formed ongoing,
outreaching church groups (I Thess. 1:5-8; Titus 1:5, etc.).

7. In Scripture we do not find that the planting of an
indigenous local church is an end in itself. It is both the
result of God's purpose in this age, as well as the means
of carrying out His continued purpose. "Mission is not an
imposition upon the church, for it belongs to her nature
and should be as natural to her as grapes are natural to
branches that abide in the vine."[28]

8. There is less possibility of church-mission tensions if
we have the same spirit which the apostle Paul had when he
wrote: "Ye are in our hearts to die and live with you"
(II Cor. 7:3); and "What is our hope, or joy, or crown of
rejoicing? Are not even ye in the presence of our Lord
Jesus Christ at His coming? For ye are our glory and joy"
(1 Thess. 2:19, 20).

      *   *   *   *   *

In terms of mission societies and local churches as
instruments in God's hands, His plan for this age could be
diagramed as follows: CHURCH----MISSION----CHURCH----
MISSION----CHURCH (etc. until Christ returns).

This is not speaking of multiplying new church denominations, but of extending the community of the King, which
structures itself in local churches, which then structures
their witness to others in missionary outreach. In this
way Christ's commission to evangelize the entire world can
be accomplished.

GUIDING PRINCIPLES IN RELATIONSHIPS

As we recognize that both the church denomination and
the mission agency are para-church organizations structured
for functional purposes to fulfill the Great Commission, we
realize that their relationship to each other is a dynamic
one. Their own maturing process and the changing context
around them produce tensions which need to be translated
into positive dynamics. The interaction of church and
mission makes evaluation and relational adjustments essential. To neglect this does as much harm as the parent-child
relation that does not change as the child matures. The
reciprocal effect of one on the other necessitates change
in relation: the father stimulates the child to mature;
the maturing child develops a different need to be met by
the father, as the child passes into adulthood.

As Winter observes, "Once the national church takes hold,
the task becomes more fascinating and delicate than ever, as
two Christian -- and culturally very different -- committees
enter into permanent symbiosis."[29]

With the studies we have had thus far in this book, we
should be able to make some practical deductions, not only
to reduce church-mission tensions, but more important, to
make possible the continued fulfilling of God's purpose in
this age.

1. A responsible church is able to govern, support, and
expand itself. The third factor must be included, or else
the first two become ends in themselves. Expansion or
propagation insures that the church is fulfilling Christ's
purpose through missionary witness. A responsible church
is able to stand on its own feet, to relate to its world,
to express and think through its convictions theologically
in the context of its society. Such maturity does not come
all at once. There is an adolescent stage when mistakes
are expected but the goal is in sight. Also the "sending
church" needs to apply these standards to itself as much as
to the "receiving church."

2. Any relationship of the mission which inhibits or denies
the responsible functioning of the church must be changed.
The mission's high visibility or its structure could, for
instance, usurp the leadership role of the church. Even as
the relation between a father and son must change if the
son is going to reach the goal of manhood which the father
has always had for his son, the parent-child relationship

must change to an adult-adult relationship. Such a relation is based on mutuality, with recognition of maturity on the part of both partners, not on the basis of one partner being weak or dependent on the other.

Although Paul had to write strongly as a spiritual father to the believers at Corinth, he took care not to dominate their faith.[30]

3. To avoid denying the church's responsibility as it matures, the mission must remove itself from all position of legislative authority over the church. There must be no foreign authoritative control over the national church.

When this transition takes place, the missionary's real authority is that which the apostle Paul had -- the authority of the teaching of the Word of God applied not by legislation but by the Holy Spirit. He used this authority for their edification and not destruction.[31] This is the strongest contribution a missionary can make, and he must not neglect it simply because he no longer has legislative authority. At the same time, his teaching gift should not be imposed by the mission, but should be recognized and welcomed by the church.

4. To make these relationship changes effectively, we must communicate with both the church and the mission, including the supporters of the mission, in order to help all concerned bring about attitudinal changes.

a. *The national church.* Many national Christians still have a colonial image of missions -- looking to them either as the paternal provider or as the imperial intruder. It is vitally important to help the national church understand the background of church-mission relations and the motives of the mission, because the church's future outlook on the gospel and her own mission outreach will be influenced by her understanding of the channel through which the gospel was brought to them. Paul implies this in his epistles.[32]

The church's readiness to be helped by the mission in the future, and the type of help the church feels she should receive will be influenced by her understanding of the previous role and motives of the mission.

b. The mission. To be able to change its relationship, the missionary body must understand the reasons for its previous relationships, the changes which are necessitated by new factors, and the future part which the mission can play in fulfilling its missionary mandate.

c. Supporters. It is also important that the supporting constituency of the mission should understand these factors, in order to stand with the mission in fulfilling its international role in partnership with a responsible national church.

d. Change should be seen as a continuing process, rather than an abrupt wrench. Church and mission relations should be a continuum of development.

5. The church of Jesus Christ is universal, and the structure of church-mission relations should be such that the gifts and calling of God's servants internationally may be used effectively under the leading of the Holy Spirit.

The church must not use the missionary as the cheapest source of labor -- which would amount to the prostitution of the missionary's calling and a lack of responsibility on the part of the church. If the church wants God to use the spiritual gifts of the expatriate missionary to help build up the body of Christ in the nation, it must recognize the following:

a. The missionary has a definite sense of the Holy Spirit's call upon his life. This call should not be an excuse for individual careerism on the part of the missionary, because it must be fulfilled within the context of God's purpose for His church. But the local church must recognize that the missionary would not be available in the first place had he not experienced a spiritual calling for the use of his gifts, and that calling may have been specific. (I know an Anglican missionary who has a calling to evangelize Hausa-speaking Muslims, and who applied to his church accordingly.) The church therefore must seek God's leading along with the missionary, and not arbitrarily assign him to just any post in order to avoid finding finance to employ a national.

Paul's ministry recognized this sense of specific call-ing. He felt he had a mandate to evangelize among gentiles, while Peter ministered among Jews (Eph. 3:7, 8). He was called to be a pioneer (Rom. 15:20) in distant parts

(II Cor. 10:16) -- to plant (I Cor. 3:6), and not build on
another's foundation (Rom. 15:20). He did not feel called
to baptize believers (I Cor. 1:17; 3:10). Yet he did not
disparage the work of others whose missionary calling was
different. He recognized the validity of Apollos' ministry
of "watering" (Acts 18:24-28; I Cor. 3:6).

b. There are two main categories of Christian workers in
mission service.

(1) There is the missionary whose gifts and calling are
distinctly evangelism and discipling. This missionary will
be greatly frustrated if the church does not recognize this,
and regards him simply as a body which can fill any post,
regardless of spiritual gifts and calling. This could be
called an *apostolic* type of missionary work.

(2) In this day of specialization and rapid travel, there
are also a number of Christian specialists who are very
happy to work with the church in another culture, in order
to help strengthen its corporate life (Eph. 4:11-16) so it
can fulfill its mandate to witness. In their own country
they would serve in their profession while being Christian
witnesses, and they are therefore happy to do so in another
country, in order to help make the church a more effective
witness. God blesses this type of witness and assistance,
whether it is through the agency of the national church, a
government department, or industry. This could be called a
diaconal type of missionary work (from *diakonos* -- one who
serves). Paul commends the Corinthians for their service
(II Cor. 9:13).

The indigenization of the work need not mean 100% of the
second group and no opportunity for the first group. True,
more of the second group may be needed as the church grows
in size and leadership than during the pioneering mission
days, but there should be continuing opportunity for the
first group as well, if the gifts within the body are to be
used properly.

Observing this distinction may help overcome the tension
which some missiologists see in the church's taking responsibility for the work. We have referred to Wagner's warning
about "the church development syndrome" and "the Babylonian
captivity of the Christian mission." When the motive of
the mission agency is to produce a church with a sense of
mission, then there will be room for expatriate missionaries
to evangelize and disciple under the leadership of the

missionary-minded church, even as there was under the
leadership of the foreign mission.

One limiting factor would be the attitudes of government
and the people. There are some countries where expatriates
are not allowed to witness publicly, and there are some
countries where direct evangelism by foreigners would block
the communication of the gospel because of its foreign
image. In such cases, missionaries with the gifts of evangelism and discipling can fulfill their calling through
helping the church with its missionary planning and its
preparation of national evangelists and missionaries.

To distinguish between the two types of Christian worker
does not imply that one is inferior or superior to the
other. Both types are urgently needed; both need opportunity for fulfilling the particular calling of the Spirit
upon their lives. For the national church to ignore this
would be a grave mistake.

c. The missionary has a responsibility to those who sent
him -- those who in response to the Holy Spirit "set apart"
the missionary and are giving of their material means to
enable him to serve the church. The church, too, is
responsible to the missionary's sending agency for the good
stewardship of the investment of person, time, and finance
represented in the missionary.

d. The missionary agency -- whether it is a church in
another land, or an organization through which a group of
churches or individuals support missionaries -- also has
its responsibilities to those who support the missionaries
seconded to the national church. As long as the national
church needs the missionary agency to recruit, provide, and
maintain personnel to serve under the church, the responsible church must recognize the responsible mission's
commitments to those who send forth personnel and finance.
The mission must not be turned into a "supply depot and
service agency."[33] It too is a responsible organization,
and the responsible church needs to work with it on a
responsible international level of mutual consultation and
planning.

6. Having recognized these principles, both the church and
mission can then mutually work out that functional relationship which will enable them to operate responsibly within
these realities. Unilateral demands and decisions in work-

ing out the relationship only deny responsible action and
cause the parties to treat each other as children.

There must be mutual respect for each other's position,
and mature negotiation on priorities and responsibilities.
The church is fully responsible for managing its affairs in
its own nation. Although each will lead in its own sphere,
in their working together one cannot dominate the other, or
be obsequious to the other, if the partnership is to be
built on responsible mutuality.

It should not be expected that any formula of church-
mission relationship will fit every situation. Church and
mission must develop their relationship together, led by the
Holy Spirit and acting on biblical principles. They must
consider the stage of development, the need, and the national context.

7. With the national church fully responsible within its
country, and the missionary agency fully responsible within
its country, what has evolved is a responsible international
partnership. The partnership functions in *mutuality*, but
not in *similarity* of role.

For instance, it may be argued that if the church has
authority (responsibility) over a ministry (e.g. a seminary), it must also take full financial responsibility --
the mission should not provide finance. Such reasoning
implies that both partners must have similar roles -- both
must have authority along with the same resources. However,
a partnership (whether in business, sports, or marriage) is
usually entered into because of the different strengths the
partners have, which together can comprise an effective
whole. And so while the church must take the responsibility
(authority) in order to be mature, its contribution to the
partnership will be different from the mission's contribution.

In developing a special project, for instance, the church
may have more manpower, and the mission more finance. This
is not speaking of pastoral and basic church support, for
which the church itself must be responsible if it is to be
a church. It refers to projects which the indigenous church
cannot yet finance but which Christians internationally can
assist with (as they would if the mission were still administratively responsible for them), without harming the self-
reliance and indigenous nature of the church.

Such international partnership projects must be the
result of mutual agreement on priorities, or else the
responsible partnership disintegrates. The missionary agency must not unilaterally impose a project on the church because of its ability to assist with funds, and the church
must not unilaterally impose a fund-raising project on the
missionary agency, whose unsuspecting supporters have not
had opportunity to weigh the priority with many other
urgent requests for help from all over the world.

8. While church and mission (or local church and overseas
church) form a "team" partnership internationally, the
relationship within the nation takes on deeper characteristics. One way of illustrating this would be by a marriage. Marriage is not really fusion, as understood in
ecclesiastical circles today. In fusion, one party completely disappears. In marriage, the two parties are made
one, but that oneness is based on the following facts:

a. The two usually assume one surname.

b. One member assumes the leadership.

c. The longer they live together, the more they think,
act, and look alike.

d. Nevertheless, the two maintain individual characteristics within the marriage relationship. By nature they
have individual characteristics which enable each to make a
special contribution to the marriage, thereby making a
wholeness which is a new entity in itself. A woman cannot
conceive a child by herself, and a man cannot give birth to
a baby. Because they are different by nature, through
marriage they can bring into existence a new life.

e. The husband and wife usually have different roles to
play in the household. There is division of duties --
which should result from mutual agreement rather than
legislation. There is a combining of strengths to aid
weaknesses on the part of both.

f. Although before marriage the single man and single
woman were complete individuals, once they have married
their new entity would immediately be incomplete without one
of the partners. The church of Jesus Christ is universal,
and no one has the authority to say that one part may not
help another.

g. A danger in such a mission-church relation is that the church may become reliant upon the mission. But in a healthy marriage, while there is interdependence, the partners are at all times able to "stand on their own feet."

h. When husband or wife fails in his/her responsibilities, the solution is not to separate and take another spouse, but to counsel with one another in love, until the partner becomes responsible. However, in some cases of personal shortcoming in a partner, the spouse may have to assume some responsibility of the partner to get the job done. This is not ideal and could be harmful to a marriage, but may become necessary.

i. The only scriptural basis for divorce is infidelity of a partner. However, even with infidelity, Scripture prefers correction, repentance, and forgiveness rather than divorce.

What relations do the relatives have?

The marriage illustration used above does not fit in every respect (for instance, need the mission-church "marriage" last "till death do us part"?), but it is useful especially to the Western mind in portraying a church-mission relationship. It avoids the possible paternalism of the father-son relationship, and yet portrays a working partnership on mutual respect and love.

Interestingly enough, however, some African leaders feel that the marriage illustration is not as culturally suitable as the father-son illustration.

"If you are talking of a Western marriage, the illustration is all right," ECWA leaders told me. "But the typical African marriage doesn't fit. The husband and wife can never work together as equals. To us, the father-son relationship is much more meaningful. A mature son can enter into partnership with his father, and even provide the leadership as the father grows older. Each contributes his own ability to the work: the father his wisdom, the son his strength."

The father-son relation certainly is a scriptural illustration. Missionary Paul used it in addressing Timothy and also in writing to local churches. To some, however, it can imply paternalism -- an attitude which must be avoided in every relationship at every stage. The father-son relationship does not mean it has to be father-child; it can be a relationship of adult father to adult son.

Another illustration I have used to show the transition from an authority role to a partnership role is the following story of two brothers, Audu and Samuel:

> Audu had been a trader for many years, even before the railway had come through to his village. He had started out by selling salt, sugar, and kerosene, and had slowly gained experience until he was able to build a large shop. He became well known.
>
> While Audu was struggling to develop his trading business, a younger brother was born and was named Samuel. Samuel went through elementary and secondary school, and while waiting to get a scholarship, started trading, too. However, Audu and Samuel had different ideas about what should be sold and how best to sell it. Audu was not always happy that his younger brother was trying to tell him how to do things. "He was not even born when I started trading," Audu said. "Now just because he has been to school, he thinks he knows what to do. He has not suffered as I have done in the early days when trading was so difficult. I have learned much by experience which he has never learned in school."
>
> Samuel was also unhappy with his older brother Audu. He felt that Audu's ways were definitely out of date. "After all, just because he was successful in the old days does not mean he knows how to trade in this modern day," Samuel said. "I have learned many things in school that he does not know, but he will not try them."
>
> As the two brothers sold in the market, Audu began to notice that his young brother still seemed strong after working all day. When Audu would become tired, he would wish for the strong arms of his younger brother. Then one day some people cheated Samuel, and he wished for the wisdom his older brother had

in such matters. After some time they realized that they really needed each other --
that each had a part to play. They worked
together more, and finally decided to combine
their shops. They put up a new sign,
"Brothers Trading Co. Ltd."

Now the brothers are thankful for each other.
Audu tells his friends what good ideas
Samuel has, and Samuel tells his friends how
experienced Audu is. The Brothers Trading
Co. Ltd. is now becoming better known than
Audu's shop was.[34]

In discussing church-mission relations, we have observed
that the mission assumes four different roles: pioneer,
parent (instruction), partner, participant (in which the
church leads). (See appendix G.) Once a stage is started,
it leads to the next stage. To maintain one stage too
long, or to refuse to move on to the next, causes frustration and eventual trouble. Each stage causes a different
relationship to be necessary in the next. The effectiveness of the relationship in each stage will depend on the
effectiveness in the previous stage. If the parent-child
relation was poor, the adult-adult relation will break
down.

I have found this (Appendix G) a useful diagram for discussing the changing dynamics of church-mission relations.
Both expatriates and nationals need to study it, to see the
end from the beginning, and how to get from start to finish.
It immediately reduces tension, because people see they are
not intended to stay in one stage forever. As they approach the next stage, they see the responsibilities and
are less inclined to jump into them hastily. They also
begin to understand reactions.

In one seminar attended by expatriates and nationals in
a Sahel country, we discussed the hostilities which may be
carried over from stage II to III, if the teacher- (or
parent-) child relations were poor. For years the missionaries had been puzzled by the church's reaction to anything
the mission suggested. In our seminar, a church leader
suddenly realized why there were tensions.

"This is exactly what is happening between the church
and mission!" he exclaimed. "The church is rejecting whatever the mission suggests and is even doing things to hurt

the mission, because of what happened in the early stages of the work -- not because of the missionaries who are here today."

Why do these hostilities develop? How can they be avoided? The closer church and mission work together, the more important it is to understand each other. In the next section we shall study the dynamics of working and living together.

STUDY QUESTIONS: CHAPTER 6

1. Discuss the nature of the church and its task, noting the views of Mellis and Snyder. How will our understanding of the biblical nature of the church reduce mission-church tensions?

2. How is the scriptural reconciliation of mission-church tensions found in the relationship to Christ?

3. Discuss the eight guiding principles of mission-church relations. How can you apply these in your Christian work?

4. Identify and discuss the four stages of developing relations between a mission and church (Appendix G). At which stage is your own organization (or one in which you are interested), and what problems or needs do you observe?

NOTES: CHAPTER 6

1. James Wong, "Missions from the Third World," quoted by Orlando Costas in *The Church and Its Mission* (Wheaton, IL: Tyndale House, 1974), p. xiii.

2. S.O. Odunaike, in sermon at the closing service at FESTAC, Lagos, Nigeria, Feb. 13, 1977.

3. *Afroscope* (Nairobi, Kenya: AEAM, Dec. 1978).

4. Gerald O. Swank, *Frontier Peoples of Central Nigeria* (South Pasadena, CA: William Carey Library, 1977).

5. P.J. Johnstone, *Operation World* (Bromley, Kent, UK: STL Publications, 1978), p. 195.

6. Word of Life Conference Report, Addis Ababa, Jan. 1979.

7.   Panya Baba, in *Asian Missions Advance*,   Seoul, Korea,
     p. 13.

8.   Asia Missions Association, Seoul, Korea, Sept. 1, 1975.

9.   Asian Leadership Conference on Evangelism (ALCOE),
     report of Nov. 1-10, 1978 meeting in Singapore.

10. *Christianity Today*, March 10, 1978, p. 66.

11. *Missionary News Service* (Wheaton, IL, Nov. 1, 1978),
     p. 1.

12. The Devlali Letter, Item 10, All India Congress on
     Mission and Evangelization, Devlali, sponsored by the
     Evangelical Fellowship of India, January 12-19, 1977.

13. *The Challenger*, May 1978, reported in *Latin America
     Pulse* (Wheaton, IL: EMIS, Dec. 1978).

14. *Church Growth Bulletin* (Santa Clara, CA: Overseas
     Crusades), January 1979, p. 249.

15. J.H. Bavinck, *An Introduction to the Science of
     Missions*, p. 208.

16. See "How SIM Helped ECWA Develop Its Mission,"
     Appendix E.

17. Charles J. Mellis, *Committed Communities* (South
     Pasadena, CA: William Carey Library, 1976), p. 81.

18. Howard A. Snyder, *The Community of the King* (Downers
     Grove, IL: InterVarsity Press, 1977), p. 161.

19. C. Peter Wagner, *Frontiers in Missionary Strategy*,
     p. 176.

20. Orlando Costas, *The Church and Its Mission*, op. cit.,
     p. 171.

21. Ralph Winter, in *Church-Mission Tensions*, op. cit.,
     p. 139.

22. Orlando Costas, op. cit., pp. 171, 172.

23. Edward C. Pentecost, "Time for Faith Boards to Change Goals and Strategies?" (Wheaton, IL: EMQ, Oct. 1976), pp. 211-217.

24. Wilhelm Andersen, *Towards a Theology of Missions,* op. cit., p. 48.

25. N. Goodall, (Ed.) *Missions Under the Cross,* op. cit., p. 190.

26. George W. Peters, *A Biblical Theology of Missions* (Chicago, IL: Moody Press, 1972), p. 195.

27. Andersen, *Towards a Theology of Missions,* p. 59.

28. Peters, *A Biblical Theology of Mission,* p. 200.

29. Ralph Winter, *Say Yes to Mission* (Downers Grove, IL: InterVarsity Press, 1970).

30. II Cor. 1:24.

31. II Cor. 10:8.

32. I Thes. 1:5-8 with Chapter 2.

33. George Peters, "Mission-Church Relations Overseas" in *Missions in Creative Tension,* p. 200.

34. W. Harold Fuller, "Church-Mission Relations," a paper presented at an ECWA D.C.C. Leaders Seminar, Nov. 3-6, 1975.

7

The
Crucible Of Culture

"We felt sorry for the Christians in --------," an ECWA
leader told me. He had just returned from a pan-African
conference in another part of the continent. "They seemed
shocked by our traditional dress. They thought it was
Muslim. But they wore Western clothes all the time. Of
course we sometimes did for a change, but they didn't seem
to have any national robes. They acted as if Christians
had to wear suits and dresses. It seems as if they have
thrown away all their culture."

Therein lies a very basic tension in church-mission
relations -- not in whether one should wear a robe or a
suit, but the whole question of culture. Clothing is an
apt illustration.

The local body of Christ, we learned in the last chapter,
must be a body on the move in fulfilling God's will to
reconcile man to himself. Reaching that objective is going
to take "the body" into other cultures. And in another
culture, "the body" will need to consider its "garments" if
it is going to enter the life of the culture.

*Cross-cultural communication is the essence of mission-
ary work.* We can pass the gospel on to our own people in
our own cultural terms -- and they will likely understand.
That is local evangelism.

But two thirds of the world's population probably will
not be reached that way, because there aren't sufficient
Christians in their culture to reach them all before they
die.[1] So they must be reached by Christians who will cross
over into their culture. Those cross-cultural evangelists
are usually called missionaries.

Because of the cross-cultural factor inherent in missions, the majority of tensions between missions and
churches center around culture. There are many excellent
books on the subject of culture, so we shall not study it
in depth in this book. However, we need to highlight the
reasons for cultural tensions and how to reduce them.

"Authenticity"

Culture is so much a part of us that it is a highly
emotional issue. Nations will go to war to defend their
culture. "Authenticity" has been the rallying cry in
several African states seeking to rediscover their identity
in traditions after centuries of abuse by internal and
external forces.

Preservation of culture is important to a nation's self-
respect. Scripture recognizes the place of culture. But
it also distinguishes between customs that honor the living
God and those which do not.

The Republic of Chad provided an example of this
distinction. In a nationwide authenticity campaign, President Ngarta Tombalbaye decreed that every citizen must
take the initiation rites of the traditional religion. He
told Christians that the rites had nothing to do with religion, but were a patriotic duty. Many Christians saw them
differently -- the rites included sacrificing to the
spirits, and an animistic "spiritual rebirth." They refused to undergo the initiation rite on religious, not
cultural, grounds.

Many endured persecution, including imprisonment and
torture; hundreds were killed, including thirteen pastors
in a group.[2]

Byang Kato, AEAM General Secretary, planned to visit
Chad to explain to the President the deep concern of
Christians throughout Africa. By the time he reached Chad,
Tombalbaye had been overthrown. The new military rulers
asked Kato to return to give instruction on the scriptural

teaching about culture.[3] Regrettably, Kato died in a
drowning accident before he could.

While many Chadian Christians (and Muslims) resisted the
animistic rites, there were others who alleged that the
opposition was fomented by expatriate missionaries who had
come to destroy the nation's culture. In fact, there was
deep tension between some missionaries and churches over
the issue. Most missionaries withdrew voluntarily or were
expelled (although after Tombalbaye's death they were
welcomed back).

Who is changing culture?

The emotion-laden allegation of changing customs is not
new for Christ's disciples. The Jews stirred up an hyster-
ical mob to stone Stephen to death by charging: "We heard
him say that this Jesus of Nazareth will tear down the
temple and change all the customs which have come down to
us from Moses!" (Acts 6:14).

The charge that missionaries have destroyed traditional
culture is a popular and almost universal allegation and
needs examination.

It is true the early missionaries, not equipped with the
anthropological and sociological insights which we have
today (and which have in part arisen from missionary research in other cultures through the years), often made
great errors in evaluating local culture. This was particularly true of Roman Catholic missionary work during the
medieval period.

However, even after missionaries became more discerning
of cultural implications, the new converts themselves reacted strongly against using traditional instruments or
tunes for worshiping their new-found Savior, when they had
previously used the same instruments and tunes in drunken
orgies to placate evil spirits. The initial reaction of
new converts was in many cases stronger than that of missionaries, who did not realize all the significance of
traditions. It takes several generations for an object of
culture to be dissociated from its religious past and develop simply an aesthetic or artistic meaning, allowing it
to be used in Christian worship. An uneducated Nigerian
told me he wondered why missionaries kept fetish masks in
their houses -- not realizing that the missionaries valued
the carvings as art objects, not religious totems.

On the other hand, far from trying to destroy culture,
some missionaries sought to identify themselves closely
with it and to preserve it.   Hudson Taylor was notable in
this, wearing Chinese dress and a "pigtail." Amy
Carmichael, who founded the Dohnavur Fellowship in India to
rescue children from being sold into temple immorality,
followed this pattern. My sister serving with Dohnavur has
always worn an Indian sari, lived in an Indian house with
no Western furnishings, sat on the floor to eat her curry
and other Indian food, and not worn jewelry (even a ring or
a watch) in order to fit in with her Indian "Bible women"
colleagues.

Dohnavur's work illustrates the gospel's two-fold approach to culture. The missionaries have preserved the
culture in worship and living wherever possible; however,
where a custom contravened God's law of sexual purity, they
strongly opposed the custom. Their stand has since been
endorsed by the Indian government, which has banned the
sale of children into temple service.

Personally, I am thankful that the gospel changed many
of the customs of my forefathers; I also realize that the
Industrial Revolution, wars, and trade with other nations
have changed my culture as much as the gospel did. For
instance, the numbering system on these pages is not traditional European but comes from Arabic! (Traditional
European numbering would use Roman numerals.)

Critics of missions seem to forget that culture is not
static, but constantly adapts, and that Third World cultures would have changed through contact with other cultures even if Christianity had never come. Certainly Islam
has radically changed animist cultures in several African
countries. In China, the Maoist "Red Guards" destroyed
more Chinese culture in a year than missionaries had done
in a century. Stephen Neill states:

> The idea that cultures can be preserved intact
> is just a dream, even if missionaries do more
> than anybody else to preserve the structures of
> these people's lives. The Tahitian Bible,
> completed in 1829, really saved the Tahitian
> language, and with it, the Tahitian culture.
> Almost certainly the language would have been
> replaced by French or English.[4]

More recently, some governments have opposed the work of
Wycliffe Bible Translators, because Bible translation helps
keep alive the dying cultures of minority tribes. Some
governments look on this as a threat to national unity,
since it is their policy to assimilate small linguistic
groups into the official language. In these cases, culture
is being changed by the government, not missionaries.

Foreign trappings

In fact, missionary zeal to keep the gospel as indigenous as possible sometimes backfired. Early SIM missionaries in Nigeria strongly opposed the introduction of Western clothing and Western language. They did not want the
people to associate being a Christian with taking on the
trappings of a foreign culture.

Their fears were not unfounded. Samuel Crowther, up-
rooted from his own culture through the slave trade,
opposed nationalist sentiment and used the English language,
English clothing, and the English *Book of Common Prayer*.

> He believed Western civilization would raise the
> cultural, economic, social, and above all the
> religious standards of Africa. This view, how-
> ever, was not shared by the new generation which
> had absorbed the awakening spirit of African
> nationalism. They gave Crowther and his African
> colleagues the nickname "Black Englishmen."
> The African minister Henry Johnson was sensitive
> to this criticism and wrote, after a visit to
> Onitsha (Nigeria) in 1877: "I hope we shall
> bear in mind the fact that the Christianity of
> Onitsha will grow weak and sickly, and that it
> will be devoid of all inherent vitality, if
> English be allowed to supersede the native
> tongue."[5]

Western dress and use of English were also foreign ideas
identified with many of the worst elements accompanying
foreign trade. Such vices as swearing, smoking, drunken-
ness, and prostitution were associated with swaggering
young clerks wearing suits and displaying their English as
they followed the railway lines from the coast into the
north. In fact, the railway itself became so identified
with destruction of tradition that one Nigerian chief (the
Chief of Oyo) refused to have the rail line pass through

his kingdom, which was the shorter route; it had to be
diverted eastward to Oshogbo.

Because many missionaries had seen the great harm done
to young Christians through rooting them out of their culture, they went to the other extreme and opposed Western
clothing and language. However, as the youth saw the advantages of education, they could not understand this ban,
and misjudged the motives. It was the colonial era, and
the attitude of some missionaries reflected this. Convinced
that the missionaries really felt superior, the youth concluded that they wanted to keep them as their fathers were,
in ignorance and inferiority. Some missionaries were therefore blamed for holding back progress and keeping the youth
from the best things of life.

The missionary motive was commendable but short-sighted
and completely misunderstood. It became the source of
bitterness which persists in the memories of many older
nationals today.

Therefore it is doubly ironic that the culture-conscious
generation of today turns around and accuses the missionaries of destroying their culture. The previous generation
had accused missionaries of trying to keep them in an
inferior position by *maintaining* their culture! The cultural call to wear traditional garments today is what many
missionaries tried to get the early Christians to do, and
at the time they were bitterly criticized for "holding the
nationals back." Today they are blamed by some anthropol-
ogists for introducing Western culture and causing nationals
to leave their traditions.

The schismatic reaction

However, it is true that the new churches in general
took on the form and structure of the foreign missionary's
church, with resultant cultural frustrations.

In the early history of the church in Nigeria, there
were several instances of revolt against the established
structure of the denomination from overseas. The Anglicans,
Presbyterians, Methodists, and Baptists all experienced
secessions or revolts, which J.F.A. Ajayi[6] calls "a basic
conflict between the old and the new." Because there were
no indigenous precedents for church forms, the early
denominational missionaries naturally expected their converts to adopt the church forms the missionaries knew.

However, the new believers chafed under these structures.

E. Bolaji Idowu, now patriarch of the Methodist Church
of Nigeria, defines an indigenous church as meaning "that
the church should bear the unmistakable stamp of the fact
that she is the church of God in Nigeria. It should be no
longer an outreach or a colony of Rome, Canterbury, or West-
minster Central Hall in London, or the vested interest of
some European or American missionary board. . . at the same
time, she should be a church the keynote of whose life is
the lordship of Jesus Christ, the church in which in all
things He is preeminent . . . [having] the unflinching
faithfulness of the church to her Lord in her conscious
preservation of 'the faith once delivered to the saints.'"[7]

Idowu adds that "to speak of an indigenous church is not
to ask that every mark of 'foreignness' attached to her
should be removed," because that would be "to deny herself
the spiritual tonic 'which the communion of the saints'
affords."[8]

Idowu points out the need for an indigenous church to
have liberty in devising its structure in administration,
liturgy, vestments, and so forth. John Wesley observed this
same principle nearly 200 years ago when he prevented schism
among Methodists in America by stating in 1784: "As our
American brethren are now totally disentangled, both from
the state and the English hierarchy, we dare not entangle
them again, neither with the one or the other. They are
now at full liberty, simply to follow the Scripture and the
primitive church. And we judge it best that they should
stand fast in the liberty wherewith God has so strangely
made them free."[9]

The uncomfortable feeling of national Christians in
Western-style church structures has already been cited as
one of the causes for the phenomenon of separatist churches
in Africa, even though their leaders proudly wear Western-
type vestments! David Barrett estimated the number of
schismatic churches to be six thousand with over seven
million adherents. Their number is expected to double by
the end of this century.[10]

While at first the movements were seen simply as a
reaction to foreign missionary work, further analysis revealed far deeper and complex causes, including historical,
political, ethnic (tribe and clan), sociological, and other

non-religious factors. Religious and specifically theological or doctrinal disagreements are seen as only minor
causes.

The tendency to fragment or splinter is not confined to
churches, and probably would have taken place to some
extent if foreign missions had not been involved. However,
church-mission tensions certainly have been one of the
factors in some cases. These are the tensions we are
interested in examining here.

> Missions were preoccupied with and often over-
> whelmed by their task of church building, and
> had little time for any real encounter with
> indigenous beliefs and systems of thought, which
> were in any case expected to disappear in favor
> of European culture and religion.[11]

Barrett's search for a common cause of the tension
amounts to an indictment which all missionaries, whether
black or white, should consider seriously:

> The root cause common to the entire movement of
> independency, therefore, may be seen in this
> one aspect of culture clash: a failure in
> sensitivity, the failure of missions at one
> small point to demonstrate consistently the
> fullness of the biblical concept of love as
> sensitive understanding toward others as
> equals, the failure to study or understand
> African society, religion, and psychology in
> any depth, together with a dawning African
> perception from the vernacular Scriptures of
> the catastrophic nature of this failure and
> of the urgent necessity to remedy it in order
> that Christianity might survive on African
> soil.[12]

Idowu gave his own analysis of the cause of separatist
movements in a series of radio talks while he was Professor
of Religious Studies at the University of Ibadan. He saw
them as essentially reaction against "the sterility of the
church's liturgical life" which "had already petrified into
a false orthodoxy." Proliferation arose from "various
factors ranging from the motive of evangelism to that of
unwillingness to accept discipline and a desire to build up
a kingdom on one's own."[13]

Idowu pointed out that the separatist churches (1) had a
fresh and appealing unconventionality, with freedom of
expression; (2) were led by Nigerians whose manner appealed
to the masses; (3) supplied a felt need for religion to be
efficacious in every part of their lives (and therefore
these movements were usually supplemented with traditional
religious belief).

> The phenomenon had a message for the church in
> Nigeria . . . . An arid, sterile church, a
> church which is failing to nourish her children
> and satisfy their spiritual yearnings, a church
> which is not speaking and ministering to the
> needs of the flock of God, is a failure; a
> church which is imprisoned within a foreign
> structure and shackled with foreign traditions
> is bound eventually to lose her appeal and
> attractions.[14]

Another Nigerian church leader, Seth Kale, Bishop of
Lagos, likewise saw a spiritual dimension to the problem of
the church as a whole, but arising from human desires
rather than foreign "shackles":

> If there is anything wrong with the church in
> Nigeria today, it is that it pays more attention
> to the external rather than the internal. They
> import more fanciful and colorful robes and new
> designs for vestments than new evangelistic
> zeal.[15]

The journalist-historian Moorhouse sees another cause.
He states that most of the schismatic members in Nigeria
came from the Methodists and Anglicans. A number were
strangely influenced by American Christian sects. These
did not send missionaries to Africa, but "were prolific in
their distribution of propaganda." Their type of religion
seemed more in keeping with the African temperament than
that of the European missionaries.

> In all the independent church movements that
> were to creep across Africa in the first half
> of the 20th century, two common denominators
> were present. One was the adherence to some
> form of belief in the God of the Christians.
> The other was a strong sense of African racial
> identity, a reaction against various manifes-
> tations of white racial superiority. Beyond

these two points the differences were very
often wide, emphasizing the prophetic quality
of the leader, sometimes being more obviously
the emotional outlet for suppressed nationalist
feelings than others, frequently owing something of both religious flavor and racial
pride to the influence upon Africa of the
United States. Where an independent movement
was not stimulated to action by a sense of
brotherhood with American Negroes, whose own
morale was fortified by feelings of kinship
with restless Africans, it was often given a
sense of religious direction by the example
and the propaganda of various American evangelists and organizations, whose style of Christian
worship was much more in tune with the nature
of Africans than anything a European missionary
can ever exhibit.[16]

Other reasons for the splintering process have been
reaction to church discipline over such matters as polygamy
and membership in secret societies, and the desire to incorporate traditional fetish with Christian worship. Most
of the schismatic groups are syncretistic.

The Bible judges culture

Evangelicals have spoken of this tension between
Christianity and culture. Byang Kato very ably treated the
question of cultural tension with the gospel in *African
Cultural Revolution and the Christian Faith*.[17]

Gottfried Osei-Mensah, a Ghanaian who has pastored a
church in Kenya and is an executive of the World Evangelical
Fellowship, told the AEAM Theological Consultation, Limuru,
1974:

Three things may be said about Christianity and
culture:

1. The culture of sinful man, insofar as it
enshrines his cherished ideals, beliefs, and
practices, his way of life, is not neutral,
but fallen. There can be therefore no "wholesale," uncritical adoption of any culture by
Christianity (i.e. by the church). We cannot
go back and say, "This is our heritage," and
then bring it out wholesale into the church.

If we do that, we will run the danger of
syncretism, as was the case particularly in
the second century church.

2. Even traditions derived from God's
revelation, God's Word, may become corrupted
by sinful man (see Mark 7:8-13). Compare the
dogmas of the Roman Catholic Church. Man has
the sinful tendency to add to or to subtract
from the revelation of God in Scripture.
Every ideal, belief, or practice, therefore,
must be brought to the judgment of Scripture.

3. Culture is not static but evolving. There
is something dynamic about culture. We find
that even language is constantly changing.
Resistance to a higher ethical standard, or
the revival of a degenerate practice (under
the guise of authenticity!) is part and parcel
of man's self-assertion against God. If we
are going to dig up some dirty things from
the past and say, "Now that is authentic
African! So let's bring that in," when over
the years some higher ethical standards have
been brought to our view, there is nothing
noble about it. We are only asserting ourselves against God. It is part of our
rebellious attitude toward God.[18]

William Ofori-Atta, a Ghanaian lawyer and Bible teacher
who was a Presidential candidate in 1979, states:

The majority of Ghanaians have accepted
Christianity in its outward form, but their
inward spirit is still ruled by the attitudes
and outlook of the old culture. . . . For
conversion to the Christian faith to be more
than superficial, the Christian church should
come to grips with traditional beliefs and
practices and with the world view that these
beliefs and practices imply . . . . Biblical
Christianity must, by reason of its nature
and mission, come into conflict with culture
wherever it is introduced.[19]

Ofori-Atta, who is from a chieftaincy line and has
studied his nation's culture in depth, goes on to explain
why an evangelical could not condone use of a certain type

of drum in church worship -- the drum is made from wood from
a sacred tree, and fetish ceremony is connected with manu-
facturing it.

The Lagos Christian Graduates Fellowship was very out-
spoken at the time of the Second World Black and African
Cultural Festival, 1977, in a pamphlet, *Return to Origin:*

> In an avowed return to origin, it is obvious
> that any cultural trait that encourages
> primitiveness in a country that wants to take
> its place in an advancing civilization must be
> dispensed with.

While decrying such evils as nakedness, human sacrifice,
and abuse of women, the article also lists good cultural
qualities, and asks:

> What is the answer to all these decaying good
> qualities of the African culture? Can we in
> the cultural revival revive these good aspects
> of our culture, or shall we leave them to die
> off? The answer is in the return of man to
> his origin. The origin of man is not culture,
> culture was evolved after man himself had
> originated. The origin of man is God. The
> return of man to God is the teaching and con-
> cern of Christianity.
>
> Christianity explains how man, originally made
> in the image and with the purity of God, debased
> himself to a level where his thoughts became
> nothing but evil. It also explains how through
> the atoning death of Jesus Christ man can be
> reconciled to God. Any man reconciled to God
> becomes a new creature. The Bible says in II
> Cor. 5:17, "Therefore, if any man be in Christ,
> he is a new creature: old things are passed
> away; behold, all things are become new." In
> becoming a new creature, he is purified in body,
> in mind, in soul, and in spirit. He becomes
> the best of every culture in which he finds
> himself.[20]

SUMMARY

In this chapter we have seen that cultural tensions are at the heart of mission-church tensions because the gospel communication is crossing cultural lines. Missionaries have sometimes misunderstood the significance of culture, and the church has also misunderstood the motives of missionaries at times. Reaction to foreign culture in the church has been one of the causes of schism, which has also been linked with syncretistic tendencies in the name of culture.[21] The final authority in the life and practice of Christians and the church must not be culture (foreign or indigenous), but the rule of the Bible. It is the judge of every culture.

Having established the importance of culture in our relations, in the next chapter we shall look at some of the causes of tension in the daily interaction of missionary and national. Later in chapter 11, we shall look at ECWA as a case study of a national church seeking to overcome cultural tensions in its own missionary outreach.

STUDY QUESTIONS: CHAPTER 7

1. Why is cross-cultural communication the essence of missionary work? Define culture (see appendix A).

2. What tensions may arise because of bicultural misunderstandings in missionary work?

3. What is the evangelical attitude to culture and the Bible? Discuss the implications to aspects of your own culture.

NOTES: CHAPTER 7

1. Ralph D. Winter, *The Grounds for a New Thrust in World Mission* (South Pasadena, CA: William Carey Library, 1977), p. 2 etc.

2. W. Harold Fuller, *Christianity Today*, Nov. 14, 1974.

3. Byang H. Kato, "Promising Future for the Church in Chad," report to AEAM, May 1975.

4. Stephen Neill, *Decision*, October 1976, p. 4.

5. Beyerhaus and Lefever, *The Responsible Church and the Foreign Mission,* p. 69.

6. J.F.A. Ajayi, *Christian Missions in Nigeria,* p. 255.

7. E. Bolaji Idowu, *Towards an Indigenous Church,* Literature Department, Methodist Church, Nigeria, 1973. (First published OUP, 1965).

8. *Ibid,* pp. 11, 12.

9. Lars Qualben, *History of the Christian Church,* p. 538.

10. D.B. Barrett, *Schism and Renewal in Africa* (Nairobi: Oxford University Press, 1968), p. 265.

11. *Ibid,* p. 156.

12. *Ibid,* p. 156.

13. Idowu, op. cit., pp. 11, 12.

14. *Ibid,* p. 12.

15. Seth Kale, *Sunday Times,* Lagos, Nigeria, June 16, 1974.

16. Geoffrey Moorhouse, *The Missionaries,* pp. 313, 314.

17. Byang H. Kato, *African Cultural Revolution and the Christian Faith* (Jos, Nigeria: Challenge Publications, 1976), p. 56.

18. G. Osei-Mensah, *Perception,* (Nairobi: AEAM, August, 1977).

19. William Ofori-Atta, "Evangelization and Ghanaian Culture," paper given at the Ghana Congress on Evangelization, August 1977.

20. *Return to Origin,* Lagos Christian Graduates Fellowship, PMB 3037, Surulere, Nigeria, 1977.

21. For a thorough treatment of this topic, see Tokunboh Adeyemo, *Salvation in African Tradition* (Nairobi, Kenya: Evangel Publishing House, 1979).

8

Tension Points

"I had no idea that southern Nigerians thought so differently from me until I went to school in the south and made a big mistake," Simon Ibrahim, ECWA General Secretary, told missionaries at a conference where they were discussing turning over responsibility for the mission's work to the church. Ibrahim, from the north of Nigeria, was illustrating cultural tension points in church-mission relations.

"I was put in charge of roasting a goat for supper. So I skinned it before putting it on the fire. The school prefect gave me a severe reprimand. Why had I ruined the meat? How could I do such a stupid thing as skinning the goat before roasting it? I got off punishment only by pleading ignorance and promising never to make such a mistake again. I didn't know that the local people roasted their goats with the skin on!"

Many nationals have never moved from their own tribe, and therefore do not understand that another tribe may have a different set of cultural values and be perfectly right in their own sight. A visitor is therefore sometimes simply tolerated, sometimes resented, but rarely understood.

If nationals can live in the same country without understanding basic cultural differences affecting behavior, how much less will national pastors understand why missionaries from another race behave as they do! They may not even see the need to understand; to them there is only one right way

to behave. A person who has not lived in an alien culture
may not be able to imagine how different people can be in
their basic attitudes to life. Not realizing that, he may
believe a person of another culture acts the way he does
because of hatred or superiority.

So those who have become biculturally aware need to take
the initiative in promoting understanding. Unfortunately,
very often the national is left to continue misunderstanding, and if it were not for his patience and God's grace,
resentment would make cooperation between missionary and
national impossible.

Logically, expatriate missionaries should be the ones to
help bridge the gap of cultural misunderstanding. They
have crossed from culture A to culture B; they have passed
through the culture shock of realizing that there exists
another culture with a complete system of thinking different from their own. The person who has not left his own
culture has not gone through this shock; he tends to
evaluate the foreigner's actions and judge his motives from
the standpoint of his own value system -- not from the
standpoint of the foreigner's value system, which he has
never experienced (see diagram 8A). He doesn't understand
how cultural differences can affect behavior.

Diagram 8A: **Promoting cross-cultural understanding**

Culture A   **Culture B**

Person A goes from culture A to culture
B. He is aware of the two cultures and
must take the initiative in promoting
understanding. He evaluates person B
from B's cultural standpoint.

Person B does not leave his own culture, and is unaware that a complete
cultural system different from his own
exists. Person B tends to judge A's actions from B's own cultural standpoint.
Misunderstanding arises.

(W. Harold Fuller, SIM, 1980)

Understanding a culture is not the same as observing it, however. An expatriate missionary may be frustrated, critical, and cause great misunderstanding in another culture because he does not understand the value system behind it. The same can happen to a national visiting the missionary's country. He can see the different way of life and yet resent it because he does not understand it.

Enrique Guang, a Latin-American educator, psychologist, and theologian, describes the problem:

> Missionaries think they know us, but I think they know little of us. Our anthropology, sociology, psychology are a world apart from North America's. And unless an effort is made to know these deeply, missionary work will continue as practiced . . . regardless of results, as beating the air (I Cor. 9:26). To know how a man lives, thinks, feels, reacts, why he reacts in a given manner, what values he possesses and how he uses them, isn't contrary to divine leading. Rather, it makes for effective communication of the gospel, it makes it easier to reach goals, it gives an "in the meantime" urgency to the work. Paul did know the man in the area where he worked and knew how to become all things to all men, that he might by all means save some. Interpreting this anthropologically, it means to know and identify with people in the area of missionary work.[1]

Ibrahim gave helpful advice to SIM missionaries who were wondering how they could identify: "Overcoming tension is not done by trying to become like each other. I'll never be a white man, even if I wear a suit all the time, and you'll never be a black man, even by wearing a robe. The way to overcome culture tensions is to understand and respect each other's culture."

Understanding each other works both ways. Victor Musa, ECWA Church Growth Secretary, wrote while studying in America: "I discovered I was making a grave mistake in judging people's motives before I really got to know them. Whenever I set aside my pride and initiated discussion, I found that a white man's face did not show his heart often. Even the stone-faced were concerned, humble, and loving."

At one time I felt, in some frustration, that missionaries and nationals could never really understand each
other. Just when we thought we did, some new tension would
arise, revealing a whole new area of misunderstanding. As
the church took over, they would be responsible for policies
-- so why try to explain the past? I concluded it was
better to forget it and move on to the future.

Then I observed that misunderstanding of the past
affected current attitudes and made barriers between us,
hindering future cooperation. In fact, it could affect the
church's attitude to the whole concept of outreach.

So I decided it was worth it for missionaries and
nationals to take time to understand each other. I saw a
minor illustration when I was drinking coffee with a group
of Africans at the International Congress on World Evangelization in Lausanne, Switzerland. My companions were
shocked to see delegates throwing their disposable plastic
cups in a large garbage can. Those cups would have been
valuable in their countries. The Congress was discussing
the need for resources for world evangelism, and was advo-
cating a simpler life style for Christians. Then why such
waste -- why not wash the cups and use them again? That
can full of plastic cups made the Congress pleas seem
hypocritical.

It took us a while to discuss the difference in the
economy of industrialized Switzerland and labor-intensive
Africa -- that it would cost more to pay for washing the
cups than the cups were worth. Using disposable cups *was*
a simpler life style in Switzerland. If the cups had been
saved and washed, it would have cost the Congress money
that could be used to promote evangelism. Happiness
returned to the faces of my friends; their impression of
the Congress improved.

Let us look at some of the cultural values that produce
tension in daily work.

Customs of etiquette

Almost imperceptible cultural differences can cause
great misunderstanding. For instance, many a new missionary has thought a national child to be dishonest because in
some African cultures children are taught not to look
directly at adults when talking to them, whereas in Western culture, downcast eyes during a conversation may

indicate an attempt to evade or hide something.

Traditionally, no African bride would gaze into her
husband-to-be's face, but Ibrahim points out that an
English hymn translated into Hausa states: "The bride eyes
not her garment, but her dear bridegroom's face."[2]

The North American habit of greeting with a hasty "Hi!"
instead of spending time exchanging lengthy greetings has
been misunderstood by many an Asian or African as a lack of
interest or friendliness. With the colonial era in mind,
the national can easily believe that the hurried greeting
really indicates that the white man feels he is superior.

A misunderstanding in the office of a Christian organization in Ghana provides an illustration. The Ghanaian
office staff said that the missionary office manager did
not love them because when he arrived at work in the morn-
ing, he rushed right into his office and sat at his desk
without greeting them properly. On the other hand, the
expatriate office manager, conscious of the donations from
Christians making the work possible, probably felt that the
Ghanaian staff were not faithfully using the Lord's time
by their prolonged greetings to each other before starting
work. So national and expatriate felt that the other was
not a very good Christian because of misunderstanding a
very minor aspect of each other's culture.

There are other customs of etiquette, minor in themselves, which can convey a strong negative message. I may
invite an African pastor to my house, when he arrives ask
him if he would like a cold drink before the meal, tell my
wife the meal is delicious, and profusely thank our guest
for coming while we shake his hand at the door as he
leaves. I may feel I have shown my sincere love for my
friend; I have acted just as I would with a guest in my own
land.

But my African guest may go away convinced I don't like
him, and that the invitation was only a cover-up for my
hostility. Otherwise, why would I set a time and date for
him to visit, instead of letting him drop in any time?
Why didn't I put a drink before him instead of asking what
he'd like -- obviously I didn't want to give him one, so
he replied,"No thank you." What was the problem between
my wife and me, that I had to tell her the food was
delicious? And why didn't I walk down the street with my
guest when he was leaving, instead of shaking hands at the

door? I must have been glad to see him go. Yet I
hypocritically bared my teeth in a big smile as he left!

The next Sunday at church, I would congratulate myself
on improved church-mission relations!

Major differences of viewpoint

If such minor matters can cause misunderstanding, think
of the major differences of time-orientation versus event-
orientation, or of a dichotomistic versus a holistic viewpoint, as found in Western and Eastern cultures.

How do a national pastor and an expatriate missionary
work together on problems when the pastor's culture has
taught him it is a sin to report someone else's wrongdoing,
and the missionary has been taught it is a sin to keep
silent about wrongdoing?

What happens when a missionary has been taught that every
coin must be carefully accounted for and money designated to
one pocket must not be used for another pocket; but the
pastor has been raised with the holistic concept of the
extended family, where anything belongs to anyone in need
and money given for one purpose may be used for another
purpose?

Tensions have arisen because of different values and
priorities which pastors and missionaries have had --
depending on whether they are church-centric or mission-
centric. Most pastors can understand the value of something
tangible belonging to the church -- like a dispensary, a
bookshop, or a school. If the missionary works in one of
these, the pastors and church members are happy -- the missionary is contributing to the success of what visibly
belongs to the church.

The problem comes with a missionary who tries to fulfill
a wider vision outside the church institutions. One missionary lady spent all her time selling Christian literature
-- often in the heat of the day in the marketplaces and army
camps. Her distribution of Bibles and other Christian
literature was phenomenal -- much more than the local bookshop. Yet some local people felt that her work was useless,
and that she was unnecessarily occupying some of the
buildings on the compound which could have been used by the
church.

Another missionary taught Bible Knowledge in government schools, instructing children who had come into the big city from rural Christian families, and who would have been prey to anti-Christian philosophies and religions. Yet the local church was very cold to him, feeling he was not really helping the church because he was not working in a church institution.

In both of these cases, the problem was not hostility against a colonial mentality on the part of the missionary, because both missionaries had the happiest personal relations with Africans. Both of them personally cared for needy African children, and had nationals living in their homes from time to time. The tension was caused by different priorities and values in the work.

"The average pastor's concept of a good missionary," says Simon Ibrahim, "is one who will personally work for him in his church. He can't understand how the missionary is doing anything worthwhile to build up the church by ministering in government institutions and selling gospel literature in an army camp. But the trouble is that many pastors are completely ignorant of what their own church work should be. So if a missionary goes to him to ask, 'What can I do?' the likely answer will be, 'Nothing today.'

"This is because the pastor has not planned ahead, and also doesn't know how to delegate to nationals, let alone to trained expatriates. When a missionary receives an answer like this a few times, he stops coming to ask the pastor, and does his own thing."

The solution here, advises Kashima Shayama of the Evangelical Churches of Zambia, is for the missionary to be seen as part of the church exercising his gifts, rather than an outsider offering his "skills."[3]

Threatening relationship

This latter tension is really part of a larger problem which can appear to be a missionary-pastor tension, or even a racial tension, but really results from an education gap. It can show up between two nationals of the same race. An older pastor may feel threatened by a newly graduated Bible college student. The older man sees his empire being challenged by the graduate's education, and so he ignores or rejects the younger man, who goes away discouraged.

"Let us face the fact," an older pastor told ECWA's
General Church Council when discussing the problem of Bible
school and seminary graduates not entering the ministry;
"we are largely to blame. When these young people come
back to their churches during school vacation, we don't
make use of them. We don't understand them, and are afraid
of them."

The threat of an educated person to an uneducated person
is heightened between people of different races. Because
of the misfortunes of history and the technological advancement of the West, people in developing nations unconsciously
think of Westerners as superior -- or if they don't, they
think that Westerners must *consider* themselves superior.
Whichever it is, the result is a deep resentment against
the rest of the world, which seems to have by-passed the
Third World -- or acts as if it has. Some nationals
instinctively, even unconsciously, think that expatriates
look down upon them or think of them as inferior. Some
expatriates do, even as some nationals look down on foreigners. But if a national feels that all expatriates are
superior, or all act superior, he will react when the
expatriate attempts to teach him something. The national
may unconsciously feel that the expatriate thinks the
national needs instruction because he is inferior!

The expatriate could teach the same thing to another
expatriate without evoking this kind of reaction; so he
can't understand the reaction. It makes him feel very
unsure of himself and adds to his tensions. The national
may interpret the instruction as motivated by a racial bias,
and the expatriate may interpret the reaction also as
racial.

The role of women in most developing countries adds to
this kind of instructional tension. Since the year 1850
approximately, women have played a major part in missions.[4]
Their dedicated work can only be viewed with gratefulness
to God. However, they have had to serve in cultures where
male attitudes are different from their own lands. It is
very disturbing to many a man to see a foreign woman pro-
ficient in activities which the *man* may not yet have
learned (typing, driving a car) -- let alone the average
woman in his society. Many tensions have developed because
of this factor -- a reality which calls for much grace and
humility on the part of national men and expatriate women.[5]
(We should add that the younger generation has learned to

accept the role of qualified women in professions such as education and medicine.)

The differing value systems of cultures also cause church-mission tensions. "All this cultural talk is simply an excuse for inefficiency!" exclaimed one frustrated missionary. He was trying to keep a radio recording studio operating -- a strictly time-oriented organization, but with event-oriented staff members. What the missionary considered "inefficiency" was the result of the clash. Time-oriented efficiency is an acquired cultural trait. Europe didn't possess it before the industrial revolution.

The very presence of an efficiency-conscious (time-and-goal-oriented) missionary may make the "inefficient" (event-and-people-oriented) national feel insecure, to say the least, and possibly inferior -- therefore resentful. A pastor may very much desire to have a missionary work with his church because of the spiritual and physical benefits resulting from his presence, and yet may feel resentful of the missionary.

It is interesting that John Mbiti of Kenya lists efficiency as one of four aspects in which the church must change its cultural attitude:

> *Efficiency* is not in our blood or not a serious concern of our traditional cultures.
>
> *Farsightedness* is difficult to acquire because the long future dimension of time is lacking in our traditional concept of time.
>
> *Experiments* should be carried out in all areas of church life, bearing in mind that it is not a sin to experiment.
>
> *Taking the risk* is another demand of change. Without risks there can be no progress.[6]

(Philip Chelilim of Kenya points out that Mbiti is speaking from the viewpoint of an acquired value system in a technological age. Traditional African culture had its own forms of efficiency, planning, experimenting, and risk-taking.[7])

Leadership tensions

Most missionaries want to see leadership develop, and
many have done a good job along this line. However, some
do not realize the demotivating influence of their own
attitude. They come from a culture which has rewarded
"talent" and hyper-activity at school, in church, and in
the community. It has taught them to be aggressive, to be
first with the answer, and to demonstrate other forms of
what is considered "leadership." After a term or two as
missionaries, they are discouraged and perhaps critical
because they don't see emerging national leadership. What
has happened?

"I have observed among evangelical missionaries what I
call the Director Syndrome," writes Wakatama. "It seems as
though a good number of missionaries do not feel their
ministry is important unless they are director of something."[8]

Guang describes the effect in more detail:

> If a missionary assumes a monopolizing role in
> the work -- i.e. he teaches, preaches, visits,
> is musical, is the treasurer-counselor-pastor-
> evangelist, sings, decides, buys, sells, etc.,
> the latent message he is sending to his
> congregation is: You are stupid, incapable,
> inept, don't know how nor are you able, you
> are the type of people who can't be put in
> charge of anything. None of this is said in
> words, but it isn't necessary to do so, for
> its sterile effects are immediate. And to
> prove it, just take a look at the scarcity of
> leaders in the Third World and the churches
> that don't produce; they were sterilized at
> the beginning of their life. If someone were
> to grade the results of that kind of teaching,
> it would be outstanding! In my judgment as
> an educator, this may be the worst error
> committed in missionary work. There has been
> unfaithfulness to the Pauline principle of
> discipleship and to the theology of the body
> of Christ as a joint work of all its members.
> And I think this error was made believing that
> here was the highest indication of total
> commitment.[9]

Guang stresses the importance of placing "various forms of leadership . . . in national hands very early in the development of the work . . . . The best reason for turning over leadership should be the aspiration of seeing a mature church . . . . The ideal is to permit gradual autonomy as a sign of coming of age."[10]

If the missionary leader is doing everything himself, nationals will feel frustrated. In fact, under any foreign leadership a national may sense tensions at times because of the expatriate's different leadership style. When nationals lead the work, expatriates working under them will have similar tensions.

Some expatriates may be used to a participatory type of leadership, in which all the staff are kept informed by memos and meetings, and decisions are reached after conferring with the people doing the work. I have seen cases where missionaries did not use this kind of participatory management with those working for them (whether expatriate or national), but fully expected it from those above them.

Some societies conceive of leadership as strongly authoritarian. What the chief or boss says must be done. A person in such a society expects to carry out orders from above without participating in forming them. Consequently when he comes into leadership himself, he does not expect to discuss decisions or have them questioned.

This may account for one tension between some expatriates and nationals. When the missionary was leading, he often did not know the thinking of staff because they were not accustomed to questioning plans or decisions stated by leaders. (A clerk told me how puzzled he was by his African supervisor at first, because the supervisor asked him what he thought of plans for the work. The supervisor had studied participatory management and had become accustomed to this pattern of leadership, but the clerk thought his solicitous attitude was some trap to get him fired!)

When the role is reversed, the national leader may be offended because the expatriate missionary questions plans. The national may look upon this as a personal attack on his decision-making ability or as rebellion against the idea. The expatriate thinks of it only as healthy examination of an idea, part of the participatory decision-making process.

An expatriate from Western countries is usually very
conscious of structures and systems. He may feel secure as
long as he knows the system and it is followed. But in a
person-to-person society, decision-making does not always
follow an arbitrary system. The structure may be completely
by-passed because the visitor or event of the moment is
considered more important than the system or organizational
structure. This will be a frequent source of tension. It
will require openness in discussing and understanding the
cause, and consideration for each other's value system.
The problem needs to be looked at from a management, not
personality, viewpoint.

Development of national leadership is one of the
greatest contributions a mission can make to a growing
church. It has not always been emphasized enough. Speaking about leadership in churches throughout Africa, Panya
Baba stated:

> Although we can claim to have control of
> leadership, we must not forget that many of
> the leaders were not prepared for their role.
> Perhaps due to nationalism, the founding
> mission had to hand over things overnight to
> the national church, thus resulting in leaders
> that were not of the ideal caliber as far as
> leadership of the work is concerned. It is
> important that we consider the qualitative
> dimensions as we evaluate where we stand now
> as far as development of leaders in Africa is
> concerned. Qualitatively, therefore, I think
> there is much more room for improvement.[11]

The tension of change

Changing a method or a means of operation often causes
reaction in one's own culture. In a cross-cultural situation, it can produce harmful tension. Introducing
Theological Education by Extension (TEE) in Nigeria is an
illustration of what can happen.

In earlier days, missionary teachers set up schools with
the classroom structure which educators were using at the
time. Until then, traditional African education had been
informal -- learning the crafts and lore of the tribe from
relatives in the compounds, out in the fields, or seated
around a fire in the evening. The classroom method was
new, and some children had to be almost bribed or threat-

ened by the government to attend school. Christians caught
on to the new system faster in their desire to study God's
Word.

Then educators gained new insights into the learning
process, and the informal extension method was adapted for
TEE. SIM hosted the first TEE workshop in Africa, sponsored by the Committee to Assist Missionary Education
Overseas (CAMEO), and led by Ted Ward of Michigan
State University. A couple of experimental projects were
set up to test the suitability of the concept locally
in Nigeria.

Missionaries felt this was a God-given tool to deepen
the life of the churches through giving Scripture input at
the grass-roots level. They also saw it as a way of
multiplying their effectiveness and giving them wider scope
for teaching at a time when visas were difficult to obtain
and their number was being reduced. The experiment came
just at a time when the churches took responsibility for
operating the vernacular Bible Training Schools (BTS), and
the mission felt it was culturally advisable for nationals
instead of foreigners to train pastors and evangelists at
that level.

However, that fact of timing was part of the reason for
the reaction that set in. "Just when we take over the
Bible schools, the missionaries start something new because
they don't want to work under us," alleged some pastors.
"Instead of teaching in our schools and using their money
to help support them, they use their money for traveling
around doing something that doesn't help us at all."

Apart from the suspicion of the motives for starting
TEE, many pastors could not understand how education could
be worthwhile if not taken within the walls of a classroom. To them, the BTS represented a visible ministry of
the church which they understood and needed. A traveling
TEE teacher wasn't building up that work. When one TEE
teacher tried to explain the advantages of the experience-
applied TEE concept over the theory centered BTS method,
pastors were furious. A TEE certificate became a threat to
their classroom-earned BTS certificate. A farmer attending
TEE sessions could eventually claim the same education as a
pastor who had earned status by sitting in classrooms for
four years. Unthinkable!

The mission and church had to reconsider the whole idea.
There was tension between the felt needs of the churches
and the need perceived by the mission. The reaction was
increased by the mission's attempt to introduce a new
method of education which clashed with what had become part
of the church's sub-culture. Motives were misjudged because of the general image of expatriates which some
pastors had. (Similar tensions over TEE have arisen in
other parts of the world.)

Missionaries are also affected by change. They may be
more sensitive to tension after the church takes leadership,
because the system they have felt comfortable in begins to
change. This introduces feelings of insecurity and loss.
Although their dedication includes willingness for major
sacrifice, such as being separated from their children,
they may not be prepared for the petty sacrifices involved
in subtle inconveniences. Disappointment and criticism
may follow when things don't function according to one's
expectations.

Demotivation can come from two feelings:

1. That the missionary's work is completed -- there is no
more need for him. In SIM-ECWA relations, the church
leaders sought to assure missionaries that they were needed
as much as ever. There was still a vast job to do. In a
few cases, however, local pastors did not know how to
relate to missionaries, and expatriates felt unwanted.

2. That it is impossible to control the work as before.
Missionaries who have been strong leaders feel this the
most. They have to realize that God can use the gifts He
has given them even if their leadership gifts are re-
directed.

Development and evangelism in tension

Missions have an outstanding record of meeting the needs
of deprived people. The pioneers treated the sick,
improved farming to overcome hunger, reduced languages to
writing, and taught people to read. It was all part of
communicating the gospel for the whole man.

As the theological base of missions changed among
liberals (see chapter 3), social activity seemed to be
emphasized more than spiritual regeneration. Evangelicals
stressed the spiritual dimension. A dichotomy arose in

people's minds: liberals and social action; evangelicals
and spiritual life. The tension was increasingly expressed
in the question: social action or evangelism? Because of
opposition to a spiritually lifeless social gospel, some
evangelicals swung to the opposite extreme and neglected
physical needs. Their position was strengthened by events
such as the Boxer Rebellion in China, when large institutions built by missions were lost and very little spiritual work continued in the major denominations.

In Khartoum, Sudan, Gordon College was built largely by
donations in memory of the devout General Gordon to provide
higher education in Sudan; it eventually became a center
for Muslim learning. Many evangelicals became anti-
institutional, feeling that it was better to invest in
lives than in buildings. This reaction produced tensions
within evangelical missions, and the young churches did not
fail to notice. They did not understand the reason for the
evangelical reaction, and presumed it was based on a Western sense of superiority and lack of concern for the
people's felt needs. As recently as 1974 this charge was
leveled by the President of Chad against some evangelical
missions.[12]

However, most evangelicals realized the proper place of
social concern and development. To them it was not a
question of "either -- or" (social action or evangelism).
To them both the Great Commission and the Great Commandment
had the same goal: to bring man into right relation with
God.

> That goal remains constant, while the strategy
> for reaching the goal changes as the context
> changes. In pioneer work, medical clinics may
> be the priority strategy; as literacy increases,
> schools become necessary; later other aspects
> of community development may be a priority.
> The messengers of the good news interact with
> these strategic needs as they aim at their goal
> of evangelizing and discipling believers.
> Evangelized people tend to become alert to
> their *needs* and potential; discipled believers
> should become aware of their *responsibilities*
> to the community.
>
> One reason for the ecumenical accusation is
> that they headline social action, whereas we

emphasize spiritual priorities while quietly
going about doing good. Liberal social
activists therefore misjudge our strategy. I
believe we have the right priorities, and we
don't need to flagellate ourselves for the
past. I can take you to a community which
threw off the injustice and oppression of a
neighboring ethnic group because missionaries
gave them the gospel -- not because they were
political activists. As to relieving physical
suffering, twenty years ago SIM, only one
evangelical mission, had more leprosy patients
(24,000) under treatment than any government or
World Council agency.[13]

The institutional tension

So evangelicals cautiously developed institutions with a
low profile to meet specific opportunities. In the 1950s
in Nigeria, missions (including all Protestant and Roman
Catholic) were responsible for 60% of Nigeria's education.
Converts needed education, and the schools were a channel
for helping others spiritually. Not to have responded to
this need would have represented a great loss to Christian
work.

Today the witness of the churches is strengthened by men
and women who were educated in these Christian schools and
are now living for Christ in government and the professions
throughout the nation. This is also true elsewhere on the
continent.

A tension arises, however, as governments begin to
assume responsibility for these services. Missions see
hospitals and schools as temporary adjuncts to the mandate
of evangelism and church planting; loss of them would not
necessarily hinder carrying out that mandate -- especially
where the church is established. In fact, in some cases
government takeover could relieve the church and mission of
pressures that hinder their primary task because of changing circumstances.

The churches, however, usually see government takeover
in a different light. To them schools and hospitals represent crucial services for their people. Also, if the mission has found the institutions to be a fruitful means of
witness, why shouldn't the church?

"Should the church be saddled with a hospital?" some
missionaries ask.

Not necessarily, because it may take the best men away
from ministries more vital to the life of the church, and
churches aren't structured to run a complex institution
like a hospital.

However, to argue that it is different for a mission to
run a hospital does not make sense to the church. It looks
upon the mission as a type of church organization. In fact,
in the public's mind, they are the same.

Dayton argues for the example which community development provides for the church: "Christian development models
what the local church should be, a community of people
helping one another, able to love because they are loved by
the maker of the universe. Christian development, therefore, has large potential to establish a church that has
the capacity to carry the gospel throughout its cultural
boundaries. One can imagine what a vital force such a
church can become! A church that sees Christianity not
just as a system of belief with a credal religious practice,
but rather as a joyous desire to share its life in every
dimension, this church will quickly become a missionary
church."[14]

"The institutional tension" is a common one in church-
mission relations. Edgar Stoesz of the Mennonite Central
Committee makes these observations about transferring projects from expatriate to indigenous ownership:

> The transition is seldom smooth. The sponsor-
> ing agency has a tendency to hold on too long
> and then leave too abruptly. The receiving
> system is inclined to underestimate what is
> involved . . . . Later, problems arise, accu-
> sations are made, and disappointment is great.
>
> Expatriate agencies have a record of intro-
> ducing innovations which are bigger than the
> receiving system's experience . . . . Managing
> an enterprise of this size may be beyond
> local competence.
>
> While indigenous management has many advantages,
> it also has some serious disadvantages . . . .
> Many cultures expect friends and relatives to

> receive preferential treatment. They do not
> permit the discipline [expatriate] employers
> take for granted.
>
> Expatriate agencies have a tendency to run
> things themselves and not give enough prior-
> ity to effectively training their successors.
>
> Finally, the transfer often reveals that the
> procedures of the sponsoring agency were not
> as disciplined as it had thought . . . . The
> system was designed to serve those who intro-
> duced it. It seldom serves the successors as
> well.[15]

What is Stoesz's solution? "The ideal is an innovation
that is under indigenous sponsorship from the outset and
does not need to go through the critical transfer stage."[16]

Some evangelicals have seen their community development
work (whether medical, educational, agricultural, or other)
as tools *they* should use in *their* evangelism and church
planting, but not for the church to have. This is a short-
sighted, mission-centric view, ignoring the tension which
will arise. The churches have been stimulated in their
expectations by the projects, but their wrists are slapped
as they are told the projects are not good for them to
have.

It may be true that circumstances have altered the
priorities for the project, or the church may be unfairly
and harmfully saddled by keeping it going. But these
factors should be anticipated and the local Christians
should be taken into confidence about the project from the
beginning. The project ideally should be kept within the
growing church's capacity to administer at all times -- and
her administrative capability needs to be developed by the
mission to keep pace with potential responsibility.

However, we must be realistic. Often, projects have
become larger than the church should take on -- perhaps as
the result of a temporary opportunity requiring a crash
program (e.g. a government asking a mission to provide
foreign expertise to operate a school system or medical
relief program). If the church is fully aware of the
heavy responsibility involved and still one day wants to
take it on, it would be paternalistic on the part of the
mission to say, "You can't." The church will have to learn

the responsibility of decision-making the hard way. That,
unfortunately, is the way most of us entered adulthood.
John Cumbers, SIM Director in Ethiopia, adds this advice:

> Every attempt should be made to weed out pro-
> grams which are not wanted by the church. This
> will tread on the toes of some missionaries who
> have started a program with zeal and enthusiasm,
> thinking that the church wants it. But here in
> Ethiopia it took a revolution for some of the
> church leaders to tell us that what we thought
> was ideal for the church was not what they
> wanted or needed all these years.
>
> All new projects should be approved by the
> church and community together and carefully
> screened by both mission and church to weed
> out the "one-man band" ideas.[17]

The horizontal administrative structure of a para-church
organization (such as most missions) clashes with the
vertical structure of many church bodies when the two are
brought together under one administration. See diagram 8B
for the cause and the solution.

"I don't know how I fit into the goals of the work" --
this frustrated statement is another aspect of "institutional tension." First of all, church and mission have to
evaluate the institutional work periodically to make sure
it is contributing to the overall goals of evangelism and
discipling. Then they have to show each staff member how
his or her part fits into those main goals.

Showing the relationship to the long-range objective
will help to reduce tension of staff. It will also help
the church and mission as a whole to look more objectively
on changes in institutions. They will see that the whole
gospel ministry is not jeopardized just because a school or
hospital is phased out or taken over. (See appendix V for
the way that SIM-ECWA illustrated the relationships of
institutions to the "main stream" of church growth.)

Property and personnel

"I'm interested in leaving a living church," a missionary said in the midst of an evacuation crisis. "I don't
care who gets the sticks and stones."

Diagram 8 B: THE INSTITUTIONAL TENSION

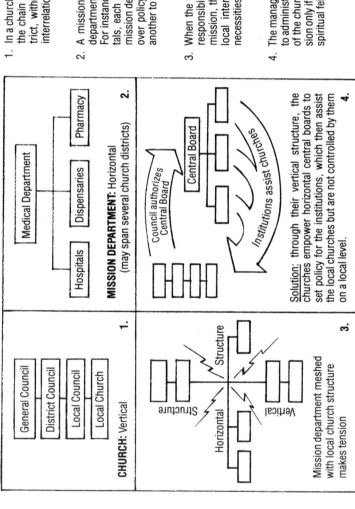

1. In a church structure such as ECWA developed, the chain of command is vertical in each district, without central authority over horizontal interrelation.

2. A mission, being parachurch, can operate a department across geographic church lines. For instance, there may be two or three hospitals, each in a different church district, but the mission department maintains central authority over policy, and can deploy staff from one to another to meet emergency needs.

3. When the vertical local church structure takes responsibility for the horizontal structure of the mission, there is tension between the two. The local interests clash with the departmental necessities.

4. The management solution is for a central board to administer each department's work on behalf of the churches; this will function without tension only if the people involved are working in spiritual fellowship.

(W. Harold Fuller, SIM, 1980)

In diagram (labels):

1. General Council / District Council / Local Council / Local Church
CHURCH: Vertical

2. Medical Department / Hospitals / Dispensaries / Pharmacy
MISSION DEPARTMENT: Horizontal (may span several church districts)

3. Structure / Horizontal Structure / Vertical Structure
Mission department meshed with local church structure makes tension

4. Council authorizes Central Board / Central Board / Institutions assist churches
Solution: through their vertical structure, the churches empower horizontal central boards to set policy for the institutions, which then assist the local churches but are not controlled by them on a local level.

Sticks and stones were what the mission buildings were made of in his area. The sentiment sounds correct, but it may reveal a dichotomous attitude to church and mission. The missionary had used the buildings as a useful base for his work, but he had not foreseen their continuing use as a base for God's work after he was gone. In the crisis of evacuation his attitude seemed irresponsible to the church. Were the buildings erected for God's work or for a foreign mission? A church-centric, mission-centric tension arose.

Lands and houses unfortunately become the basis for much tension between church and mission.[18] This should not be surprising to expatriate missionaries if they consider the importance of property in their own countries. How much more in nations where durable buildings are scarce. When turnover of property seems imminent, a scramble for it can ensue -- not so much to take it from the missionary as to make sure a rival doesn't get it first.

The solution would seem to make sure that the "sticks and stones" belong to the local church early in its development, with the understanding that the mission will have use of the buildings as long as needed.

Most churches will agree to this. Years before SIM turned over leadership in Nigeria to ECWA, I was surprised to find a mission house kept vacant by the local church -- to which it had been given. "We're keeping it vacant for a missionary," the pastor explained, although it was unlikely that an expatriate missionary would be stationed there again, in view of the church's ability to handle the work and because of greater priorities elsewhere.

That is an unusual case, though. While churches understand the need for expatriate missionaries to have housing if they are to work in the country, the sight of an empty house is difficult to understand. The church may happily agree that a national tennant will move out as soon as an expatriate can be found -- but at the time of "eviction" a new tension will arise. Careful planning and agreement have to be carried out between church and mission to avoid irreparable harm to relations over property.

The role of missionary personnel also needs to be specially considered. In one sense he is "the man in the middle," between the national church which has asked for his service and his home church which has enabled him to go to serve. David Hesselgrave points out that "it will

require some concern and care on the part of all responsible
men of missions if [the missionary] is not to become 'the
man in the muddle.'"[19] The national church must regard the
sense of the Holy Spirit's calling with which the missionary comes, and must also realize his responsibility to
those who have enabled him to serve. It is a serious
undertaking for the church to utilize a person's gifts in a
responsible way. To use him simply as "the church's cheapest form of labor" could be demoralizing to the missionary
and irresponsible to those who sacrificially support him.

Finance: Root of much tension

Finance is a basic need of both church and mission. I
remember a visitor to Africa who was critical of the concern
over money which he noticed in the churches. However, when
he took part in a discussion with missionaries, most of
their questions centered around support and other material
needs. Their questions were quite legitimate, but I hoped
that the visitor would realize that national pastors had
their legitimate concerns too.

Some church-mission tensions center around differences
of opinion about the use of finance. While most church
leaders may be aware of their responsibilities in finance,
some people can have a "cargo cult" attitude, expecting the
arrival of vast material possessions from overseas through
the mission agency.

A few foreign missions have almost encouraged such
attitudes. A graphic illustration occurred in Zaire:

"Up to the 1940s a group of churches in the Bandundu
Region of Zaire were self-supporting and spiritually alive.
The missionary society with which they were associated was
an interdenominational one with few material resources.

"The work was 'taken over' in the mid-forties by a well-
meaning denominational mission. 'We have relatively much,'
they said, 'and you have so little. Let us help you pay
the salaries of your pastors and evangelists.' The church
received -- and still receives -- money from overseas; and
the spirit of self-help and evangelism has gone."[20]

That is an extreme, not a mature relationship between
two responsible partners in the work of God. The church
should be self-reliant in supporting its pastors and con-
ducting its normal activities. However, at times there are

major opportunities in which Christians in other lands can
help the national church without becoming a crutch and
weakening the indigenous nature of the church. People have
supported missions in making special projects possible; a
change in leadership (the national church assuming responsibility) does not suddenly make it wrong to continue
assisting. The question is whether the church can bear the
financial responsibility itself, and whether foreign assistance in the particular project will weaken or strengthen
the church. Will it stimulate or discourage local giving?

But as to the use of funds channeled through the mission
agency, agreements need to be worked out mutually and carefully to prevent tensions arising. The churches need to
realize that unless they have an adequate accounting
system, the confidence of those who give (whether nationals
in the country or foreigners outside the country) will be
lost, and giving will diminish.

Edward Dayton depicts the missionary agency as "being
stretched between two poles." On the one hand, the national churches feel they should decide the priorities of
financing, and how the finance is going to be spent. On
the other hand, the missionary agency is only a channel for
the gifts of churches and individuals, who have their own
perception of the need. The donors can be educated as to
the need, but if they do not feel that their money is going
to meet real priorities, the agency will soon have no funds
or personnel with which to help the national church.

"We are thus faced with four different realities,"
Dayton points out. "First is the national church's view of
reality. Second is the ministering agency's view of reality. Third is the donating or sending church's view of
reality. Fourth is the true reality. The task of all
concerned is to bring those four 'realities' into as close
a proximity as possible."[21]

The resultant tensions call for maturity on the part of
all. "Perhaps the day has come when the mature need to
say, 'Brothers and sisters in Christ, this is our situation.
Accept us as we are, forgiven sinners, stretched between
two poles.'"[22]

The Evangelical Alliance Commission on World Mission
offers the following guidelines on finance:

Whatever method is used for allocating funds, the essential thing is that they are given in such a way as not to undermine the receiver's self-respect and direct loyalty to and dependence on God, or the giver's sense of stewardship and of responsibility to God for the use to which money given is put. Usually people think this means "aid without strings"; but if "aid without strings" is taken to mean that the donor asks for no account of how his money has been spent, it can be corrupting, and is in fact another subtle form of patronage. It is because the donor looks on the receiver as being less than an equal that he reckons he will be offended if he is asked to say how he used the money.

Bishop Stanway from Tanzania writes, "Accountability should be asked for, so that the money given for specific purposes is used for those purposes." Mr. Gottfried Osei-Mensah from Ghana suggests that "the responsibility of donors to ensure wise spending can be carried out through a local committee." In the long run, however, the donor himself is responsible to God to decide whether to continue his grant: to do so he needs to know how it is being spent. If we are really talking of dealing between equals, this should be fully accepted.[23]

As mentioned in chapter 7, there is a cultural factor in the use of money. Mission donors live in a very structured society where money is categorized specifically. (The annual income tax questionnaires illustrate that!) People give for specific projects; governments insist that grants are used according to budgeted needs.

In non-industrialized cultures, however, money and possessions are looked at very holistically. Produce belongs to a community; the extended family shares with its members according to need, not individual ownership. When a holistic-oriented person takes a job in an office where money is strictly accounted for, he often gets into trouble. He "borrows" money from the cash box to meet an urgent need; the money is not being used, and he will replace it before it is needed, he reasons. However, his holistic optimism over replacing it does not materialize in reality, and he finds himself unaccountably charged with embezzlement!

This is one aspect of culture which will have to change as it changed in Europe -- simply because of changing society. The holistic rural economy is changing to a world of account books. National teachers and industrial employees live in that world, and they want to know how their church offerings are used.

A mission needs to help the church develop its economic base. Too often we have prided ourselves on evangelism and have neglected to equip the resultant churches so they, too, will have a strong financial system. We could not evangelize effectively without that kind of base, and neither can they.

Often we criticize the church for lack of giving, sloppy financial management, and wrong methods of raising funds. We may be partly to blame. I was asked to speak at a church district conference on Christian giving -- the Christians did not understand the joy of giving; they were legalistic about it. After speaking, I discovered that the pioneer missionaries used to deduct the tithe from their employees' salaries before paying them. The pattern of legalism had been set 40 years before!

Missions can help the financial scene in several ways:

1. Teach Christians joyous giving -- and set an example.

2. Train bookkeepers and accountants.

3. Help the church set up adequate financial management systems.

4. Get Christian laymen with business experience involved in finance committees.

5. Show how some departments (e.g. literature) can be made self-supporting.

6. Discuss legitimate ways of increasing church support.

7. Enlighten the church about world economics and the mission's wider commitments, so that local needs will be seen in realistic perspective.

People: Most important resource

A resource more important than money is people. And
people are the products of their culture. A church taking
over responsibility for the work of a mission must realize
this. Happy is the mission that can relate to church leaders who have had a bicultural experience. Otherwise there
will be difficulty in working together.

Expatriate missionaries can be expected to learn local
customs and understand the culture. They should be prepared for self-denial; physical conditions may not always
be ideal. But a national may not readily understand some
cultural implications, such as the relationship of a missionary to his or her spouse. A couple with one mission
resigned because the church assigned husband and wife to
separate stations 200 miles apart -- where their professions could be better used. This was culturally acceptable
to the church, but unthinkable to the mission.

Relationships to one's children, the needs of missionary
children's education, personal psychological problems --
all these are deeply affected by culture and need the understanding of someone of the same culture. A solution is
for the church to set up a Services Committee which is
responsible for missionary care. A Liaison Officer should
have the prerogative of objecting to an assignment made by
the church if he feels it would be injurious to the missionary. In this way both the church and the missionary
are protected from problems of personnel welfare.

Agreements: Written or verbal?

Matters of personnel, property, and finance all need
careful consideration. Mutual agreements need to be in
writing because both mission and church personnel change.
However, signed legal agreements seem to be an obsession of
the Western mind, and can themselves create misunderstanding in holistic minds. To put a discussion in writing as
a record of an agreement is one thing; to present it as a
legal document to be signed by two parties can be very
threatening. People unaccustomed to such documents may at
best feel unsure of themselves in the presence of legal
procedures, or at worst they may suspect some trap.

Bates observes this in his analysis of the agreement on
housing with the Free Methodist Church in Burundi. "Why do
we need it in writing?" church leaders asked in effect.

"We'll always provide housing for missionaries." The debate over the wording of the agreement was heated and
extensive.[24]

W.E. Mulwa, former leader of the Africa Inland Church,
noted the same apprehension when the Africa Inland Mission
was turning responsibility over to the AIC:

> The church never could understand the reason
> for signed agreements because to the African
> the church is a living organism and as such
> the relationship between white Christians and
> black Christians must never be legislated in
> a signed piece of paper but must be regulated
> by the living spirit of Christ . . . . Because
> of misunderstanding in this important "African
> thinking," negotiations were weakened each time
> the Joint Committee met . . . . In many ways
> the church has resented the mission's philos-
> ophy of existence by signed agreements.[25]

In a person-to-person culture, the more acceptable way
of recording agreements is by a letter referring to the
points discussed and agreed on. This is not threatening,
and yet provides a record which can inform those who take
up office in later days.

Choosing friends

There is one other tension point we should mention.
Because of its constitution and also its constituency, a
mission may not be able to enter into certain affiliations,
over which an indigenous church may not have the same
qualms. If the indigenous church does make such an affiliation, it may harm the mission agency and therefore ad-
versely affect the work it is seeking to do on behalf of
the church in recruiting personnel, encouraging prayer, and
raising finance for special projects. Yet the indigenous
church may be irritated by the mission's mentioning this,
feeling it is interfering and importing foreign divisions
which do not concern it. The indigenous church may infer
that it is still "tied to the apron strings" of the
mission.

Only a deep respect for each other and confidence in
each other can stand the stress of this kind of strain on
relationships. Church and mission will need to study the
situation together in the light of God's Word, and see

whether the affiliation really contravenes scriptural
principles or is simply based on a foreign historical
problem.

Instead of reacting emotionally, a mission may need to
give time for the church to realize the harmful results of
its decision; and in some cases the church may need to refrain from a decision which it has the right to make, but
which would harm its international partner, the mission.
In the same way, a husband and wife may forego something
legitimate which either could do; but because of its adverse effect on the beloved partner, each refrains from
doing it. Working together may involve giving up some
things for each other.

Reciprocity

Ted Ward of Michigan State University points out the
tension which arises from "acts of kindness" if they are
limited to giving and training. They can make the recip-
ient dependent and ultimately resentful. Ward recommends
a relationship of reciprocity: "the mutual dignity of both
parties offering themselves to the needs of the other."
Barnabas and the relationship developed between the
churches in Jerusalem and Antioch illustrate reciprocity,
Ward states.[26]

SUMMARY

Cultural misunderstandings will never cease, but through
close personal fellowship between nationals and expatriates,
confidence can be increased. This overcomes suspicion and
misjudging of motives. When people of different cultures
pray and play together, they make allowances for each
other's differences instead of criticizing them. Expatriates need to take the initiative in this, because they
have the advantage of already having crossed cultural
lines. They should realize that people of different
cultures are very different because of value systems.

Only the Holy Spirit can bring us together in true harmony. As He does so, He will also help us -- national and
expatriate -- to see those things in our cultures which
will need to change in us, in order not to hinder His work
through us. Systems and agreements are necessary, but only
the Spirit of Christ can enable us to work together as one.

In discussing problems which have arisen in the past, we must realize that the people concerned acted in the context of their day. We must remember that we likely would have acted the same. Rather than being negatively critical, we should seek to learn from the past. As Hay states:

> It is easy for those of us living in the late
> 20th century to be critical of the past gen-
> erations' failures. Our vantage point in
> history perhaps does permit broader vision.
> The tragedy is not so much what happened in
> the past; it occurs when we who work today try
> to maintain those same types of relationships,
> or when we are so busy confessing the sins of
> our forefathers that we fail to note the
> errors we ourselves are now making. The next
> generation will not fail to point them out to
> us!27

"We should not evade problems but rather face them in the strength of the Holy Spirit and in humility," states Charles Salalah of the Africa Inland Church. "Locating and working on problems immediately can save us from heartache.

"However, the present complicated problems of church-mission relationships need more than this. They need men of God who will be willing to come before the Lord with all their failures and normal clash of personalities. The attitude of a white and a black man should be completely eradicated.

"My approach would be prayer. Senior church leaders and mission leaders should meet together for prayer alone, without first trying to solve the problems. Unity should be the theme of the prayer meetings. Does not the Bible say, '...being diligent to preserve the unity of the Spirit in the bond of peace' (Ephesians 4:3)? Financial matters and cultural differences have taken the first place in our lives instead of diligence to preserve the unity of the Spirit.

"This I believe is a solid foundation where other plans of working together can be built. It is not something which can be done once for all. It is a continuing process."28

STUDY QUESTIONS: CHAPTER 8

1. Why must a missionary take the initiative in adjusting
   his thinking culturally (see Diagram 8A)? Discuss
   what this would mean to you personally.

2. What are major areas of cultural difference which
   can create tension between a mission and a church?
   What illustrations can you think of? What can be done
   to promote understanding and reduce the tensions cited?

3. How does a dichotomous outlook (church-centric vs.
   mission-centric) add to cultural misunderstanding based
   on different value systems?

NOTES: CHAPTER 8

1. Enrique Guang, Latin-America Pulse, vol. Xl, No. 4,
   Oct. 1976, p. 3.

2. S.A. Ibrahim, "Cultural Barriers to Communication of
   the Gospel," a paper presented at the Nigerian Congress on Evangelization, Ife, August 1978.

3. Kashima Shayama, General Executive Committee member,
   Evangelical Churches of Zambia, in a comment on this
   text during a Missions course at Columbia Graduate
   School of Bible and Missions, December 1979.

4. Ralph D. Winter, *The Grounds for a New Thrust in World
   Mission* (South Pasadena, CA: William Carey Library,
   1977), p. 19.

5. The author speaks from personal knowledge, having an
   unmarried sister who has served as a missionary in
   Asia for 35 years. For a study of the role of women
   missionaries, see R. Pierce Beaver, *All Loves
   Excelling* (Grand Rapids: Eerdmans, 1968).

6. John Mbiti, *The Crisis of Missions in Africa*
   (Kampala: Uganda Church Press, 1971), pp. 3, 4.

7. Philip Chelilim, Africa Inland Church, Kenya, in a
   comment on this text at Columbia Graduate School of
   Bible and Missions, Dec. 1979.

8. Pius Wakatama, *Independence for the Third World Church* (Downers Grove, IL: InterVarsity Press, 1976), p. 41.

9. Enrique Guang, *Latin-America Pulse*, vol. X1, No. 4, Oct. 1976, p. 4.

10. *Ibid*, p. 8.

11. Panya Baba, "Prospective of Solidarity of A.A.A. Leadership," in *Asian Missions Advance*, Seoul, Korea, January 1979, pp. 13, 14.

12. As related to the author by Chadian refugees during Tombalbaye's persecution of the church 1973-1975.

13. W. Harold Fuller, "Evangelicals and Community Development," in *Consultation on Theology and Mission* (Grand Rapids, MI: Baker Book House, 1979).

14. Edward Dayton, "Development as Evangelism," *Marc Newsletter*, January 1979.

15. Edgar Stoesz, Associate Executive Secretary for Overseas Program, Mennonite Central Committee, Mimeographed paper December 1976.

16. *Ibid*

17. John Cumbers, letter of March 21, 1979.

18. Gerald E. Bates, *A Study of the Processes of Conflict Resolution*, unpublished dissertation, Michigan State University, 1975.

19. David J. Hesselgrave, "The Missionary of Tomorrow," *Missiology*, June 1975.

20. Rurcon Newsletter, January 1976.

21. *MARC Newsletter*, World Vision, Monrovia, CA., March 31, 1976.

22. *Ibid*

23. *One World, One Task* (London: Evangelical Alliance, 1971), pp. 132, 133.

24. Gerald E. Bates, op. cit.

25. W.E. Mulwa, address to AIM missionary conference,
     Nairobi, Kenya, November 1978.

26. Ted Ward and Kathleen Graham, "Acts of Kindness:
     Motives and Relationships," a study paper, Institute
     for International Studies, Michigan State University,
     East Lansing, MI, 1977.

27. Ian M. Hay, *Church Mission Tensions Today* (C. Peter
     Wagner Ed.), 1972, pp. 203-204.

28. Charles S. Salalah, Africa Inland Church, Tanzania, in
     an unpublished paper, "A Church in Transition,"
     Columbia Graduate School of Bible and Missions,
     Columbia, SC, Dec. 1979.

Part Three

Dynamics
Of Responsibility

9

A Current Case Study

Neill referred to SIM as "the largest single Protestant
missionary organization in the world" at the time he wrote.[1]
What kind of mission is it? What policies has it followed
in relation to the church? What tensions have arisen between it and its churches? How have the tensions been
handled?

SIM's oldest work is in Nigeria. Let's look at it as a
case study of the principles we have discussed in earlier
chapters.

SIM beginnings

SIM was not the result of some church desiring to du-
plicate itself in another land. Its beginnings were not a
reaction to the slave trade. SIM started as a result of
the Christian concern of a mother in Canada who had been
reading about the great area south of the Sahara between
the Niger and Nile Rivers, which was then all called "the
Sudan." She and her praying friends were thankful they had
the Word of God themselves, but were burdened for those in
the vast Sudan area (then estimated to be between 60 and 90
million) who had not had opportunity to hear God's Word
and its message of salvation. The Great Commission had not
been fulfilled in the area now known as northern Nigeria.

Finally in 1893, the mother's son, Walter Gowans, and
two companions, Thomas Kent and Rowland Bingham, prepared
to go. When they could find no mission to send them, the

three young men decided to set out on their own, and arrived in Lagos December 4, 1893. Gowans and Kent died
while trying to reach the far north, and the third, Rowland
Bingham, became ill and had to return to Canada. He found
other volunteers, and finally in 1901 SIM missionaries established a base for preaching the gospel in the Nupe town
of Patigi on the Niger River. Progress was very slow because of the small number of missionaries, illness, the
need to learn local languages, and the opposition of other
religions to the entrance of the gospel.

SIM from the beginning was an interdenominational mission simply because the young men were unable to find a
church to back them. The mission attracted evangelicals
from different denominations who were desirous of communicating the gospel to people who had not had the
opportunity of hearing it. They were conscious of a strong
sense of responsibility to fulfill the Great Commission.
All subscribed to the SIM biblical doctrinal statement.

Since the first station was not opened until the turn of
this century, Bingham and his colleagues were able to
benefit from the experience of other missions. They were
aware of some of the pitfalls of the colonial era. The
Mission carefully followed many of the basic indigenous
principles developed by Henry Venn, Rufus Anderson, and
Roland Allen, especially those of the local church being
self-governing, self-supporting, and self-propagating.

Although the missionaries worked in the colonial era,
many government officials did not appreciate their work.
Some were critical of the missionaries' friendliness with
the people, and their living right in the villages. Finally, the missionaries had to move outside the towns when
the government prohibited foreigners living in the towns
and cities of the far north.[2] The officials were afraid of
upsetting the status quo, upon which they depended for
their policy of indirect rule. Some were also hostile to
Christianity, even though they were Englishmen.

Professor Ayandele also states: "In the judgment of the
missionaries, the chief reason why most of the Residents
(top government officials) proscribed missionary propaganda
in their areas of jurisdiction was the latters' fear that
missionaries would not condone many of their actions."[3]

The colonial mentality of government officials and commercial agents affected missionaries as well -- it was the outlook of their world at the time. Even though missionaries came with a genuine desire to help Africans, there were some who could not believe that a black man could really be equal with a white man. Africans, therefore, must be kept in their place; too much education would make them proud, they felt.

While such attitudes cannot be condoned, we must remember that they were not peculiar to white people. They were the result of man's sin -- the same sin of pride that caused one African tribe to look down on another and even enslave its members. Ethnic pride continues to affect us today. A Nigerian government officer once told me how he admired the missionaries he had seen living among the people of a remote village. "I'm sure I couldn't accept those bush people as the missionaries do," he admitted.

It is also true that many missionaries came without any feelings of superiority, as humble servants of God. They were convinced that Africans were in no way an inferior race, and could take their place as equals with any peoples, given opportunity. Such missionaries were criticized by some government and commercial officers.

The early SIM missionaries were also aware of the danger of introducing foreign culture with Christianity. They had heard of the reactions in China, India, and in southern Nigeria -- where younger Christians had called the older African pastors (including Bishop Crowther) "black Englishmen." They knew that the younger African church leaders had strongly criticized the use of English in worship services (see chapter 7).

SIM pioneers therefore sought to contextualize the gospel in such cultural aspects as traditional clothing and local languages. So concerned were they to make the work truly indigenous, that they opposed the wearing of Western clothes and the use of English.

However, the entrance of the gospel to village life awakened the expectations of the oncoming generation, and the young people could not understand the missionaries' attitude. In view of the colonial image of the superior white man, this opposition to what seemed "progress" confirmed the young Nigerians' suspicion that the missionaries really wanted to keep them backward.

An African friend told me recently that he had heard the missionary with whom he lived 35 years ago say he wanted the Christians to live as their fathers did. My friend took this to mean that the missionary wanted to keep them in a state of ignorance; my friend was still reacting against nearly everything the mission suggested.

Dress sometimes became a complex issue. Take for instance tribe X. Fifty years ago the animistic culture forbade women to wear clothes. Irate pagans would rip the dresses off Christian women, fearful that the clothing would bring the wrath of the spirits on the whole tribe. The pioneer missionaries were careful not to make clothing an essential of the gospel -- the decision to wear clothes must arise from a convert's personal conviction, not a church regulation.

When a convert decided to don clothes, the next question was what kind to wear. If Western clothes were uncultural, the alternative was to adopt the dress of the predominantly Muslim neighbors. The missionaries did not object to men wearing the basic shirt and trousers, but when converts added the voluminous robe and fez, they looked more like Muslims than Christians. In those early days, it appeared like instant Islamization of the community!

Then some of the missionaries had a good idea, they thought. Back in their own lands men were throwing out their shirts when the starched collars frayed. If the worn collars were cut off, the rest of the shirt had a lot of good wear left in it. And besides, African traditional shirts didn't have collars either. So the missionaries' friends sent their collarless shirts to Africa to be passed on to evangelists, pastors, dispensers, and others.

The missionaries thought the problem had been nicely solved, but there was a communication gap. Their motives were misunderstood. The impression passed down to today's generation half a century later was that the missionary wanted to keep the black man in his place and therefore opposed the wearing of both Western and national dress. The people supposed that when the missionaries did pass on Western shirts, they first ripped off the collars so the wearers would not appear to be on the same level of society as missionaries -- who wore shirts with collars!

The pioneers did not realize that this was the impression given, and missionaries who have since served among those people could not have guessed the background to some of the church-mission tensions which have resulted.

"If the missionaries had other reasons, they did not communicate them," a church leader recently told the author; "they rather gave the impression of keeping the black man in his place."

"We had no idea of such feelings," one of the pioneers commented. "The matter of dress was discussed by the church while we were on our first furlough, but we did not know what was said. When we returned, the believers were wearing simple clothes -- the men shirts and shorts, the women homespun cloths tied around the waist. As far as we knew, the Christians developed their own acceptable styles."[4]

A theological lecturer in another part of the country told me that his father had often talked about the local missionary's opposition to the use of English and Western clothes. His father, a pastor, had been very bitter about it. "Although the people loved the missionary and still speak of him as their 'father,' some have never forgiven him for opposing those things," the lecturer told me. "And only now have I come to understand the missionaries' motives."

A number of pastors left SIM over the issue at the time. When one of them returned to SIM, he was abused by the others, who said they were going to fight out the issue.

During the time of this reaction Bingham revisited Nigeria. The missionaries asked his advice because their well-intended indigenous culture policy was causing such problems. Farsighted Bingham said, "You may as well try to stop the ocean tide coming in on the seashore in Lagos!" He advised the missionaries not to oppose the trends, but rather to help the new Christians understand the proper use of the new ideas coming in. The new enlightenment could be channeled to God's glory.

The memory of those early policies, however, has lingered until this day. There was a time when young men preparing to go overseas for study would keep the matter secret until they actually had their acceptance, passport, and ticket in hand. One told me he was convinced that if

he had informed the missionaries, they would have written
to the government to cancel his passport! A missionary who
showed interest in the higher education of nationals was
said to "love the people," in contrast to other missionaries who did not seem to display such an interest.

In spite of such feelings, many villages trace their
entrance into the modern era from the date of the arrival
of their first missionary. Until recently the Nigerian
town of Kagoro celebrated "Kagoro Enlightenment Day" -- the
anniversary of the arrival of the first resident missionary.
The churches where "the collarless shirt" misunderstanding
took place, recently celebrated the 55th anniversary of the
gospel's arrival. They gave thanks to God and the missionary pioneers. Christian love has overcome the tensions,
even though the early actions are still misunderstood.

As the number of Christians increased, the mission saw
the need for training them as Christian citizens as well as
church leaders, and so continued to raise the level of
their schools from the early "Classes of Religious
Instruction" eventually up to the level of secondary
schools and teachers colleges. ECWA Theological Seminary
at Igbaja, Nigeria, is a post-secondary school. A schol-
arship program has produced graduates trained in the
country and overseas, who are now playing their part for
the Lord in both church and government service.

Other departments developed under the mission to take
care of medical work, literature and radio, Christian
education, evangelism and church growth, and rural development.

ECWA's formation

Meanwhile, toward the end of the 1940s SIM and church
leaders had seen the need for the churches to be formed
into a body recognized by the government as an indigenous
organization, with the authority to fulfill church
responsibilities. Consultations of church and mission
leaders were held in the early 1950s and a constitution
was ratified in 1954.

"Most Nigerian delegates wanted a name that would link
them with SIM," recalls Raymond J. Davis, SIM West Africa
Director at the time, "but it was our belief that with
nationalism growing, this would militate against the
church. Also, the delegates invited me to be the

President, but we felt that the church executives should all
be Nigerians. After much insistence by the Nigerian
members, we agreed that a missionary, Douglas Blunt, could
be Vice-President for the first year."[5]

The Association of Evangelical Churches of West Africa
(ECWA) was the name chosen. Two years later ECWA was
officially registered with the government.

Davis points out that SIM was constantly pressing the
churches to take more responsibility than they thought they
could bear, with the beneficial result that the church did
not have to demand anything that the mission was not willing to give.

"But this produced a reverse tension," says Davis. "The
pastors feared to stretch themselves and step out in
assuming responsibility. They felt we were too aggressive;
we felt they were too slow. We could see nationalistic
feeling arising in the country, but many of the older pastors in the villages did not. Even in the case of reg-
istering the new church name, it was easier for them to
continue sitting in the mission's shadow. But as we
assured them and pressed a little, they took on responsibility well.

"There were also tensions in the new church denomination
between the various districts, which were formed around
ethnic communities. They had different attitudes to
discipline, marriage ceremonies, education, and such things
as eating kola nuts. Some of the tensions became great as
they discussed the constitution. They solved the problem
by agreeing to latitude in secondary matters, within the
guidelines of Scripture, while all agreed on the major
doctrines."[6]

The formation of ECWA helped to fulfill the goal of the
pioneers, to see the Holy Spirit raise up an indigenous
church which would be self-reliant, not depending on the
mission as a crutch. The problem of remote control by a
"mother church" overseas, described by Idowu and Mbiti, did
not arise with SIM and ECWA; as churches overseas sent missionaries to Nigeria, the sending churches did not exert
authority over the new churches in Africa (as Paul was sent
out by the church at Antioch, but Antioch did not exert
authority over the young churches formed by his converts).

SIM and ECWA have also avoided the problem which Idowu
raises about foreign vestments and other elements in church
worship.[7] SIM did not come to plant a church like itself,
because it did not represent any one church overseas. It
therefore did not have denominational traditions to pass on
to the church. It came to give the Word of God, so that
the Holy Spirit would raise up the body of Jesus Christ
within the context of the nation.

Missionaries encouraged the new Christians to develop
their own worship forms. Although at first missionaries
supplied the need for hymns by translating from their own
English hymnbooks, later they encouraged the writing of
indigenous hymns set to local tunes. There were individual
missionaries who frowned on the use of local instruments,
especially drums. But generally speaking, ECWA and SIM
have avoided the major tensions which have been so loudly
denounced by some other national churches, arising from
foreign customs being imposed in the churches.

In fact, Nigerian churches have at times taken on
foreign customs against the personal desires of the missionaries. Ian Hay remembers advising a new city church he
attended in the late 1950s not to spend their meager resources on a non-cultural accessory, choir gowns. As soon
as Hay left, the church bought the gowns anyway!

A humorous sequel occurred when Hay showed an SIM film
at an American school. The film included a scene of the
robed choir. The anthropology professor denounced the
mission for imposing Western choir robes on the church in
Africa! Fortunately, Hay was there to give him the facts.
Missionaries have had to realize that a Christian sub-
culture has now arisen in many lands, as it has in Western
countries.[8]

Because missionaries have had no constitutional or
administrative function within ECWA, they have been welcomed as colleagues and counselors -- except in cases where
misunderstandings have hurt relations.

SIM and ECWA have avoided the schismatic phenomenon seen
so much in Africa, perhaps because foreign church forms
have not been imposed upon the churches. In one or two
cases small groups have left over the question of polygamy
or "charismatic" extremes; others have left because of

personal ambition (one group even taking on SIM's initials!). The Yoruba pastors who left over the English language misunderstanding in the 1930s joined other churches.

The relationship of SIM and ECWA was one of partnership of the two separate organizations. SIM's motive was to encourage the church to rely upon itself, and not a foreign organization. At the same time the mission helped the church through SIM departments. There have been advantages to this system as ECWA gained experience in running its own affairs.

TENSIONS OF GROWING

Dichotomy

However, there were also harmful reactions. ECWA members could not understand why their churches were not called SIM churches, not realizing the foreignness of the name. Today it is actually a misnomer for the mission itself, because most of the area is no longer called the Sudan and the mission is not working only in the interior of the country. In some countries there has been political reaction because of the use of a country's name -- Sudan, a geographic term to SIM.

Another reaction was the tendency toward strong dichotomy. Some missionaries took the attitude, "Now you have your own church, so you look after your business and we'll look after ours." There were also some pastors who said to missionaries, "This is our business, so you stay out of it." There were both missionaries and pastors who felt rejected by each other.

Ian Hay well remembers the feeling. He and his wife, June, had recently taken up church-planting work among the Gbari people of Nigeria. His father had pioneered the area.

"I sincerely felt I was doing the right thing by pushing the Christians to take responsibility and not depend on me, the foreign missionary," he recalls. "The church was now formed, and I mustn't weaken it. However, the pastors had been used to working closely with my father. The change was too abrupt, and they felt hurt. Some reacted. There was misunderstanding because of a communication problem."

Hay and the local pastor, Gagara, prayed together, and
both learned how to overcome the tensions of that transitional period. Elsewhere also, both church and mission
have come to realize their need for each other in order to
edify the body of Christ unitedly.

People outside the church had difficulty in understanding
the relationship. The Nigerian *Daily Times* printed an
editorial accusing the Roman Catholics, Ahmadiyyas (a
Muslim sect), and SIM of not indigenizing sufficiently. We
discovered that the editorial was actually an attack on the
Roman Catholics for requesting an increased number of expatriate priests for the churches, but the editor included
the Ahmadiyyas and SIM to make his editorial seem un-
biased! The *Daily Times* printed our reply in which we
pointed out that ECWA, the churches arising from SIM, were
already indigenous, with not one expatriate pastor.[9]

Hay and SIM's U.S.A. Director, Trevor Ardill, found the
same misunderstanding when they talked with the Nigerian
ambassador in Washington. "We don't need any more foreign
priests in Nigeria," he said, explaining his refusal to
grant visas at the time. Fortunately the Nigerian vice-
consul was also present, and turned out to be a member of
ECWA, trained in SIM schools. "You don't understand how
SIM and ECWA work," he told the ambassador, explaining
that the missionaries were not coming in as pastors but to
help ECWA develop her potential. The mission got more
visas.

However, the people continued to have a problem in
understanding the division of authority between SIM and
ECWA. We illustrated the problem in terms of umbrellas.
In much of Africa, an ornate, tasseled umbrella is associated with the authority of a chief -- it shades him at
official ceremonies. Originally the people saw only the
SIM umbrella. Later, when the church was registered, they
saw two "umbrellas": one marked SIM, and the other marked
ECWA (see appendix H). ECWA pastors continued to look to
SIM when they needed something, instead of to church headquarters. More than one SIM district superintendent was
bluntly told by pastors that it was his business to get
them such and such, when their requests should have been to
church headquarters.

As ECWA took on responsibilities for some institutions,
such as dispensaries and schools, discrepancies developed
in such things as conditions of service and other policies,

affecting staff serving under mission or church. Besides labor tensions, there were also feelings of "our work" and "their work," sometimes producing an atmosphere of rivalry, divided loyalty, and suspicion.

Some pastors asked, "What is the mission doing for us now?" -- not understanding the responsibilities still being carried by the mission, because the departmental budgets did not appear on the church budget. Also, they saw SIM only in Nigeria; they did not see the churches and work in nine other African countries, for which SIM also had responsibility in varying degrees.

Finance

As we saw in chapter 8, misunderstandings over finance are the most common in mission-church relations, and ECWA-SIM proved to be no exception. In fact, the very formation of ECWA caused suspicion that SIM wanted to keep the church separate so that the mission could withhold finance from the church.

While ECWA leaders knew SIM's financial policies, most church members did not understand the mission's financial structure or all that was involved in the giving from overseas. They did not know about funds being designated for a certain purpose, which could not be used for any other purpose. They did not understand the system of individual support for the missionary, or how he obtained his car or equipment as donations from churches to enable him to do a better job as a missionary. Most ECWA members were not aware that the missionary's salary was only a fraction of the salaries of other expatriates they saw in the country working for government or industry. Unless they were very close to a missionary, they simply presumed he must be as rich as any other expatriate.

Neither did they realize that the government operating-grants paid on the basis of missionary teachers in post-primary schools were not touched by the missionary teachers, but were put into a fund to provide scholarships for ECWA men and women, and to help keep the fees low at the Bible colleges and seminary.

They did see that a missionary was often able to help the Bible school where he was teaching, or the work he was engaged in, and they were thankful for that. But when the missionary was moved to another station, usually that help

went with him. They therefore felt that the missionary
must be keeping the money to himself for "his" projects,
instead of encouraging his Christian friends overseas to
continue sending it to the work. The supply of finance
seemed related to the presence of the missionary.

Actually, many missionaries were able to interest their
friends in continuing to give to the work after they moved
on to some other station. That help would then be channeled through the department responsible for that aspect of
the work, and so the local Christians would not realize
that help was in fact continuing from the missionary's
friends. However, there were some cases where help did
cease simply because Christian donors are human, and they
like to give to the work in which their representative,
their missionary, is actually engaged.

Later on, when ECWA had its own missionary organization,
ECWA members began to realize this was not a practice confined to a foreign mission. ECWA would support a Nigerian
missionary in a village, but when the local Christians had
developed sufficiently to support their own pastor, the
national missionary would be moved to another village.
Naturally, support for him had to move with him so he
could evangelize in the next village. That support could
not be made available to the Christians in the first village where he had been, or he would not be able to continue
his ministry of evangelism elsewhere.

Another suspicion was that SIM was keeping its overseas
friends to itself. Byang Kato reported that some Christian
university students confronted SIM and ECWA with this
challenge: "SIM has been supported from its foundation by
overseas churches. One would have expected the mission to
introduce ECWA, the fruit of the mission work, to overseas
churches, but there seems to be no effort made to this end;
in fact, one would suppose that SIM acts as a deliberate
barrier between ECWA and overseas churches interested in
it."[10]

What the students had expected to see was money coming
directly to them from overseas. When Kato later joined SIM
staff in North America for several months on a speaking
tour, he discovered the following:[11]

>   1. Evangelical churches represent a minority
>   of Christians, and they are besieged by pro-
>   jects from many missions and Christian groups

around the world. They therefore are
properly cautious in taking on support, in
order to be good stewards of God's finances.
Because they had confidence in a mission through
long years of contact, and the mission was
based in their country, they preferred to give
to ECWA projects through SIM.

2. The North American system of granting
income tax deductions for gifts to missionary
organizations or other charitable work meant
that people had to give through North American-
based organizations, such as SIM, if they wished
to receive receipts which would enable them to
make income tax deductions. Without these
deductions, many Christians would have less
money to give to the Lord's work.

3. Because of their convictions about
indigenous principles, and because some independent fund-raisers had misused donations,
churches very rarely gave directly to individuals unless they were fully endorsed by
a well-known organization, such as the mission.

4. SIM in fact was "introducing" ECWA to her
friends. SIM had full-time speakers telling
churches about ECWA as well as the other SIM-
related churches in other parts of Africa.
One of their objectives was to build up confidence in the indigenous church, so that
Christians in North America, Europe, and elsewhere would give to projects of the church
as well as supporting SIM missionaries. Had
it not been for such donations through the
years, the help which SIM was providing to
ECWA through the departments would not have
been possible. However, since ECWA members
did not know all that was involved in the
budgets of the departments, they did not
realize the extensive help which Christians
overseas were providing for ECWA through SIM.

5. Money did not automatically come in when
an African spoke in churches in North America.
In fact, the donations which came in as a
result of Kato's speaking tour amounted to

$2000 less than the expenses of his tour.
(Some ECWA pastors had thought that if they
could send delegations overseas, they could
raise a great deal of money, but they did not
reckon on the expenses involved, which would
use up that money.)

Kato found that the benefits of the speaking
tour could not simply be added up in finance,
but that the spiritual benefits had to be
recognized as well. Several Americans and
Canadians came to know Christ as Savior during
his tour, and a number of lives were challenged
for Christian service. This is also part of
the ministry of the full-time SIM staff in
"home countries."

6. Finances which came into the mission had to be
divided among a number of countries in Africa
to meet the needs of the work from Liberia
right across to Ethiopia. ECWA therefore had
to remember that she was only one church
needing assistance.

As more Nigerians have gone overseas, they have come to
understand some of this background, and as the church and
mission have come closer together there has been greater
understanding of the actual situation. Three senior pastors
who visited Britain and North America returned not with
demands for more aid, but with thanksgiving for the prayerful backing of missionary work they saw in many churches.
"Christians who have never seen our country are praying
for us!" they reported in amazement. "Even small churches
support a missionary. If they can, so can we!" They then
challenged every ECWA church to support a national missionary.

Kato commented on attitudes to finance as follows:

'Bread-on-the-Plate' type of aid may not be
the only reason for a stagnating church, but
churches that have been taught responsibility
and sacrifice are the most evangelistic and
growing churches in Nigeria. If foreign aid
is to help rather than hinder the work of
the Lord, it must be given as unto the Lord
and received, too, as God's money.

> There must be a strong element of trust all
> around. To by-pass the existing mission
> agencies is not going to be the solution . .
> . . As to actual programs in which foreign
> aid could be directed without any fear of
> stifling growth, it is hard to lay down a
> general rule, because situations differ.
> However, partnership of mission and church
> to determine the priorities should be a
> safe rule."[12]

Independence

Not only was ECWA developing, but the whole national
context in which SIM found itself was changing. Nigeria
was approaching independence (1960). The attitudes which
some missionaries unconsciously carried over from the
colonial era waved like red flags in the new "winds of
change" blowing across Africa.

William (Bill) Crouch, then SIM's West Africa Director,
challenged Council members with the urgent need for the
mission to adapt to the new circumstances. He remembered
the colonial era, when missionaries sat on the church plat-
form and pastors had to sit below. He warned of allegations of racial discrimination arising from extreme dichotomy. He pointed out the need to prepare the church to take
responsibility:

> From being in complete control at the beginning,
> the missionary must gradually step down until
> he finds himself one with many others working
> with and under the national leaders. The
> great problem is in ascertaining the time and
> method of this withdrawal in order to achieve
> the greatest help and blessing to the work.
> If Christianity is to become truly African,
> it must do so through the labor of an autono-
> mous African church. Yet few people would
> say it is time for missionaries to leave and
> go home. There is much to be done and all
> available help is needed to accomplish the
> task while there is still opportunity. The
> need then is to unite the home church (rep-
> resented by the missionary, financial means,
> and technical knowledge) with the African
> church (with its numerical strength, racial
> advantages, and natural zeal and ability).

Can we do this in a way that will bring about
fellowship in the work rather than separation?[13]

The earlier formation of ECWA as an autonomous body in
1954 was a major step toward this goal. That made the
churches responsible for their local church life. But the
mission was carrying on the major part of the work, and the
churches understood very little about what was happening.
They were grateful for the results, but they wished they
could be involved in bringing them about. Instead, in some
aspects the church and mission seemed like rivals.

Fortunately there were several factors in Nigeria which
helped the mission to make the transition.

When political independence came (1960) it was not
accompanied with the hostility to foreigners which has
marked the end of colonial rule in some countries, and ECWA
was already a registered autonomous body.

Unlike East and South Africa, the climate of West Africa
had never been conducive to settling by European farmers.
Also, other than Lagos colony, Nigeria was a protectorate,
and Britain would not permit settling by foreigners. So
Nigerians did not develop a general resentment of expatriates. By the time political sensitivity had increased, the
British administrators had learned colonial lessons the
hard way in India and elsewhere; Nigerians saw that, for
the most part, the British were working hard to prepare the
country for independence.

Nigeria's educational program, largely developed at first
by missions, had prepared a large cadre of professionally
trained men and women -- unlike Zaire (Congo), which had
only 16 university graduates at the time of independence.

Nigeria's large population and relatively stable
economy in the 1960s, aided by oil production, gave the
nation a sense of self-confidence. The civil war actually
added to this feeling. Unlike some African states,
Nigeria did not feel paranoid and did not have to espouse
anti-foreign causes to create an image.

Nigeria's government leaders were realistic. Unlike Idi
Amin's frenetic nationalization by force in Uganda, Nigeria
gave time for foreign countries to train nationals and form
indigenous partnerships -- a policy fair to nationals and
expatriates. When indigenous contractors failed to fulfill

their contracts, thus wasting government funds and slowing development, the government openly turned to foreign contractors to get the job done. The nation saw that as long as Nigerians were in charge, they could utilize foreign expertise without endangering their independence.

The national climate made the indigenization task of missions easier than in countries where there were few trained nationals -- especially Christians -- to draw on, and where reaction to foreigners increased problems.

MOVING INTO THE NEXT STAGE

During the 1960s SIM and ECWA worked jointly in departmental committees. (See appendix I.) ECWA executive increasingly participated in SIM Council meetings as advisers. But there was still considerable dichotomy, and obviously the time was approaching to move into the next stage of church-mission relations. The topic was discussed during the SIM's 75th anniversary "furlough seminars" (1968)[14] and in subsequent Council meetings. In 1974 ECWA and SIM held a seminar[15] to discuss their roles and relations, and the insights from this helped to prepare the way for subsequent changes.

"When I see the tensions between churches and missions in some parts of Africa, I feel that complete fusion is the only solution," said Byang Kato, when he later became General Secretary of AEAM. "Then when I return to Nigeria and see how well SIM-ECWA partnership is working, I feel better."

However, Kato advised ECWA and SIM to enter into a closer relationship in view of increasing trends in Africa. At the same time, developments in Ethiopia underlined the need for new relations. In June 1975 SIM's General Council (its top international body) set forth the following guidelines for all SIM work:

1. To pursue prompt integration of activities for church and mission in outreach and development.

2. To encourage the adoption of mutually agreed structures and timetables for ever-closer fellowship, consultation, and administration.

3. To implement mutually agreed plans that
encourage the leadership role of the church,
recognizing that missions were never, from
their start, intended to be permanent
structures.

4. To channel facilities, personnel, and
finances as available to perform authorized
assignments within the policy framework of
both church and mission.

Changes like that could not be brought about overnight.
They involved not only structure but also attitude -- on
the part of both national and expatriate. Church and mission proposed a two-year period during which there would be
full discussion, trial of proposals, council review, and
final ratification.

A complex organization

For one thing, ECWA had to rethink her constitution because in the original no provision was made for the work of
departments or their administration. ECWA was seen, as its
name implies, as an "association" of churches, each one
congregationally self-governing, but provided with a loose
structure for fellowship, communication, and common planning, through the system of Local Church Councils, District
Church Councils, and ultimately a General Church Council.

In the initial thinking, this Association was considered
to be such a loose "fellowship" that the only full-time
officer needed throughout the whole work, apart from full-
time church pastors, would be a general secretary to handle
correspondence and some bookkeeping for central office
functions. The initiators were well motivated and did not
wish to contribute to the building up of a strongly
hierarchical system, with power invested in an "arch-
bishopric." Also, the churches at first lacked finance to
support more full-time executive officers. However, the
following realities soon became evident:

1. The Association had become very complex, involving many
ethnic groups spread over a very wide geographic area.

2. Pastors and members from these varied ethnic groups
were mobile, so that ultimately a policy set up by local
churches in one ethnic group could come into conflict with
churches of another ethnic group in a city to which members

of the various ethnic groups and their church had moved for
employment.

3. Some central coordination would be needed, which
constitutionally was to be provided by the General Church
Council. However, since that body met only once a year,
and it should be concerned with the review and approval of
policies and not local details, the actual coordination
needed to be delegated by the GCC to the executive:
president, vice-president, general secretary, treasurer.
As the complexities of the work increased, obviously one
full-time man (general secretary) could not begin to handle
the work.

4. The numerical growth of the churches also increased the
amount of work at headquarters.

5. Because of traditional attitudes, there could be a
tendency for division and separation within the Association,
unless there were some strong and visible leadership. This
tendency was increased by two factors.

a. SIM missionaries, coming from different countries and
different denominations, and by their nature often being
extremely independent, tended to instill a sense of independency in local churches. In fact, at the time of
ECWA's formation, a few had opposed the idea and had discouraged their local churches from joining because this was
against their Congregational convictions. Such missionaries
bequeathed to local churches a legacy of individualism,
which often made it difficult to bring about a sense of
oneness within the Association.

b. During earlier days SIM itself provided an overall
"umbrella" which gave a family sense of oneness to the
individual congregations. Even though there had been no
constitutional recognition of the fact, SIM in essence
actually provided a unifying sense. This was missing when
SIM stepped out of the leadership role among the churches,
so that there was a danger of factionalism increasing.

It has taken time for ECWA to build up a central leadership role, which is part of African culture; but in doing
so ECWA has sought to keep it from going to the other
extreme of an authoritarian hierarchy. Kato used to
describe ECWA's church government structure as a compromise
between the Baptist and Presbyterian structures. "I don't

know if we are Baptist Presbyterians or Presbyterian
Baptists!" he used to say.

6. If the church should take responsibility for the
departments which had arisen under SIM leadership, there
were several viewpoints to consider:

a. Some of the departments were transitory, and would not
be needed as soon as the government or private groups took
responsbility for such things as medical treatment and
education of the population.

b. The church would start similar departments where they
felt the need (such as evangelism and literature): the
mission departments would then ultimately phase out.

c. Some departments might not be essential to the church's
life, and would only be a burden. The mission had often
entered into such ministries as educational work because
the government or private organizations were not meeting
the need, and the mission used these ministries as
opportunities for the advancement of the gospel during a
certain stage in the country's development.

The church's attitude was that if the mission had found
these ministries to be of blessing to the work, the church
should continue them as well. The mission realized the
church's need to minister through the departments; so as
the church became ready to take on responsibility for
individual institutions, they were transferred to ECWA.
These included schools, dispensaries, bookshops, and the
publishing department.

7. Wherever possible, expatriate missionaries should move
out of a management or supervisory role into an advisory,
counseling, or training role. The following advantages
were seen in this:

a. It could reduce cultural or racial misunderstanding
in staff relations.

b. It relieved expatriates of administrative pressures,
giving them more opportunity for spiritual ministry.

c. It could enrich the church by developing gifts of
administration among its members.

d. It could increase prospects for continuing the projects, through providing national leadership and responsibility for the future.

e. It could make the project more relevant to the needs of the church, thereby causing the church to think of the project more as its own.

f. It followed the New Testament method of training others for the work of the Lord.

Because of these developments, the churches came to realize that the number of full-time executive members had to be increased, and they had to be provided with adequate staff at headquarters in order to carry out the responsibilities delegated to them by the GCC. The constitution also needed to be reworded to include the relationship of departments, which would come under the authority of the GCC through the executive, and would provide their specialist services to help the whole church.

ECWA's aspirations

ECWA had her own goals in considering taking on the responsibility of SIM work. In the November 1975 SIM Area Council, the ECWA Executive outlined "Some of ECWA's Aspirations":

1. To build a virile responsible church committed to the fulfillment of the Great Commission.

2. To develop/mobilize personnel to meet the challenge of open doors for Christian service in different areas.

3. To promote a sense of responsibility at all levels of ECWA's structure.

4. To establish reliable and constant financial resources to maintain the work with minimal dependence if necessary on outside help.

5. To bring into effect a functional structure which will ensure goal achievement.

6. To revise ECWA's constitution to accommodate new trends.

7. To insulate the mission against any political and ecclesiastical implications.

8. To avoid any loss of mission property to the government.

9. To establish a built-in system of mature advice from the parent mission.

10. To promote healthy and fruitful unity in ECWA.

11. To promote cooperation between missionaries and church.

12. To ensure a good spiritual harvest through the ministry of each department.

Explaining self-reliance

What was the average pastor's concept of the departments? Did he look on a dispensary or bookshop as a money-making asset to support his church? Or as a ministry for the overall good? Did he understand how the departments worked as a team to help develop the spiritual capabilities of the church for witness?

ECWA established a team which toured the districts, using an adaptation of Engel and Norton's Spiritual-Decision Process chart[16], to show how the departments had differing roles to play on the team. They explained what turnover of responsibility would really mean.

Simon Ibrahim outlined some of ECWA's concepts in a paper, "ECWA Today: The Need for Self-Reliance." (See appendix J.) This was discussed with the churches in district conferences.

During this transitional stage, ECWA was greatly helped by an expatriate management expert, Kenneth Hansen. A Christian with a spiritual outlook, he made four trips to Nigeria, at his own expense, to consult with ECWA on developing the church's organizational structure and management capability. He and colleagues who accompanied him conducted seminars which helped the various management levels to understand their responsibility. Without this kind of management input, ECWA would have had much more difficulty in taking on responsibility for the mission's complex work.

To help coordinate and develop the work, ECWA set up a bi-monthly department heads meeting. Another concept developed by ECWA was the district level "task force" made up of local departmental officers. Perhaps a bookshop

manager, Christian education coordinator, evangelism coordinator, and dispensary supervisor would discuss with the
district church leaders ways in which the work could be developed.

"In the past we waited for the churches to decide what
to do," explained the ECWA executive; "but most of the pastors were busy with their local church problems and were
not innovative in their thinking. Task forces of departmental men and women can stimulate their thinking and make
recommendations. The pastors and elders can think the
ideas through and make the final decisions on matters affecting their own churches."

Missionary concerns

Missionaries also needed time to discuss the SIM General
Council guidelines thoroughly, and to participate in im-
plementation. Discussion papers were circulated, and for
two successive years nearly every missionary was involved
in conferences where issues were frankly debated. Nationals
with bicultural experience participated in these.

In an interdenominational mission such as SIM, there is
a great cross-section of views on church-mission relations.
The background of some is strongly dichotomistic and
mission-centered. Others are holistic and church-centered.
Most have well-thought-out convictions which cannot be
lightly brushed aside.

When the SIM Council first proposed turning over responsibility to ECWA, one council member estimated that in his
opinion 30% of the missionaries would strongly oppose such
a move, because of their conviction that church and mission
should work separately. However, after a year of discussion
at all levels, during which missionaries better understood
the principles involved, only 4% opposed the turnover, 10%
were not sure, and 86% were in favor. As to timing, 72%
felt it was just right, 16% said "too fast," and 12% said
"too slow!"[17]

"Last year I said the proposal was crazy," commented one
missionary. "Maybe it could work in five years, or ten.
But now I ask myself, why didn't we do it sooner?"

"I think we have moved as fast as the church was ready,
maybe faster, and yet from the government's viewpoint,
probably not fast enough," said another.

Each missionary was already assigned to one of eight
departments: Education (including Theological), Medical,
Media, Evangelism, Church Growth, Finance, Rural Development, Services. The relation of the missionary to his department did not change at the time of turnover. The major
difference was that his department head reported to the
ECWA executive instead of to the SIM director. The director would become a consultant to the executive (see
appendix L).

Since local pastors would not usually know the professional requirements of a department, a strong departmental
board composed of professionally experienced members
(national and expatriate) was to set policies for the department. In essence, this had already been done with the
literature department (although to meet government regula-
tions for publishing and distribution, it had to be registered as a company). Where a strong central board was not
formed right away, tensions became evident.

For a missionary assigned to work with local churches
directly, the pastor was to draw up his goals and help in
writing the missionary's job description. In this way the
pastor was supposed to think through what he wanted the
missionary to accomplish, and both he and the missionary
were supposed to know what was expected.

"We want SIM missionaries working with us," said ECWA
leaders. "We'll be responsible for their job assignments
through the departments. But SIM should continue to look
after their welfare -- their salaries, furloughs, children's
education, and so on. Those are cultural needs you understand better than we; so you look after them."

To do this, a Services Committee of expatriates and
nationals was set up to look after the care of expatriate
personnel serving with ECWA. It also handled other aspects
of help to the whole work, such as guest houses and
aviation. (See appendices M, N, O for procedures for
secondment and stationing.)

The role of the SIM director changed to that of consultant to the ECWA executive. His title became International
Liaison Officer (ILO), and ECWA saw him as a vital link
with the SIM international organization, conferring about
recruitment of overseas personnel and special project funds
as mutually agreed between church and mission. The ILO
also would be ultimately responsible to SIM internationally

for the welfare of SIM missionaries working with ECWA. If
he saw a major problem, it was up to him to point it out to
the ECWA executive and to work with them on a solution. The
ILO and church executive met together as colleagues, for
prayer and fellowship as well as business.

The former SIM district superintendent role was no
longer necessary, since the ECWA districts had their own
officers. However, to help the Services Committee in its
care of expatriate personnel, Local Personnel Counselors
were elected by the missionaries. Since they had no line
authority but were experienced and spiritual people, ECWA
leaders felt that they could play a useful counseling role
with local pastors as well. They reported to an Area
Personnel Officer (APO) on the Services Committee, who in
turn discussed personnel problems with the ECWA executive
and the SIM ILO. Expatriate stationing recommendations
from the department heads were coordinated by the APO,
discussed with the executive and ILO, and processed through
the Services Committee.

One of the main concerns of missionaries was the shortage of trained leaders for the departments. "We aren't
opposed to working under church leadership," they said.
"But what happens if the department head is ill, or dies,
or goes for further training? Are there others able to
take his place?"

This is a common problem in rapidly developing countries,
and Nigeria was no exception. ECWA saw the problem and
realized the need for developing leadership. Meanwhile,
they felt there was no point in placing unqualified people
in office just for the sake of nationalizing. The fact
that ECWA was now legally responsible for SIM's work in the
country helped the standing of the work in the eyes of the
government, and beyond that, Nigeria was used to the concept of using expatriate specialists.

"We want to have the right man for the job -- whether he
is black or white," the executive said. They asked several
missionary department leaders to continue leading until
suitable nationals could be developed. Where an expatriate
was in charge, they appointed a national assistant. Where
a national was in charge, they appointed an expatriate assistant. In this way they benefited from a bicultural
team, each member providing the strengths of his background.

Although finance is usually among the first topics discussed in church-mission relations, at the time of the turnover ECWA was in no hurry. The executive wanted to think
through their whole financial structure before taking on
more responsibility for financial management. They made
good use of the experience and talents of church lay members
by appointing an advisory finance committee.

A year after the turnover ceremony eventually took place,
ECWA finally said she was ready to take on financial management of the departments. The SIM and church accounting
systems were amalgamated in one finance department, and SIM
Nigeria accounts became ECWA accounts. SIM International
accounts, including missionary salaries, were cared for in
the SIM International ledgers within the one department.

SIM pressed ECWA to appoint a Nigerian as head of the
finance department, but ECWA asked SIM to allow their
expatriate accountant to carry on for at least two years.

"We don't have anyone for the post yet," ECWA explained.
"We want the right man -- he should understand the churches
in the districts and be a spiritual man, not just anyone
with accountant's training."

Answering the questions

SIM constituencies, who had helped to make it possible
for ECWA to grow to its present maturity, also needed to be
informed about what the transfer of responsibility involved.
The mission's magazine, *Africa Now*, and staff representatives helped in this communication process. Most supporters
favored the turnover, but there were questions which naturally arose and needed answering:

*1. Since ECWA is taking responsibility for the work, is
SIM phasing out of Nigeria?*

Answer: There are several roles which missionaries have
played in the past, only one of which is that of leadership,
or having administrative responsibility. It is wise that
ECWA, desiring to be a responsible church, should take the
responsibility role. But other roles such as counseling,
teaching, evangelizing, church planting, and ministering
through special services will still be needed. ECWA is
asking for SIM missionaries to help her in these roles.

Thus, SIM is not phasing out in Nigeria in the sense of discontinuing work, but is continuing to be as active as ever. The difference is that this work is now under the leadership of the churches, which are strongly desirous of SIM's participation. Now the work in Nigeria is led by ECWA, but SIM and ECWA continue in an international partnership.

2. Has SIM lost its evangelistic vision, and is now only ministering to a church?

Answer: Not at all. SIM still has the vision which the pioneers had: evangelizing the part of Africa then known as "The Sudan." The early missionaries developed this primary goal into the twofold scriptural goal: evangelizing and discipling; winning people to Jesus Christ and then building them into the body of His church. However, the goal was not complete even there -- it involved raising up and equipping the local body of Christ to be an outreaching, missionary-minded church.

The SIM General Council stated in 1975:

> The overall objective of the mission in evangelism can never be accomplished by missionary personnel alone. The goal of the mission, therefore, is to mobilize and teach believers as quickly as possible so that they will assume their responsibility of proclaiming the gospel to all men and discipling them for Christ.[18]

With the church taking legal responsibility for all such work, missionaries from other lands can continue to fulfill their primary goal of evangelism and discipling, but now they do so through a missionary-minded church indigenous to the country. In some cases, this goal may be fulfilled directly. In other cases, it may be fulfilled indirectly as the missionary helps to equip believers to do this themselves. Not to do so would be a disaster -- irresponsible. It would mean that the original goal had only been partly fulfilled, and that the church had been left to stagnate.

Therefore missionaries and their supporters should not think of themselves as "serving a younger church," but as fulfilling the Great Commission through and with a younger church. ECWA leaders have stated: "We don't want to

think of you as serving under us, but alongside us in the
church of Jesus Christ."

SIM and ECWA are very conscious that an estimated 25
million people in Nigeria have not heard the gospel.[19]
Reaching them is the evangelistic vision of church and mission working together.

*3. Now if there are so many churches in Nigeria, and they
are responsible for their work, why is it necessary for
overseas churches to help financially?*

Answer: The church is working on trying to be self-reliant.
It has been for many years, as far as its pastors are concerned. This has always been the policy of SIM and ECWA --
except in exceptional cases such as following the Civil War,
when pastors in the affected area were completely destitute.
They were then temporarily assisted.

The churches are supporting their pastors and sendingout
missionaries. They are also contributing to some ministries, such as radio evangelism over ELWA. They are beginning to contribute to the support of their vernacular
Bible schools. However, there are still major projects for
which support is needed, and which the churches (most of
them rural) cannot yet undertake -- if they did, it would
harm their support of their own missionaries and pastors.

These projects include the development of the seminary
and operation of both the seminary and the Bible colleges,
and Theological Education by Extension projects. These are
projects for which the vision of local churches and their
ability to support them will need to be developed. Meanwhile, the church as a whole would be weakened, instead of
strengthened through improved pastoral care and leadership,
if Christians overseas did not join in assisting financially.

Finance is only a resource, but it is a resource which
overseas churches can use to help the younger church develop. It needs to be used with discretion so that the
work will be strengthened instead of weakened. The main
way is through theological and church leadership training
programs, which do not detract from the indigenous support
of the church, but in the end help to make it more strongly
indigenous.

Hay points out how this can work: "In the administration of the New Life for All program, 90 percent of the main office expenses were met from outside sources, whereas on the local level, where evangelism actually took place, 95 percent of the finances came from the church."[20]

Part of the mission's ministry in Nigeria is what Paul refers to in I Thess. 3:10: "Night and day praying exceedingly that we might see your face, and might perfect that which is lacking in your faith."

4. Is it possible for a national church to avoid dependence on a foreign mission, and yet integrate the work of the church and mission?

Answer: We believe it is. In the relations being developed by SIM in Africa, the mission and the national churches form an international partnership. In the sending countries, SIM takes the leadership in encouraging prayer, recruiting missionaries, and raising finance for projects which the churches cannot yet undertake. In Africa, the national churches take the leadership for the work, depending on their level of development. Where the church can take the responsibility (as with ECWA), missionaries work under national leadership.

As this international partnership is worked out in practical detail, it should strengthen the indigenous church. The mission's contribution, instead of being an obviously foreign, separate ministry, should become more relevant to the spiritual and cultural needs of the national church. The "indigenous church" belongs to the country; its life is relevant to the nation; nationals administer its work -- including that done by overseas missionaries. Its indigenous nature does not exclude using the gifts of the Spirit brought by missionaries from other lands. Their work is integrated with the national church, in keeping with its indigenous character.

SUMMARY

The ECWA-SIM experience is an example of a church and mission working out their relationships as they have grown together. No one formula will fit all situations, and the relationships of missions and churches in other lands will need to be formed in the context of each nation and the level of development of each church.

SIM pioneers came to fulfill the Commission of Jesus
Christ to preach the gospel and disciple believers. In
order to help achieve that goal, the mission developed
departments of the work. ECWA, which has been autonomous
(self-governing, self-supporting, and self-propagating)
since 1954, is now taking leadership for the departments in
order to continue meeting the same goals, with SIM
assisting her. Neither church nor mission knows all the
problems or needs that there may be in the future, but because of mutual trust and mutual goals, they will be able
to work together as the relationship develops. God willing,
as long as SIM is needed, she will continue to work with
the church to help her fulfill the Great Commission, not
only in Nigeria, but in other lands as well. (See appendix
P for chart.)

STUDY QUESTIONS: CHAPTER 9

1. In this case study, how did the SIM seek to avoid the
    tensions observed in some church denominations, over
    non-indigenous practices?

2. What tensions arose as the ECWA church grew and became
    a recognized body?

3. What realities did the new church denomination (ECWA)
    need to recognize?

4. What adjustment in thinking was needed on the part of
    the expatriate missionaries and their supporting
    constituency?

NOTES: CHAPTER 9

1. Stephen Neill, *History of Christian Missions*, p. 459.

2. R.V. Bingham, "Britain's Crisis in Missionary Policy,"
    Evangelical Christian (Toronto, Ontario: Evangelical
    Publishers, June 1919), p. 165.

3. E.A. Ayandele, *The Missionary Impact on Modern
    Nigeria, 1842-1914* (London: Longmans, 1966), p. 151.

4. Facts gathered from interviews by the author with
    nationals and expatriates who have been involved in
    the area.

5. R.J. Davis, in a letter to W.H. Fuller, April 25, 1977.

6. *Ibid.*

7. E. Bolaji Idowu, *Towards an Indigenous Church* (London: Oxford University Press, 1965), p. 5.

8. Comment of Rev. Simon Ibrahim (ECWA General Secretary) on the matter of choir robes (in a note to the author on the manuscript draft): "Whereas SIM discouraged the use of the choir robes, there were other missions which promoted it. ECWA learned some Western practices from other missions and thus got itself into problems for which SIM is not to blame. The introduction of the choir robe is not only a financial drain but has also led to formalities against which some members are crying. 'Why do we have to stand up when the choir marches in? Is it to honor the uniform or the Lord?' ask many ECWA members."

9. *Daily Times,* Nigeria, Feb. 25, 1974, p. 19.

10. Byang H. Kato, "Aid to the National Church" (Wheaton, IL: *Evangelical Missions Quarterly,* Vol. 8, No. 4, 1972), pp. 194, 195.

11. Byang H. Kato, discussions with the author.

12. Byang H. Kato, "Aid to the National Church" (Wheaton, IL: EMQ Vol. 8, No. 4, 1972), pp. 197-199.

13. W.G. Crouch, "SIM-ECWA Relationships," message to SIM West Africa Council, 1960.

14. SIM Furlough Seminar Lectures, 1968 (Scarborough, Ont: SIM Archives).

15. Church-Mission Seminar papers, March 11-13, 1974 (Scarborough, Ont: SIM Archives).

16. James F. Engel, and H. Wilbert Norton, *What's Gone Wrong with the Harvest?* (Grand Rapids, MI: Zondervan, 1975), p. 45.

17. From research conducted at area conferences in 1976 and 1977 by James E. Plueddemann, SIM-ECWA Research Office, Jos, Nigeria. See appendix K for one of the summaries, dated May 1976.

18. SIM Manual, 1976, p. 43.

19. Researched by SIM's Gerald Swank for the Nigerian
    Evangelical Fellowship, Ilorin, Nigeria. See also
    Gerald Swank, *Frontier Peoples of Central Nigeria*
    (South Pasadena, CA: William Carey Library, 1977).

20. C. Peter Wagner, *Church/Mission Tensions Today*
    (Chicago, IL: Moody Press, 1972), p. 207.

10

On Target

The government official shook hands with SIM's General
Director Ian M. Hay after the ceremony marking the turnover
of responsibility to ECWA November 19, 1976.[1]

"I thank God for this day," he said, tears in his eyes.
"We have done it without war between Africans and the mission."

The official was Zechariah Gaiya, Commissioner for
Internal Affairs, Kaduna State, who had formerly been principal of an SIM secondary school. He chaired the turnover
ceremony, and his statement to Hay referred to the fact
that the turnover was not the result of a crisis or confrontation between church and mission.

Church and mission saw it as the continuation of a
turning over process which began with the establishment of
ECWA in 1954. "We are grateful that in 1975 the SIM
General Council made the decision without pressure by the
government or ECWA," stated ECWA General Secretary Simon
Ibrahim, "and that SIM has continued to take the initiative
in finalizing the passage of control to the national
churches."

In his acceptance speech, ECWA President David Olusiyi
said: "We are making history today. This will be a great
joy to our parent, SIM, that her baby has grown to the
state of manhood to take up her full responsibilities."

Hay stressed the significance of SIM's continuing participation in Nigeria. "We have a new vision," he said,
"of ECWA growing in every sector, aggressive in evangelism
and church planting. We are happy to assist ECWA in the
achievement of these goals."

In an article in *Africa Now*, I explained the transfer
like this:

> A while ago I was riding in the back seat of
> ECWA General Secretary Simon Ibrahim's car.
> He was at the wheel. SIM missionary Gordon
> Beacham sat beside him.
>
> I thought about the fathers of those two men.
> Gordon's father had been a pioneer SIM mis-
> sionary among the Tangale people of Nigeria.
> Simon's father had been one of the first
> Tangale preachers. They often traveled to-
> gether in the missionary's car. Gordon's
> father sat at the wheel; Simon's father sat
> beside him.
>
> That's the way it was in the work, too. Of
> necessity at that time, Gordon's father was
> the driver. Today, their sons have changed
> places. The church is in the driver's seat,
> and the mission sits alongside.
>
> That's what has happened in the transfer of
> responsibility. The team members are still
> the same; they're still traveling together
> to the same destination, but ECWA is now be-
> hind the wheel.
>
> That transfer of responsibility to ECWA does
> not mean that SIM is winding up its work in
> Nigeria. Taking over responsibility means
> taking over the leadership. It doesn't mean
> suddenly being able to finish the task all by
> oneself. It's a change of leadership, of
> authority, of responsibility, but it's not
> the completion of the work.
>
> We've often said, perhaps glibly, "We're here
> to work ourselves out of a job." That's good
> from one standpoint -- it says we don't have
> a colonial mentality of remaining forever in

charge. Unfortunately the statement has also come to imply that as soon as a missionary finds an African replacement, he can quit. Further, some people think that as soon as the national church takes responsibility for some phase of the work, the mission should move out. That's not necessarily so.

It's true that we missionaries should all be working ourselves out of *a* job, in the sense of training someone else for a particular post, but we aren't working ourselves out of *the* job of evangelism and discipling.

There are some who feel that the mission and church should remain entirely separate. That view is known as dichotomy. It means that when a church takes over responsibility from the mission, the mission withdraws completely.

Then there is the fusion viewpoint, in which the mission is absorbed into the church. The thought behind that is that the church is the only valid factor, and once it is established, there is no more place for the mission as a separate entity.

It is interesting that ECWA doesn't see it either way. What we have in our relationship is the church as the continuing structure, and the mission as a sort of task force working with and through it. Both are distinctive organizations that are knit together very closely because of their mutual goals. As I have reviewed mission-church relationships in various countries, I have been convinced that God has given SIM and ECWA a very precious and unusual relationship.[2]

As Commissioner Gaiya said, SIM and ECWA arrived at this relationship "without war." However, that did not mean that there had been no tensions, or that there would not be tensions in the future. In fact, since the turnover, ECWA and SIM have experienced most of the tensions which we have discussed in chapter 8.

"My people have a proverb," Simon Ibrahim once told me
with a grin; "you can't be true friends unless you fight!"
The closer the relationship, the more opportunities there
were to test our true fellowship in the midst of the tensions. In that way tension could become creative. All tension is not harmful; in the field of dynamics, tension is
essential to operation. But it has to be handled in the
right way.

Transferred tensions

When SIM was in leadership, missionaries did not realize
the tensions which nationals felt. Nationals were working
under a leadership style from another culture. For the
most part they quietly put up with the misunderstandings,
looking upon them as a necessary complement of the missionary's bringing the gospel -- for which they gave thanks.

Occasionally there was a minor explosion, but the missionaries usually did not realize what deep feelings lay
under the surface. After turnover, nationals felt much
more free to express their frustrations, ECWA leaders
found.

Since the church took responsibility for the work, it
has been the expatriates' turn to work under a different
leadership style. So they have felt tensions more than
they did before.

Turnover of responsibility does not remove all tension
-- it transfers some of it. For instance, during a leadership skills course, when we discussed why missionaries may
feel isolated, a Nigerian asked, "Why should missionaries
feel isolated now? Don't they realize that many of us
nationals have felt isolated from them all these years?"

However, without turnover, other tensions would become
increasingly harmful to the work, as we have discussed in
previous chapters.

In the new SIM-ECWA relationship, some of the tensions
arose from circumstances unrelated to turnover -- such as
the inefficiency of a person not suitable or not trained
for the post. Some such appointments at times had been
made unwittingly by SIM before turnover, and in a few cases
had involved expatriates. It was one of the unfortunate
results of staff shortage, and could be demoralizing.

Organizational matters accounted for some frustrations.
The loose association of ECWA could not exert the strong
central control which missionaries were used to when SIM led
the work. Some priorities were different, sometimes affecting stationing, housing, and projects. The system at
times bent to culture. (However, we noted that missionaries sometimes by-passed the system too!)

Not only expatriates, but also ECWA leaders were frustrated by some problems as ECWA gained experience. After
one conference, the Church Growth Secretary told the department heads' meeting:

> The haphazard planning of the conference has
> betrayed our inefficiency . . . . We have lost
> a valuable opportunity that can cause a steady
> decline for as long as an apology does not go
> out to our pastors . . . . If nothing is done,
> it will be comparable to laying eggs that will
> hatch for our successors.[3]

The horizontal-vertical tension (see chapter 8, diagram
8B) was felt most in the medical department. The
horizontally structured network of dispensaries and hospitals came into tension with the vertically structured
local churches. Staff were caught in the middle of the
tension.

Communication problems seemed to account for most frustrations. Missionaries had been used to communication
flowing from Council through a district superintendent to
their stations, and vice versa. When the Mission Council
and the district superintendent roles were changed, they
felt isolated. Did their departments really know anything
about them or their work, they wondered. Communication
channels needed improving. ECWA pastors also felt some
tensions. They sensed lack of communication with some missionaries. "We don't know what the missionary is doing or
where he is traveling," they told ECWA headquarters; "yet
you say we should help them if they run into problems. Do
they want our help only when they are in trouble?"

Some felt that SIM was still directing the work because
they did not understand the departmental structure, even
though the departments now reported to ECWA and not SIM.
At times an enthusiastic missionary would make a unilateral
decision, giving the impression that SIM was in charge.

In chapter 8 we discussed the suspicion over the TEE
program -- pastors thought that missionaries developed it
so they would not have to work under the church. The same
suspicion was voiced over some missionaries who taught Bible
Knowledge (BK) as a subject in government schools. Christian students preferred to have their own Sunday service in
the school and not in the local church -- they felt more
comfortable in their student sub-culture. BK teachers were
sometimes accused of encouraging this in order to maintain
their own areas of control, separate from the church.

Many streses arose from the fact that individuals gave
different interpretation to the turnover. The average local
pastor's attitude was influenced by (1) his previous relations with missionaries; (2) his personal expectations; and
(3) his whole concept of what SIM was and how it operated.

Housing was an example. The concept of ECWA HQ, and the
agreement in the turnover, was that SIM would register all
property under ECWA, but that ECWA guaranteed the use of
residences needed for housing SIM missionaries, since ECWA
wanted those missionaries to continue serving in Nigeria.

When a local pastor heard that SIM had turned houses over
to ECWA, he might think the house was to be "auctioned off"
and that he should put in his bid before someone else did.
To the missionary, this looked as if the pastor wanted to
have the house more than to have the missionary.

Depending on the concept the pastor had of turnover, when
he saw missionaries caring for local housing (as agreed by
ECWA HQ), he could feel that the turnover was all a hoax --
that SIM hadn't really turned over responsibility to ECWA.
The ECWA President had to write the districts to clear up
these misconceptions.[4]

Mission and church leaders came in for their share of
criticism at times. Even before turnover, some missionaries
felt that the officers at headquarters were unaware of their
local problems, and therefore lived in an "ivory tower." We
sought to help overcome this feeling in a conference discussion paper:

> Some missionaries feel that way, when we at
> headquarters try to be positive in what we say.
> They think we are naive, or super-optimistic,
> or unrealistic. I don't know how to assure
> them that we do understand, without saying

some things that would not be at all helpful.
Actually, we understand not only *your* local
problem, but the local problems of many a
missionary in different parts of the country
-- so we have an overall picture. You hear of
problems in your village church; we hear of
them all over. Besides this, both ECWA and
SIM Executive members can see the problems in
their own local churches.

I'm saying this so that you will know that you
aren't alone in facing problems, and that we
are not ignoring them. But it simply would
not help if we went around telling everyone what
problems Pastor X or Missionary Y are having, to
prove that we don't live in an ivory tower! When
we hear of problems, we try to get action through
the right channels -- and in some difficult
cases we are "shut up to prayer." Right now,
ECWA leaders are trying to overcome communication blocks which keep church problems from
being dealt with.[5]

Some ECWA members criticized their leaders for "dancing
to the missionaries' tune," while at the same time some
missionaries felt mission leaders were being "pushed around"
by ECWA. "Sometimes we feel like a rope in a tug-of-war,"
Ibrahim once said, "We are pulled this way and that."

Few realized how frankly both mission and church leaders
leveled with each other about problems, and how they prayed
together for God's solution. Their goal was not to see what
each could get for "his side," but rather they sought each
other's good and the good of the Lord's work in the nation.

"If I had known as much as you, I would have walked right
out of some of those tense sessions I remember in Jos,"
Victor Musa wrote us. He was ECWA Church Growth Secretary
at the time of turnover, and since has studied Missiology
overseas. "It is obvious that all we are grappling with in
church-mission relations, the indigenous church, and personnel development, you have been wrestling with for years!
I couldn't have stood discussing a subject I knew so well
while novices like 'Victor' discussed sometimes foolishly
and even misrepresented these issues. This is not to say
some of the difficulties were not heavy or tough and
nasty."[6]

"Victor, do not feel that we were upset as we discussed many issues in Jos," I wrote in reply. "We ourselves did not feel that we had superior knowledge, even though we did have access to information through books and our own experience. We realize that our knowledge and experience had to go through the process of Nigerian thinking, and had to be matched with the practicability of Nigerian experience. It was therefore helpful to us to have to debate issues with you and others, because that enabled us to think through more carefully and adapt our thinking."

While it would not be honest to overlook the tensions which church and mission have experienced since turnover of responsibility, it would also be misleading to give the impression that all was tension, or that there was an atmosphere of animosity. To the contrary, the general attitude of missionaries and pastors was one of fellowship and concern for each other. People prayed about the problems as they continued their work.

The spiritual dimension

"Our experience has been both joyful and painful," Simon told me. "Missionaries shouldn't expect everything to work smoothly. They should be prepared to weep at times, to pray at times. They should not allow their hearts to ache because the work may not seem to be theirs. The work isn't ECWA's. It isn't SIM's. It is the Lord's. We are only His instruments to get it done.

"The path we have followed hasn't always been as straight as we planned. We've gone to the left and the right. Our visions have taken much longer than we thought, to organize the turnover properly. Patience is the key -- we all need to trust the Lord as we work out the problems together."

As we have noted elsewhere, although structure is important, *attitude* is even more important. No system can succeed if attitudes are wrong. The dynamics of ECWA-SIM relations caused many a missionary and pastor to examine the spiritual dimension in his own life. Larry Fehl, International Liaison Officer for Nigeria, tells of one conference:

> How does one begin to tell about something that is beyond human comprehension? God did a wonderful thing through the ministry of Ray and Anne Ortlund.[7] We were prepared beforehand

for a work of the Holy Spirit; we were expecting God to do something in our lives.

We had three full days, with three sessions
each day. The Ortlunds stressed the need to
have the three priorities straight in our
lives: right relations with God, others, and
the work. They stated that missionaries often
go from priority 1 straight to priority 3,
without putting the second priority into
proper focus.

Each day we discussed one of the priorities.
After exposition we put into practice in small
groups what we learned. On Friday we learned
how to worship and put God first in our lives.
On Saturday we learned how to begin a discipleship group.

In the evening we were told how to begin to
love one another. The first step is to tell
another person that you love him and why you
love him. At the end of the service we were
asked to tell five people personally that we
loved them and why, before we left the chapel.

For a minute everyone just looked around. Ray
said in fun: "Lock the doors!" Then the ice
broke and people went up and down the aisles
telling why they appreciated and loved one
another. Some people later said no one ever
had told them that they were loved.

The Lord started right then to put a love in
our hearts for one another. This type of
appreciation and concern continued for the
rest of the conference.

On Sunday we studied the miracle of the
paralytic (Mark 2), seeing how evangelism is
teamwork. If our commitment to God is first
and our commitment to each other is right, our
third commitment to our work becomes natural
and easy and a joy.

Sunday afternoon and evening were "body life"
sessions: sharing from the Scriptures, sharing
where we hurt, where we had a need, where there

was need for restoration and confession.

People began to share areas of their lives that
were hidden. It was not a morbid confession of
sins that should have been confessed only to
God. It was confession of sins that we all
knew about, and that should have been confessed
publicly. People took off masks and asked one
another to pray for specifics.

We prayed; we shared; we confessed; we wept --
we all were brought very low before God. This
went on until after 10 p.m. Sunday. It would
have gone on half the night if Ray Ortlund
hadn't suggested we stop. He then warned that
we were on a mountain, and tomorrow we would go
down to the valley where we live.

On the last night an ECWA leader stated that he
had had his priorities mixed up -- the work
came first many times, and he hadn't taken time
for God or for people. He said: "I want all
of you missionaries to know that I love you and
want to work with you." Several people then
prayed for the ECWA leaders and their families.

We are all praying that the renewal will not be
an event, but an ongoing way of our relating
to God, to one another, and to our work. There
have been dramatic breakthroughs in many of our
lives as poor relationships have been made
right.

Beneficial results

Spiritual re-evaluation under the pressure of changing
circumstances was one beneficial result of the turnover.

An obvious benefit was the opportunity for ECWA to gain
experience in problem-solving while SIM missionaries were
still available to assist, and without the pressures of any
crisis in the work or nation. ECWA was already experienced
in administering her actual church life, but shouldering
the complexities of the departments was something new.
ECWA did not fully realize all the implications -- one
usually learns best by actually doing a job.

A new sense of responsibility developed. Pastors realized that development of the work depended on them and their
members, rather than the missionary. Educated young men and
women began to ask how they could help.

Since turnover, ECWA's image as a Nigerian organization,
not a foreign subsidiary, has increased. ECWA officials,
not missionaries, have been the ones to confront the government on issues affecting the work. Increasingly Nigerian
leaders of thought have asked ECWA leaders their opinions on
national issues.

The most encouraging result was a greater sense of responsibility for unreached people. Other factors were involved in this, including greater awareness of the need as
a result of research and greater capacity to meet the need
as the income of Christians increased. The turnover coin-
cided with these developments.

"What were the goals of SIM before turnover?" Simon
Ibrahim asked in a joint executive consultation one day.

"To win people to Jesus Christ and disciple them into
local churches," we replied.

"Are those goals being met today, in spite of the
stresses some people find in the work?" Ibrahim asked next.

We agreed that ECWA was meeting those goals, and that was
the most important factor in evaluating our relationship.

Evangelism and missionary outreach were not new concepts
to the churches. As the early converts studied the commands of Christ, they responded by taking the gospel to
others. In 1937 five Nigerian couples were sent as missionaries by the Tangale churches. This was only 21 years
after the gospel first entered a tribe known for ritual
murder and cannibalism. In 21 years missionaries had
learned the language, put it into writing, and translated
the New Testament, while establishing churches. In that
period these new converts had also learned to read the Bible
in Hausa, a language foreign to them, so they could go
across their cultural boundaries with the gospel. These
were in reality "foreign missionaries," supported entirely
by very young churches. Those same churches also took up an
offering in 1937 to help SIM go into the Sudan (then known
as the Anglo-Egyptian Sudan).8

EMS -- A CASE STUDY OF A THIRD WORLD MISSION

In December 1948 a committee of Nigerian pastors and SIM missionaries met to form the African Missionary Society -- later renamed the Evangelical Missionary Society (EMS) to avoid confusion with another group called AMS. The society was approved by the SIM Council in 1949. Its goal was to send national missionaries across ethnic and cultural boundaries, as distinct from the evangelists who were already working out from local churches.[9]

Meanwhile, further south, three Yoruba young men were challenged by the need for missionaries among the people of neighboring Dahomey (now Benin). At the Annual Conference at Egbe, January 1949, they volunteered and an offering for their support was taken on the spot. After the conference they left for Dahomey with an SIM missionary returning to his work. The Egbe area churches promised regular support.[10]

In 1950 the EMS supported 27 Nigerian missionaries, most among other ethnic groups in Nigeria, and 3 in Niger to the North.[11]

It was not until four years later that the SIM-related churches formally joined together under the name ECWA, and in 1956 ECWA was officially registered with the government. EMS became the mission society of ECWA.

The number of EMS missionaries has steadily increased, until in 1979 there were 130 couples, or 260 missionaries, counting husband and wife. Since 1950, more than 300 missionaries have been sent out, serving in 50 distinct language groups. The ECWA church base for this operation numbers 1400 local congregations, but many of them are small subsistence-level groups.

To encourage Nigerian Christians to support their own missionaries and not depend on foreign resources, SIM missionaries contributed to EMS support only through church missionary offerings -- not directly. Donations from an expatriate missionary direct to EMS were supposed to be only for such additional needs as travel and EMS children's hostel support.

EMS has had to be concerned about the care of her missionaries working in different cultures. For several years EMS provided a hostel and school for the children of mis-

sionaries working in areas where there were no schools, or
where Islamic pressures made schooling difficult for their
children. This project was eventually abandoned in favor of
having such children live with Christians in villages where
they can attend school, if at all possible. Sometimes
school-age children have to be left with relatives in their
"home culture."

The support figure for EMS missionaries has been minimal.
For the first 20 years it was so low that a missionary could
not support his family without farming -- and that took a
lot of his time. When there were general wage increases
throughout the country in 1975, ECWA took a realistic look
at the situation and doubled the monthly salary. In 1978 it
was again doubled. However, it still was only two-thirds of
the government scale for unskilled labor; the EMS calling is
still one of sacrifice. The salary fluctuates monthly, as
EMS is dependent on how much comes in.

In spite of this, EMS missionaries rarely complain. At
a gathering of church leaders from across Africa, one leader
asked the EMS Secretary, "How do you keep your missionaries
from complaining about poor living conditions?" The
Secretary hardly knew how to answer because he hadn't had to
handle such complaints.

EMS has more calls for workers than it can meet. Requests have come from Ghana, Chad, Sudan, Benin, Niger,
as well as from other tribal areas in Nigeria.

"We could place 17 missionaries right now, if we had the
people and support," reported Panya Baba, EMS Secretary.

EMS is trying to watch her "indigenous principles." As
soon as a church is formed and can support a pastor, EMS
moves the missionary to a new station. In one recent year,
six missionaries were thus restationed.

Until recently few EMS workers had any primary schooling
-- only four years of vernacular Bible training. Now EMS
is attracting men with more education. One resigned from
the police force, took Bible college, and signed up with
EMS. This year a primary school teacher and a school head-
master gave up their government salaries and went to work as
missionaries, for one-tenth their previous salary. A
government mechanic handed in his resignation in order to
work with EMS; the government thought he resigned because of
money, so promoted him and offered him a car. When he would

not be dissuaded, his boss was so amazed that he sent a
government truck to transport his family and possessions to
wherever he might be stationed.

Nigerian Christian businessmen donated to EMS four bicy-
cles, two motorcycles, and two cars within a 12-month period.

In one recent year the EMS income was twice the income
for ECWA Headquarters expenses. Although ECWA always could
use more money to provide central services for the churches,
the Executive really are thankful for the emphasis on giving
to missions.

"When we lack money for administration, we cry, but we
don't get it!" ECWA's General Secretary said jokingly.
"When our EMS Secretary tells us that missionaries are
lacking support, the money starts coming in. Evangelism
[missions] is the only department which gets money by asking
the churches for it!"

EMS has experienced the kind of problems which most missions face. Raising support is one we have mentioned. Lack
of trained staff for office functions has been another. It
sounds great to have 260 missionaries out in the work, but
ECWA has only recently come to realize the kind of supportive staff needed to keep them out there.

"I don't have a secretary," EMS Secretary Panya Baba said
on one occasion; "so I can't keep up with my correspondence.
I know I should spend time planning strategy, but I'm tied
down to office details."

Pastor Panya and ECWA leaders asked SIM for accounting
help. "We don't have trained people," Panya explained.
"As a result, we had to use an untrained clerk who really
messed up the account books. People haven't been getting
receipts; we can't trace some of the gifts. You know how
bad that is for giving -- our donors will lose confidence.
We need help fast!" (See appendix E, "How SIM helped ECWA
develop its mission.")

Cultural clashes

EMS has also faced the cultural clashes that expatriates
face. Many of the missionaries have come from ECWA's most
responsive area, which has an animistic background. When
these recruits cross ethnic lines into Muslim areas, their

accent, dress, eating habits, and other customs often form
a stumbling block.

Nigerian missionaries in Benin at one time had to withdraw. There were tensions over their different culture and
living standard. The local people felt that some of the
Nigerian missionaries were tending to dominate the work and
were introducing Nigerian customs. It was hard for the
enthusiastic supporting churches in Nigeria to understand
this. Eventually the Nigerians were unable to get re-entry
permits because the government was suspicious that they
might stimulate political activities.

Kantiyok Tukura, a Nigerian missionary to neighboring
Ghana, found he had to study the customs and beliefs of
Muslims in Ghana before he could witness to them effectively.
He found a cultural backlash when he wore his customary
robes from Northern Nigeria. Muslims in Ghana equated
Christianity with Western suits and the English language.
They became annoyed when he wore traditional clothing and
preached in their vernacular language (both of which were
customary for Kantiyok to use in his own country)!

The Tukuras felt very lonely at first in an alien culture. The people wondered what were their real motives in
living among them. They also found that Ghanaians looked
upon Nigeria as being rich. The Tukuras, therefore, dressed
more simply than they normally would in Nigeria, so as not
to be a stumbling block.

In neighboring Chad, ECWA learned more missionary lessons.
During the persecution of the church in Chad in the early
1970s, ECWA, with SIM relief assistance, had enabled 10
Chadian refugees to take Bible training in Nigeria. When
the persecution stopped, ECWA responded to a chief's request
to set up a small vernacular Bible school. The refugees
and Christian villagers were enthusiastic. They felt this
would help rebuild the decimated church. ECWA leaders had
no expansionist motives, but saw this as an opportunity to
help fellow Christians in need. They planned to send two
Bible teachers for two years.

"When we sent over to set up the program, we really ran
into trouble," said Victor Musa, ECWA Church Growth Secretary. "We had a good idea and worthy motives, but some
church leaders misunderstood. They wanted to do things their
way, and we had to be patient and let them. Through this

experience we learned a lot about missionary problems. Now we can understand some of the tensions SIM has faced!"

ECWA saw the need for cultural adaptation among different ethnic groups in Nigeria itself. When the Hausa Maguzawa people recently started coming to the Lord in numbers, ECWA used the local custom of holding a community feast to celebrate an important occasion. Instead of announcing their faith singly (a Western individualistic custom), new converts studied together until a number were prepared for a corporate announcement. Christians gathered from surrounding villages, bringing food with them and joining in a "Feast of Repentance." Muslim neighbors looked on in amazement but could not object to the culturally acceptable demonstration.

Somewhat as the Jerusalem Council had discussed the gospel's entry to the gentiles, ECWA leaders discussed the phenomenon of thousands of Maguzawa coming to Christ. They decided to open a separate Bible school for Maguzawa converts -- so they would not be affected by the Christian subculture which characterized the other Bible schools.

"Such things as using drums to accompany hymn singing are out," EMS Secretary Panya stated. "And they should be allowed to sit on mats rather than benches, if that would be more cultural."

The EMS has been an inspiration to churches in other developing countries. Panya has described the work at conferences in Asia, Europe, and America. The cross-pollination of ideas between Third World mission agencies is proving mutually helpful.

ECWA realizes the need to develop both her missionaries and her missionary support base in the churches. Seminars on evangelism are held in the church districts, using such texts as Gerber's *God's Way to Keep a Church Going and Growing*.[12] ECWA is developing a missions study center. ECWA Media has produced a filmstrip to encourage churches to support the work of EMS. *ECWA News*, the churches' journal, constantly reports on missionary work and local witness. Evangelism is discussed more than any other topic at Department Heads meetings and Councils.

ECWA is taking her responsibilities for cross-cultural and local evangelism seriously. When her leaders accepted the challenge of the Nigerian Congress on Evangelization to reach everyone in Nigeria with the gospel in a two-year period, they calculated they would need 150 evangelists for their part. They mobilized 50 vernacular Bible school seniors to start with. For the remainder they called on 100 churches to release their pastors for a one-year "sabbatical" to evangelize unreached people.

"But how will we support these?" asked the local overseers.

"Aren't they supported now?" the Executive replied. "Let the churches continue their salaries."

"But who will pastor the churches while they are away?" was the next question.

"The elders and deacons have the gifts of the Spirit," was the reply. "They can do the pastor's work while he's away. We've got to give this priority!"

ECWA realizes that her missionaries will need to learn new languages and cultures to reach most of the unevangelized groups. Some of these have no church among them; some have churches which cannot yet cope with the size of the task.

Recently an Ibo Christian businessman was invited by Yoruba churches to speak to them on ways in which Christian businessmen can help the church. Chidi Abali was very impressed by what he saw of church growth in the Yoruba area.

"The SIM pioneers did a great deal to help establish the churches here," he told the Yoruba pastors. "Now why don't you send missionaries over to help us in the Ibo area, where we are short of workers?"

The pastors replied that they did not speak Ibo.

"When the foreign missionaries came to your towns, could they speak Yoruba?" Abali asked. "They had to learn the language before they could preach. Why don't your pastors come over and learn the language and teach our people, as the early missionaries did among your people?"

This was an indigenous challenge to missionary outreach!

SUMMARY

Even though a number of changes have taken place in the way the work is being done since SIM turned over leadership responsibility, the original scriptural goals of the work are still being pursued. The results are even more culturally relevant now than before.

The church organization has not become an end in itself but the means to an end -- an instrument to pass on the gospel to other unreached people. In doing this, ECWA is experiencing the same types of tensions that SIM passed through. Although SIM missionaries now feel certain cultural stresses more than they did before turnover, they have been spared the most frustrating tension a missionary can face -- impasse over reaching the unevangelized.

Evangelism and missionary outreach were not new concepts transferred to ECWA at the time of turning over responsibility. They were not a foreign idea imposed by the mission, but were central to ECWA's goals -- something that belonged to ECWA.

"Evangelism is at the heart of ECWA," declared ECWA President Olusiyi at the April 1978 General Church Council. "When evangelism dies, ECWA is dead!"

Olusiyi was speaking from his heart. He was one of the three young men who volunteered as missionaries at the Egbe conference in 1949.

STUDY QUESTIONS: CHAPTER 10

1. What "transferred tensions" were observed after the church assumed responsibility for leading the work? What were the major causes?

2. What were the beneficial results of transfer to church leadership?

3. What tensions did the indigenous mission (EMS) experience as it started church planting in other cultures? Relate these to mission-church tensions experienced by the apostle Paul and missions ever since his day.

4. In what ways was SIM able to help EMS develop as a mission, without harming its indigenous character (see appendix E)?

NOTES: CHAPTER 10

1. For Turnover speeches and documents, see Appendices Q, R, S, T, U.

2. W. Harold Fuller, *Africa Now*, (Scarborough, Ontario: SIM, March–April 1977), pp. 8–11.

3. Victor Musa, ECWA Church Growth Dept., Jos, Nigeria, memo for Department Heads Meeting, Sept. 6, 1977.

4. David Olusiyi, ECWA Headquarters, Jos, Nigeria, letter to DCC leaders, Nov. 28, 1977.

5. W. Harold Fuller, "A Discussion Paper for SIM Area Conferences in Nigeria, 1976," SIM, Jos, Nigeria, p. 11.

6. Victor Musa, letter to the author, December 25, 1978.

7. Raymond Ortlund is pastor of Lake Avenue Congregational Church, Pasadena, CA, and has an extensive Bible teaching ministry. He and Mrs. Ortlund spoke at conferences in West Africa in 1979.

8. *Evangelical Christian* (Toronto, Ontario: Evangelical Publishers, Sept. 1937).

9. SIM Nigerian Field Letter No. 5, Feb. 1949.

10. Sophie de la Haye, *Tread Upon the Lion* (Agincourt, Ontario: SIM, 1973), pp. 109, 110.

11. Raymond J. Davis, "A National Missionary Movement," a paper presented at the EFMA–IFMA Executive Retreat 1964.

12. Vergil Gerber, *God's Way To Keep a Church Going and Growing* (Glendale, CA: Regal Books Division, G/L Publications) (South Pasadena, CA: William Carey Library, 1973).

11

Responsibility
Of
The Future

Political and economic crises have forced us to recognize
the interdependence of the nations around this globe. We
have become painfully aware of the relation of raw materials, politics, and even religion, and the way in which
events halfway around the world can bring dramatic changes
to our own local communities.

Developments in Asia, Latin America, and Africa will
continue to affect the future of the rest of the world.
For instance, Africa has 25% of the world's states, giving
her enormous voice in world bodies.

The influence of the Third World also has great potential
in spiritual matters. Since our case studies are chiefly
from Africa, let us look at the significance of the continent.

Out of a total Africa population of around 800 million
predicted for the end of this century, 350 million may call
themselves Christian -- about 46%[1]. This would give
Christianity a majority over any other religion in Africa.

What does this mean to churches and missions?

Responsibility within Africa

For Africa, the prediction is both exciting and frightening. Barrett says such "growth could become catastrophic." He quotes Hastings: "By [AD 2000] there will have been a widespread breakdown of the church in Africa, simply clogged by numbers. . . . Such figures are frankly terrifying, at least when no one is doing the church planning such an increase demands."2

The explosion of church growth in Africa provides a challenge to evangelicals, who believe in personal salvation and scriptural discipling. Barrett's figures include every type of "Christian" sect. Less than 10% could be considered to have accepted Christ as Savior in the biblical sense of the new birth.3

Consequently the majority are misled by a syncretistic or at least nominal Christianity, and are still outside the kingdom of Christ. They exert a deadening effect on the churches, leading them into unscriptural views and practices -- all in the name of "African Christianity." In fact, there is the danger that the results of the sacrificial labors of gospel messengers, black and white, over the past century, could be dissipated in this generation.

"Many evangelical churches are busy winning converts who are not properly discipled," warns Stephen Akangbe, an ECWA leader. "As a result, they become Christo-pagan. A lack of dedication on the part of many believers and the great desire for further education leads some to study at any cost, even if the true Scripture basis of the fundamental teaching is undermined."4

Akangbe listed training of church leadership as the number one way in which expatriate missions could assist national churches in evangelizing their countries. ECWA's Theological Education Secretary projected the need for 62,854 leaders (including lay leaders such as elders and Sunday school teachers) to be trained to match an expected ten-year growth rate of 200% in ECWA churches.5

"The Lord has a purpose for His church in this country," said Bitrus Gani, a Nigerian physiotherapist who is also a lay evangelist. "The job of the mission is to help bring out the leadership in the church, which under God will fulfill the purpose the Lord designed for His people. I would like to hope that you will find practical ways to develop the leadership in the church, so that it can serve God's purpose. There are too many missionary societies on their way out who have developed a leadership that is serving the purpose of Satan. This is true of many missionary societies. I know one church where they have nationalized beautifully, and what was started by missionaries has now ended up to be at best a political setup -- very well ordered in its hierarchy, but by and large useless to God and a problem to the nation."[6]

"Within the continent of Africa some exciting things are happening in the church," Kato stated. "But on the other side of the ledger, there are things that are frightening, indeed threatening the very existence of evangelical Christianity in Africa. In the year 2000 will the vast number of Christians in Africa be truly Bible-oriented? Or will there be a very vast number who do not yet have the light -- the biblical faith?"[7]

Kato wrote a ten-point proposal for safeguarding biblical Christianity in Africa:

1. Adhere to the basic presuppositions of historic Christianity.

2. Express Christianity in a truly African context, allowing it to judge the African culture and never allowing the culture to take precedence over Christianity.

3. Concentrate effort in the training of men in the Scriptures, employing the original languages to facilitate their ability in exegeting the Word of God.

4. Carefully study African traditional religions as well as other religions, but only secondarily to the inductive study of God's Word.

5. Launch an aggressive program of evangelism and missions to prevent a fall into the error of the doctrinal strifes of third-century Christianity in North Africa (at the expense of evangelism).

6. Consolidate organizational structures based on doctrinal agreements.

7. Carefully and accurately delineate and concisely express terms of theology as a necessary safeguard against syncretism and universalism.

8. Carefully present apologetics toward unbiblical systems that are creeping into the church. This calls for more leadership training.

9. Show concern in social action but bear in mind at all times that the primary goal of the church is the presentation of personal salvation.

10. Following the steps of the New Testament Church, Christians in Africa should be prepared to say, "For to me to live is Christ, and to die is gain" (Phil. 1:21). Africa needs her Polycarps, ready to contend for the faith at any cost.[8]

Tokunboh Adeyemo, AEAM General Secretary, likens the problems of Christendom in Africa to the early church in North Africa: "Aren't the churches in Africa confronted with similar problems today?"[9] He writes:

We need to rediscover what I call "agressive evangelism." The Christian faith is always a missionary-oriented faith. We should not let the fire of evangelism die out of our churches today. We should not get preoccupied with what we are going to eat -- what we are going to clothe ourselves with and how we are going to renovate our churches at the expense of what is really essential, the salvation of the soul.

It is not enough just to brainwash our audience -- we need to establish them and mature them in faith. Aggressive evangelism must be backed up with adequate teaching -- what I call discipleship. We need to discover the spirit of the apostles and also the pioneer missionaries and nationals in Africa. We need to go forth with a thoroughgoing biblicism and a thoroughgoing evangelism, confessing Jesus Christ as Lord and confronting the world with the claim for repentance and faith in Jesus Christ.

> We cannot afford to compromise. If we do not
> take this seriously, I can guarantee you that
> aggressive Islamic evangelism will one day
> overpower our churches and we will become a
> museum.[10]

The church in Africa needs to take seriously the task
within her continent: reaching those who still have never
heard of Christ (only 190 out of 1700 languages south of
the Sahara have the New Testament; many have no Scripture
translation) and discipling those who have turned to Him.
The task is so vast that the church needs to mobilize the
gifts of all God's people -- whether from Africa or other
lands.

Responsibility worldwide

While fulfilling her responsibilities within her own
territory, the church in Africa must share in the worldwide responsibility to fulfill the Great Commission, because
she is part of the body of Christ. What about the 2.8
billion unevangelized? At least 80% of these will be
reached only by cross-cultural missionary work.[11] Their
need rests upon the church of Jesus Christ, whether in
Africa or Indonesia or Europe or America.

Even as the Asian inclusivistic approach to theology has
greatly influenced the World Council of Churches,[12] so has
thinking from Africa. Unfortunately many of the theological
views expressed in Africa really came by way of liberal
seminaries in Europe and America. Expatriate liberal theologians now applaud these as "the voice of the African
church." It certainly has not been the voice of evangelical
Africans, as we saw at the end of chapter 3.

"The African Church is called to make a theological
contribution to the universal Church," Kwame Bediako told
the 1977 Ghana Congress on Evangelization.[13] Over half a
century before, his fellow Ghanaian, James Aggrey, pled
with mission leaders: "God grant that you . . . will give
us a chance to make that contribution to the world which is
the design of God."[14] That time has certainly come.

A strong biblical theology expressed by evangelicals in
Africa will reverberate throughout the world, strengthening
others who are wavering before the onslaught of unbiblical
philosophy which has been falsely named theology (it has
nothing to do with God's views).

"The church in Africa is of importance not only to
Africa but also to the whole world," stated Francis
Schaeffer. "Dr. Byang Kato understood the issues very
well."[15]

Historian Roland Oliver stated in 1956, when black
Christians in Africa numbered only 25 million: "If 100
million Africans were Christians, it would change the world
outlook. What is more, it would change and revitalize the
outlook of Christianity itself as a world faith."[16]

The revitalizing effect that churches in Africa have on
their own continent and the rest of the world will depend
on their spiritual life -- on whether they can say with
missionary Paul: "I am not ashamed of the gospel of Christ,
for it is the power of God unto salvation to everyone that
believes." The gospel is the dynamic (power) to fulfill the
churches' responsibility worldwide.

Dynamic realities

In this book we have sought to examine the tensions
involved in church-mission relations. There are many other
related topics which need studying, such as the nature of
the church and the mandate of missions. However, these are
outside the scope of this study, and we shall have to leave
them for others to examine.

The Bible, history, and current case studies have demonstrated how the tensions of church-mission relations can
be turned into the dynamics of extending Christ's kingdom.

In summary, there are a few salient realities which we
should keep in mind:

Reality 1. Christ's commission to His disciples applies to
us today. Jesus forewarned His disciples that they would
face tensions with religious leaders in fulfilling His
command. Today liberal theologians may preach "another
gospel,"[17] but as long as there are people who have not
understood that God has provided eternal life in Christ
Jesus, His followers must "persuade men."[18]

There is scriptural support for the concept of a special
task force commissioned by the church to spearhead missionary outreach. History bears out the need for an organized
body, or mission, to make sure that the outreach goals are
achieved. Tension between church and mission can develop,

but with prayerful understanding can be changed into dynamic teamwork.

Reality 2. Missionary outreach will involve tensions of cross-cultural communication. As much as possible an ethnic group should be evangelized by Christians of that culture. However, there are countless people who will die before they hear the gospel from someone of their own culture -- there are not enough believers in their particular ethnic group to complete the task in time. There are other massive numbers who have no Christian witness in their culture. In all these, Christians of other cultures must bear witness to Christ's salvation. That means cross-cultural communication.

Cross-cultural communication will involve tensions which must be overcome through patience and understanding. The cross of Christ will at times judge culture and cause reaction; its message cannot be compromised in any way. But the messenger of the cross must be flexible and humble,[19] not causing resentment because of pride, lack of love, or lack of concern for local culture and felt needs.

Cross-cultural missionary work is not easy at any time, but it is doubly difficult now, because of the historical background of missionary work. There is a colonial missionary image in the minds of some people which arouses hostility. The solution is not to withdraw or change names, but to demonstrate the true servanthood of the messenger of the cross, revealing Christ himself in the face of suspicion, opposition, hatred.

Reality 3. The "Third World Church" is a vital part of the world missionary force. Missions must not overlook the strategic potential of the national church to reach out in further missionary work. This scriptural concept should be taught from the earliest stages.

When we think of "mission" in the future, we should not be thinking simply of expatriates from "developed countries," but missionaries from developing countries also. Whereas in the past the flow of missionary work was chiefly from the West to the East (or from the North to the South), God will use men and women from East, West, North, and South to minister as His Holy Spirit empowers them.

"The desire of most churches in the non-western world is
for a true partnership," stated Patrick Sookdheo at the
1979 meeting of the Evangelical Missions Alliance in
Britain. "They would like missionary agencies to act with
complete integrity, total honesty and utter frankness in all
their dealings with national churches. They would like the
us/them mentality to cease and instead a recognition that we
have all been called by God to serve Him in this His
world."[20]

"Is the day of the western missionary coming to an end?"
asked Isabelo Magalit, M.D., Associate General Director of
the East Asia Office of the International Fellowship of
Evangelical Students (IFES), speaking at Urbana '79. "No,
but definitely no. World evangelism is the responsibility
of the whole church, no less of the older churches of Europe
and America than of the younger churches of Asia and Africa
and Latin America. But not more the responsibility of the
one than the other. In fact, the dimensions of world
evangelism are so awesome that only the whole Church
throughout the world working in proper partnership can get
the task done. No, the day of missions from the West is
not over."

However, Magalit stressed the need for true partnership:
"My North American brothers and sisters in Christ, can we
ever be partners? Is it at all possible for you to come to
us and say: 'I have come in obedience to the Great Commission. How can you and I fulfill it together?'"[21]

There are encouraging signs of this kind of cooperation
taking place. An example is the response of the Overseas
Missionary Fellowship and the Far Eastern Gospel Crusade to
the request of the Association of Bible Churches of the
Philippines (ABCOP), an indigenous Filipino mission, to
work together in a three-way partnership. In Japan,
churches asked if they could send their Japanese missionaries through the agency of FEGC, after the churches found
a high rate of attrition among their national missionaries.
"We need your experience in helping missionaries cope in
different cultures," church leaders told FEGC.

Reality 4. The gospel witness will face hostility. Satan
is totally opposed to it, and he will make use of every form
of opposition: physical, political, ideological, religious,
demonic.

Persecution and opposition in some countries has caused church leaders to realize the urgency of the task. David Olusiyi of Nigeria stated: "The church has the greatest opportunity it has ever had. We may not have it long; if the church in other countries has been persecuted, it can happen to the church here. We have been commanded to preach the gospel. Like Paul we say, 'Woe is unto me if I preach not the gospel.'"[22]

There may be closed doors in some nations, but we must remember that Christ is both opening and closing doors: "These things saith He that is holy, He that is true, He that hath the key of David, He that openeth and no man shutteth and shutteth and no man openeth."[23] The prophet Zechariah was also reminded: "Not by might, nor by power, but by my Spirit, saith the Lord of hosts."[24]

Kato refers to the opposition Paul and his missionary colleagues met in Ephesus, as recorded in Acts 19. "In the midst of this tremendous success was strong opposition. Detrius raised the public conscience against Christianity through the use of economic (v. 25), religious (v. 26), cultural (v. 27), and political (v. 34) arguments."[25]

Action Steps

There are several definite steps which a mission (from any land -- East or West, North or South) can take to stimulate a young church to be missionary-minded:

1. Involve the believers in missionary outreach from the beginning. Make missions a vital part of the life of the church from the start.

2. Teach the whole Word of God concerning the lost state of the world and the responsibility of believers to witness to the unreached.

3. As a mission, set an example of continuing concern for unevangelized peoples. Keep the facts of worldwide needs before the church.

4. In demonstrating concern, do not dichotomize the work, leaving indoctrination up to the national church while the expatriate mission does the pioneering. Show that preaching the gospel

and discipling go hand in hand; involve mission and church in both.

5. Avoid setting up structures and projects beyond that which nationals can administer, within a reasonable time. Keep them all related to the overall goal of evangelism and mission-minded church growth.

6. Develop the gifts within the church so that it will have the capability to sustain missionary outreach as well as deepen its own life.

7. Encourage missiological studies at top levels of church leadership, to provide insight into current issues and ability in strategic planning.

8. Do not dominate the church's outreach, but seek to motivate it through "cloud-seeding" (a term describing the process of causing cloud formations to precipitate by "seeding" them with chemical crystals). Unobtrusive assistance in strategic ways can stimulate a church to act without becoming reliant on outside help.

AUTHOR'S EPILOGUE

In this book we have examined tensions between mission and church since the apostle Paul's day. In it I have sought to suggest not only the reasons but also the solutions.

However, if the book has done only that, it would be as if I had shone a light in a tunnel so that we could avoid tripping over the rubble strewn along it -- without showing the objective at the end of the tunnel.

My purpose is not to show us how to reduce bicultural tensions so we can congratulate each other and feel comfortable.

I would rather each reader feel uncomfortable. Uncomfortable, but also challenged, until the task is accomplished.

This book arises from a burden and a challenge. I have
been burdened as I have observed dedicated missionaries and
pastors at loggerheads -- their spiritual fellowship broken
and their practical effectiveness impaired. Too often the
result has been that the mission has withdrawn from the
area in frustration, only to start a new round of mission
activity that will end up with the same impasse. At the
same time, the national church has been equally frustrated
and often demotivated.

My burden does not end there. I am fearful that both
church and mission may lose something very vital. The
church may miss its birthright of missionary outreach, and
the mission may miss utilizing the potential missionary
vigor of the young church. The loss on both counts would
be tragic.

My greatest burden is for those multitudes who do not
know that Jesus Christ is the Savior of the world. If we
believe that Jesus is what He claimed to be -- the way, the
truth and the life[26] -- then we must feel very uncomfortable. If there is no other name given among men whereby we
must be saved,[27] we must be burdened to reach out to the
25,000 "people groups" which are considered unreached,[28]
and especially to the 2.5 billion men, women, and children
who will hear only by means of cross-cultural missionary
communication.

Their number is staggering. But I believe there is hope.
If Jesus Christ's commission really does apply to us today,
if it is God's will that all should hear the truth, we must
believe that in each age He has provided the means and the
strategy to accomplish His will. That is the challenge.

In the days of Roman imperialism, He raised up the
apostles to make use of the Empire's communication channels
to spread the gospel around the Mediterranean and then
further afield.

In the European colonial era, Christian men and women
from Western nations became concerned for the spiritual
condition of other nations of which they heard. God used
the world situation as an opportunity to send His Word
around the globe.

Now in a new era of exploding population and constantly
changing power balance, He is raising up a worldwide force

to accomplish the task of missions in this generation --
missionary witnesses from every part of the globe.

God has once again brought together the need, the
opportunity, and the instruments to do His will. "Third
World" missions are a strategic part of His plan for this
era. To neglect their potential will be to imperil the
completion of the task. In fact, with world attitudes as
they are today, the gospel may be unable to enter certain
ethnic groups apart from Third World channels.

That's why missions and national churches need to
understand each other and join in meeting the challenge of
the new era before us.

It is true that some missions have become enamored with
their offspring, the national church, and are pampering it
instead of challenging it to be a missionary witness.

It is true that some churches are self-centered,
concerned only with getting fatter instead of multiplying.

It is true that some churches have no burden for unreached people in other cultures. That is true in churches
in all lands, unfortunately.

But the solution is not for a mission to give up the
national church as a bad job. These problems have sometimes
arisen from the way we have gone about our missionary work.
The relations we have had at various stages may have produced reaction and retarded spiritual offspring. We need
to get back to scriptural principles in order to produce
virile sons and daughters who will do God's will in their
own lands and also join hands with the rest of Christ's
body to reach around the world.

The potential of Third World missions has been well
documented.[29] This book does not need to convince the
reader. But we face the practical problem that missions
and churches find themselves locked into petty tensions that
prevent their planning and implementing strategies for
further missionary outreach.

This book has sought to help both missions and churches
to transform those enervating, demotivating tensions into a
dynamic partnership of believers of every culture fulfilling
Christ's commands.

Not only do missions and churches need to understand what has happened. Supporting churches need to understand also, so they can get behind the worldwide thrust which God has opened to His people.

We are on the threshold of an exciting new phase in world missions. Changing bicultural tensions into dynamic missionary outreach can help us enter it.

That's the challenge!

THE END

STUDY QUESTIONS: CHAPTER 11

1. What factors should spur evangelicals of every nationality to pursue missionary outreach all over the world?

2. What factors point up the importance of discipling in depth?

3. What should be the ultimate goal of understanding and reducing mission-church tensions?

4. What continuing realities concerning missions should we keep in mind?

5. What action steps need to be taken by any mission (of any nationality) to help a young church fulfill its missionary responsibility?

6. How can you use tools found in this book to help mobilize people of different cultures to reach out to unevangelized peoples?

NOTES: CHAPTER 11

1. David B. Barrett, "AD 2000," in *International Review of Mission*, Vol. LIX, No. 233, January 1970, p. 47. See also *Time* magazine, Jan. 21, 1980, p. 44.

2. *Ibid*, pp. 48-49.

3. P.J. Johnstone, *Operation World* (UK: STL Publications, 1978), p. 159.

4.   Stephen J. Akangbe, "Three Major Ways That Mission Societies Can Effectively Assist National Churches in the Evangelization of Their Countries." (SIM Archives).

5.   James E. Plueddemann, "Leadership Needs in ECWA," a paper for ECWA General Church Council 1976.

6.   Bitrus Gani, "It's Not Time to Pack," a message to ECWA and SIM leaders in Jos, Nigeria, May 6, 1976.

7.   Byang H. Kato, *United Evangelical Action,* June 1975.

8.   Byang H. Kato, *Theological Pitfalls in Africa* (Nairobi, Kenya: Evangel Publishing House, 1975), pp. 181-184.

9.   Tokunboh Adeyemo, *Evangelical Missions Quarterly* (Wheaton, IL: EMQ, 1978), p. 153.

10. Tokunboh Adeyemo, "The Church of the Future and the Future of the Church," a message given at the Liberia Evangelical Fellowship meeting, Monrovia, August 1, 1978.

11. For statistical support, see "Hidden Peoples 1980," a chart published by the U.S. Center for World Mission, 1605 E. Elizabeth St., Pasadena, CA, 91104, U.S.A.

12. J.A.E. Vermaat, "The WCC's Programme of Dialogue," in *Beginning op Berrijding in de Oecumene* (Hilversum, Holland: Evangelisher Omroed, 1975).

13. Africa Christian Press Newsletter, Accra, Nov. 1977.

14. Edwin W. Smith, *Aggrey in Africa,* p. 88.

15. Francis Schaeffer, "What To Do When the Flood Comes," SIM Film, 1977.

16. Roland Oliver, *How Christian Is Africa?*   London, 1956, p. 5.

17. Galations 1:8,9.

18. II Cor. 5:11.

19. Matthew 20:25-27.

20. "The Opinion of Overseas Churches about Continued Activity of British Missionary Societies," a paper presented at Evangelical Missionary Alliance, High Leigh, England, November 20-22, 1979.

21. Missionary News Service, Wheaton, Il. Jan. 15, 1980, p. 2.

22. David Olusiyi, in a message at ECWA-SIM Area Conference, Miango, Nigeria, January, 1977.

23. Revelation 3:7.

24. Zechariah 4:6.

25. Byang H. Kato, "Evangelism Opportunities and Obstacles in Africa," in *Let the Earth Hear His Voice* (J.D. Douglas, Ed.) (Minneapolis, MN: World Wide Publications, 1975), p. 155.

26. John 14:6.

27. Acts 4:12.

28. Edward R. Dayton discusses the "people group" concept in *That Everyone May Hear* (Monrovia, CA: MARC, 1979), published for preparatory study groups for Consultation on World Evangelization, Pattaya, Thailand, 1980.

29. For studies of Third World missions, see James Wong, Ed., *Missions from the Third World* (Singapore: Church Growth Study Center, 1973). Also, Marlin Nelson, *The How and Why of Third World Missions* (S. Pasadena, CA: William Carey Library, 1976).

Appendices

DEFINITIONS

So that we all understand the use of terms in the same way, we should define four main terms used throughout this study:

1. Church

The simple dictionary definition is "the collective body of Christians;
a religious society having the same creed, rites." The Greek term
ekklesia simply means "a calling out, a congregation." It may be considered "a calling unto" -- emphasizing purpose.

In Scripture we find two main definitions:
a. Mystical, ("essential"), invisible -- Heb. 12:23
(1) Established by Christ -- Matt. 16:18; Col. 1:24
(2) Headed by Christ -- Eph. 1:22; 5:23; Col. 1:18
(3) Universal -- Rev. 7:9,10 (prophetic)
b. Organized and visible -- Acts 14:23
(1) Organized, structured -- Titus 1:5; I Tim. 3:15
(2) Local assembly of believers -- Acts 11:22; Col. 4:15
(The context will indicate when we are speaking of the organized local
church and when the mystical universal church.)

2. Mission

The dictionary defines this as "organized missionary work." Scripture
does not define any structure for such work, but we note the following:
a. Workers were set apart with prayer -- Acts 13:1-4
b. Workers were trained and sent out to plant churches -- Titus 1:5;
I Tim. 3:15.
c. At times missionaries were supported by a church -- I Cor. 9:13,14.
d. Laymen (other than church leaders) were involved in witnessing biculturally -- Acts 11:19-21.
e. Missionaries reported to the sending churches -- Acts 14:27; 21:19,20.
("Mission" can mean an organization or a ministry or purpose. It is used
in both senses in this study. When the distinction is not clear, the term
"mission society" is used to indicate the organizational definition.)

3. Missionary

The dictionary defines this as "one sent on a mission" -- especially
"one sent to propagate religion." The actual word is not used in the New
Testament, but a number of other words are used which define what we refer
to in this study as "a missionary."

(George W. Peters in his book *A Biblical Theology of Missions*, Moody Press, provides a thorough and scholarly study on this topic, pages 248-253, 261.)

A missionary is one who:
a. witnesses concerning the gospel of Jesus Christ as a result of a personal experience -- Acts 4:20;
b. is sent by Christ himself -- John 17:18, 20, 21;
c. is obedient to Christ's command -- Matt. 28:18;
d. responds to Christ's empowering -- Acts 1:8;
(Boer points out that it was this response rather than just obedience to Christ's command that caused the disciples to witness -- Harry Boer, *Pentecost and Missions*, Grand Rapids: Eerdmans, 1961, pages 119, 120);
e. feels the compulsion of the need of a lost world;

Paul:	I Cor. 9:16	responsibility;
	II Cor. 5:11	sense of judgment;
	10:16	realization of unreached peoples;
	Rom. 1:14	sense of debt;
	10:13-15	necessity of proclamation

4. Culture

"A culture is an essentially complete and detailed plan embracing all aspects or needs of human life, whatever the responses to these needs may be."

"A way of coping with a particular society's physical, social, and ideational environment. It is a complete and more or less successful adaptive system, which includes the total content as well as the organization of the content." -- Louis Luzbetak, *The Church and Cultures*, William Carey Library, pages 62 and 64.

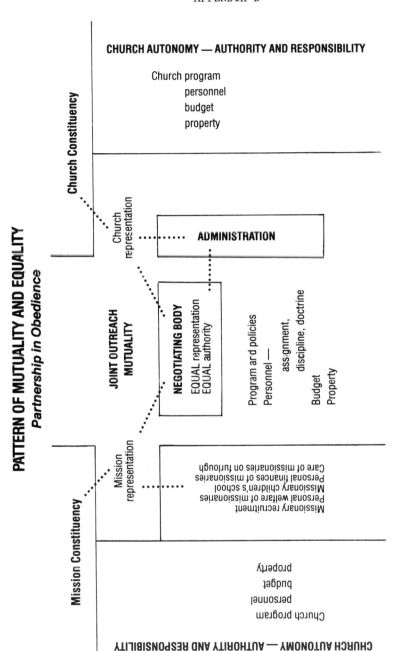

PATTERN OF MUTUALITY AND EQUALITY
Partnership in Obedience

CHURCH AUTONOMY — AUTHORITY AND RESPONSIBILITY

Church program
personnel
budget
property

Church Constituency

Church representation

ADMINISTRATION

JOINT OUTREACH MUTUALITY

NEGOTIATING BODY
EQUAL representation
EQUAL authority

Program and policies
Personnel —
assignment,
discipline, doctrine
Budget
Property

Mission representation

Missionary recruitment
Personal welfare of missionaries
Missionary children's school
Personal finances of missionaries
Care of missionaries on furlough

Mission Constituency

Church program
personnel
budget
property

CHURCH AUTONOMY — AUTHORITY AND RESPONSIBILITY

(George Peters, from *Missions in Creative Tension*)

REDEFINING THE TERM "INDIGENOUS"

At the turn of this century evangelical missions were concerned about the dependency of young national churches on the missions from which they arose. The relation of colonies to the imperial powers was the backdrop for the relation of national churches to the denominations which founded them. To avoid this, evangelicals stressed the need for the national church to be indigenous -- self-governing, self-supporting, self-propagating.

This emphasis has produced a number of indigenous churches. However, the resultant separation of church and mission has led to a different problem at the other extreme.

An *apartheid-like* relation of totally separate development has arisen in some cases. The church has its structure, its departments; the mission also has its own structure and departments. There has developed a feeling of "our work" and "their work." This has sometimes produced an atmosphere of rivalry, divided loyalty, and suspicion. But more so, the church has not understood the implications of responsibility carried by the mission. Neither church nor mission has benefited as much as it could have, from the interchange of spiritual gifts and experience God has given each.

That's why we need to redefine the term indigenous. Is it possible for a national church to avoid dependence on a foreign mission and yet integrate the work of church and mission? We believe it is. In the relations now being developed by SIM in Africa, the mission and the national churches form an international partnership. In the sending countries, SIM takes the leadership in encouraging prayer, recruiting missionaries, and raising finance for projects which the churches cannot yet undertake. In Africa, the national churches take leadership in the work, depending on their level of development. Where the church can take the responsibility, missionaries work under national leadership.

As this international partnership is worked out in practical detail, it should strengthen the indigenous church. The mission's contribution, instead of being an obviously foreign, separate ministry, should become more relevant to the spiritual and cultural needs of the national church. Redefined, the "indigenous church" belongs to the country; its life is relevant to the nation; nationals lead its work -- including that done by foreign missionaries. Its indigenous nature does not exclude using the gifts of the Spirit brought by missionaries from other lands. Their work is integrated with the national church, in keeping with its indigenous character.

Thus the indigenous principle does not become an excuse for *apartheid*, or separateness, but the basis for international partnership of church and mission.

W. Harold Fuller

Memo to SIM Council Members,
Jos, Nigeria, 1976

APPENDIX D

EXCERPTS FROM THE FRANKFURT DECLARATION ON THE

FUNDAMENTAL CRISIS IN CHRISTIAN MISSION

Today organized Christian world missions are shaken by a fundamental crisis. External opposition and weakening spiritual power of our churches and missionary societies are not solely to blame. More dangerous is the displacement of their primary tasks by an insidious falsification of their motives and goals.

We oppose the current tendency to determine the nature and task of Mission by socio-political analysis of our time and from the demands of the non-Christian world.

We oppose the false teaching (which has circulated in the ecumenical movement since the Third General Assembly of the World Council of Churches in New Delhi) that Christ himself is anonymously so evident in world religions, historical changes, and revolutions, that man can encounter Him and find salvation in Him without the direct news of the gospel.

We oppose the universalistic idea that in the crucifixion and resurrection of Jesus Christ all men of all times are already born again and already have peace with Him, irrespective of their knowledge of the historical saving activity of God or belief in it.

We refute the idea that "Christian presence" among the adherents to world religions and a give-and-take dialogue with them are substitutes for a proclamation of the gospel which aims at conversion.

Christian world mission is the decisive, continuous saving activity of God among men between the time of the resurrection and second coming of Jesus Christ.

HOW SIM HELPED ECWA DEVELOP ITS MISSION

Here are 10 ways SIM has sought to assist the mission of ECWA in the past, including ways SIM anticipates helping in the future:

1. Stress missions in Bible schools, so that graduates will either respond to the missionary call themselves, or develop missionary-minded churches.

2. Maintain the concept of indigenous support. This does not mean that expatriates cannot give to EMS (Evangelical Missionary Society, missions arm of ECWA) -- believers from one culture can always help believers in another. But to avoid dependency on foreign resources, and to encourage local financial responsibility, expatriates give through the local churches, as part of the missionary offering.

EMS feels a responsibility for missionary finance -- setting the support figure, raising support, dispensing it. Even though funds are currently insufficient, the EMS board is recommending to ECWA a further salary increase. "We must be faithful to those who are sacrificing to be missionaries," the leaders say. "Their expenses are increasing."

3. Maintain the principle of indigenous administration. SIM seconded an expatriate missionary for the first few years, to help in the administrative structuring of the work. Such skills have to be learned. SIM took the initiative in turning over the expatriate's work to a Nigerian as soon as possible; EMS wanted the expatriate assistant to continue. Leadership is completely Nigerian.

4. Build up the work through a continuous training program, at both the leadership level and the staff level. To upgrade their skills, EMS leaders have taken in-service training (such as seminars in management) and also residential study courses in Nigeria and overseas.

Periodically national missionaries are brought together for short refresher courses or seminars on specific aspects of missionary work (e.g., Approach to the Fulani People, Cross-cultural Communication). ECWA has an increased awareness of the help SIM can be in providing resource personnel for such seminars.

5. Aid EMS in developing strategy and equipping missionaries through research. Where are the greatest areas of need? Why is a tribe proving so resistant? Is the missionary's approach blocking communication? In-depth research can help provide the answers and make EMS more effective. SIM helps ECWA with research skills.

6. Assist communication through media tools. SIM has provided ECWA Media Department with staff and equipment to produce materials which will not only help EMS communicate to unbelievers, but also to their own supporters. ECWA Media has just produced a filmstrip for showing in ECWA churches -- to stimulate praying and giving for missions.

7. Assist in special projects. Raising monthly support is still a precarious matter. To introduce large special projects to the churches at this stage might detract from the limited support funds.

Two years ago when a Land-Rover was needed by EMS headquarters to take missionaries into isolated villages, Christians in Germany raised the money. The project did not detract from local missionary support.

SIM gave a hand with two new outreach ventures which would have been impossible to launch with normal EMS finance. When Ghana asked for a missionary couple, EMS knew the costs would be several times more than normal for placing a missionary. The project was undertaken by a three-way partnership: a Nigerian church undertook the couple's support, Ghanaian Christians underwrote their house rent, SIM missionaries raised their passage money.

When Chad asked for two Bible teachers to help build up the church after the years of persecution, ECWA provided the men, SIM provided funds for their travel and support for a two-year period.

8. Help the church with key personnel until staff can be trained. EMS was using an untrained bookkeeper at one time, and was having problems. ECWA saw the problem but was helpless to correct it without skilled assistance. SIM helped restructure ECWA's accounting procedures and relieve EMS's problem.

9. Set an example of missionary concern. This can fail to motivate if the expatriate missionary does his evangelistic work in isolation. National believers can wrongly look upon the expatriate as the outreach person and the national as the one who cares for local church matters.

The example of the expatriate missionary must involve the national; missionary outreach must be done together, as colleagues. The missionary must avoid the image of Livingstone being assisted by load-toting nationals. Goals, strategy, and activity must be planned and implemented together. Where there is a local church, missionary work should ideally be conducted as an outreach of the church. After ECWA's General Secretary visited SIM supporters in North America and Britain, he returned to challenge Nigerians: "Every ECWA church should support a missionary."

10. Missionary principles must be inculcated from the beginning. If they are introduced after the church has come of age, they may be seen as an imposition -- the foreigner trying to pass his burden off on the national. ECWA doesn't see it this way. "Evangelism is at the heart of our church," David Olusiyi, ECWA President, told this year's Council meeting. "When we stop evangelizing, ECWA will be dead."

W. Harold Fuller

From a paper presented to the IFMA Annual Meeting at Dallas, Texas, Sept. 1977

HOW TO RECONCILE THE TWO EXTREMES

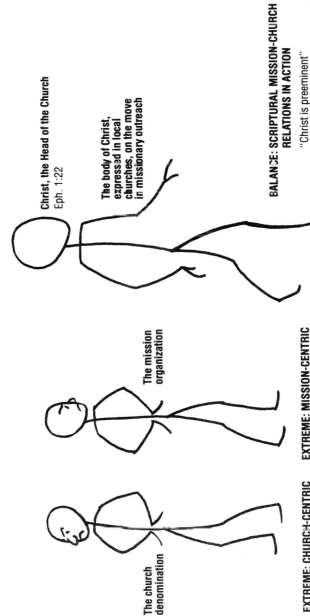

EXTREME: CHURCH-CENTRIC
"The church denomination is preeminent"

The church denomination

EXTREME: MISSION-CENTRIC
"The mission organization is preeminent"

The mission organization

Christ, the Head of the Church
Eph. 1:22

The body of Christ, expressed in local churches, on the move in missionary outreach

BALANCE: SCRIPTURAL MISSION-CHURCH RELATIONS IN ACTION
"Christ is preeminent"

(W. Harold Fuller, SIM, 1978)

MISSION-CHURCH RELATIONS: FOUR STAGES OF DEVELOPMENT

Notes: A. The attitudes developed in each stage affect the succeeding stage.

B. Missionaries whose strong leadership gift made Stage I possible, need to know how to change role to that of a counselor in Stage IV or may need to move to another area where their pioneering ability can be used.

C. The main goal of mission and church should be the same, if both are doing God's will.

MISSION'S ROLE:

STAGE I: PIONEER

Requires gift of leadership, along with other gifts. No believers — missionary must lead and do much of the work himself.

STAGE II: PARENT

Requires gift of teaching. The young church has a growing child's relationship to the mission. But the "parent" must avoid "paternalism."

STAGE III: PARTNER

Requires change from parent-child relation to adult-adult relation. Difficult for both to change, but essential to the church's becoming a mature "adult."

STAGE IV: PARTICIPANT

A fully mature church assumes leadership. As long as the mission remains, it should use its gifts to strengthen the church to meet the original objectives of Matt. 28:19-20. Meanwhile the mission should be involved in Stage I elsewhere.

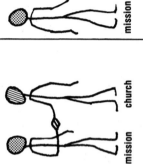

mission

mission church

mission church

mission church

ORIGINAL MOTIVATION:

Matt. 28:19-20 "Preach, disciple"

Matt. 28:19-20 until Christ's return

W. Harold Fuller, SIM, 1978)

HOW THE NIGERIAN PUBLIC SEES THE TRANSITION OF AUTHORITY

STAGE I

In some cultures, the chief's umbrella represents authority. In the first stage of SIM's work in Nigeria, the Mission had to take full responsibility, because the church was only beginning to grow. Nigerians could easily understand this — one organization was responsible for all the work.

STAGE 2

When ECWA was formed, it became responsible for the churches. SIM continued being responsible for the departments, because sufficient Nigerians were not yet trained to be responsible for them. The departments helped the churches. This worked well, but Nigerians were confused when they saw two organizations with responsibility and authority working together. They could not understand the relationship.

STAGE 3

As the churches grew and Nigerians were trained for the departments, SIM turned over the departments to ECWA. Now all the work in Nigeria comes under ECWA's leadership. Nigerians can understand this — one organization has responsibility for the work. They are also glad to see that this does not mean SIM has left the work. The Mission is still there to work with ECWA, even though it is no longer in charge. ECWA has assumed responsibility, and SIM is working with ECWA to help develop her gifts so ECWA can fulfill the Great Commission.

(W. Harold Fuller, as presented
to ECWA General Church Council, May 1977)

SIM-ECWA'S ORGANIZATIONAL RELATIONSHIPS IN FOUR PHASES

PHASE I

The period from the arrival of SIM pioneers in 1893 to the consultations in 1953 which led to the formal establishment of ECWA as an autonomous church organization.

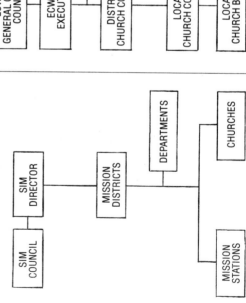

PHASE II

The period from the formation of ECWA in 1954 until 1975, when ECWA and SIM jointly discussed the next phases of development in relations following SIM General Council of June 1975.

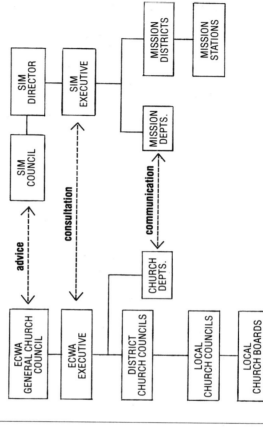

(Continued on next two pages)

(Continued from previous page)

PHASE III:

An interim phase to help in the transfer of the departments to ECWA administration, by giving a period of trial and adjustment for both mission and church.

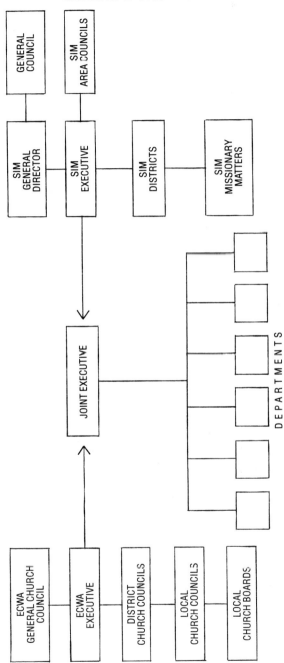

(Continued on next page)

(Continued from previous two pages)

PHASE IV: **ORGANIZATIONAL CHART SHOWING SIM-ECWA RELATIONS AS OF NOVEMBER 19, 1976**

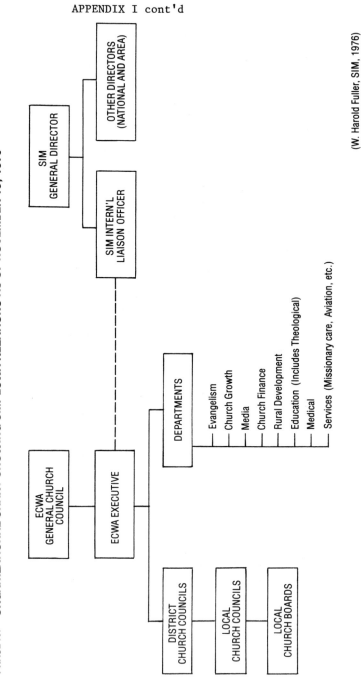

(W. Harold Fuller, SIM, 1976)

ECWA TODAY: THE NEED FOR SELF-RELIANCE

by Rev. Simon Ibrahim, General Secretary, ECWA

There are many internal and external factors which point to the need of self-reliance. I want to name a few.

1. Internal factors

    a. Dependency syndrome: Although ECWA claims to consist of 500,000 adherents organized into 16 districts, 142 LCC's, and 1342 local churches, it is amazing how many people do not understand why SIM does not pay ECWA's bills, give grants to our institutions, provide money for scholarships, provide teachers for secondary schools and teachers colleges, etc. Every shortage of personnel and finances is blamed on the mission. Because the mission had to provide these at the beginning, our people seem to think that it is a good tradition to keep; after all, missionaries come from developed countries. I suspect there are those who equate white skin with affluence. It is time every member of ECWA knows the realities of the situation: the personnel and funds are here in Nigeria, the mission should only supplement what we provide.

    b. Stewardship: A sense of stewardship needs to be developed in ECWA's local churches. It is not uncommon to find a local church with reasonable income while the pastor is on poor salary. Many elders consider themselves successful if they can have good reserves, while pastors and evangelists starve on meager wages. Self-reliance should result in mature and faithful stewardship of the Lord's money in the local churches and at all levels of church administration.

    c. Nationalism: Since Independence, it has become unfashionable to have a white man in a position of any type of leadership, as "this would violate our freedom and selfhood." If leadership is now the sole prerogative of nationals, it follows, therefore, that nationals must assume the role of planning. This carries with it the financial and personnel responsibilities required for successful execution of the plan. A right attitude to nationalism is a positive one, recognizing that it is in God's providence that Africans must lead Africa both politically and ecclesiastically.

2. External factors

   a. Reduction of missionaries: Some missionaries have left for illegitimate reasons. Some argue that since the church is growing, missionaries are no longer needed. Nothing could be further from the truth. Right now there are 900 students in a certain town waiting for only one Bible teacher, but there is none to be found. Some missionaries have to leave for legitimate reasons, such as family responsibility, retirement, etc., and they leave with our full blessing. Our prayer is that they may motivate others to come. We, too, need to motivate and mobilize our members to get involved, so that the work does not suffer because missionaries leave.

   b. World economic crisis: This is affecting the sending churches. The more any currency loses buying power, the more it will lose sending power too. We must face realities and build our church work on our economy.

   c. The call for moratorium on missions: One of the most shocking experiences I had in the United States was to learn that some African church leaders are calling for a moratorium on missions. Apparently many supporting churches have been waiting to hear such a call. One denomination seems to have responded quickly by reducing their missionaries from 1700 to only 400. Scherer made a true observation that the tragic cry arising from the midst of the [sending] church for most of its history, was not, "Missionary, go home!" but, "Missionary stay at home!" The call for moratorium will undoubtedly affect missionary support. The sooner ECWA is alerted to this the better.

   d. International politics: Changing foreign policy from either side may affect the missionary enterprise. The problem of obtaining visas is not unconnected with international politics. The changes are so rapid that we need to make adequate preparation for the future. I cannot conceive of any better preparation than for ECWA to become self-reliant.

3. Implications of self-reliance

   a. In order for ECWA to be self-reliant, it must have adequate personnel and financial resources. ECWA must understand its responsibility to raise funds and develop personnel.

   b. In order to achieve personnel self-reliance, ECWA must mobilize dedicated men and get them involved right now. We should form the core of the army, and missionaries should back us up.

   c. Our motive is not to lord it over missionaries, but to learn to be on our own. Our desire is to learn to do everything the mission is doing, while missionaries are here to criticize, advise, and back us up.

Let us have confidence in ECWA despite its weaknesses, which we want to identify and try to overcome. The most helpful thing a missionary can do is to have full confidence in ECWA and pledge his or her support and cooperation.

> *(A study paper prepared by the General Secretary for ECWA churches to help them understand the implications of taking leadership responsibility for SIM work in Nigeria. Jos, 1977)*

SIM Area Conference

SUMMARY OF DATA

By the SIM-ECWA Research Office, May 1976

The following is a list of questions from the *Attitude Survey*. They are listed in order of amount of agreement. (The figures in parentheses refer to the original questionnaire numbering system.) Missionaries were given these questions in each of the Area Conferences and were asked to state their amount of agreement with the statement. (Strongly agree, agree, neutral, disagree, strongly disagree.) Thus the statements high on the list had the most agreement, and the last statements on the list had the least amount of agreement with the statement. (Score = average post-survey.)

Strongly Agree

1. (23) An area conference such as this one is a good idea.

Agree

2. (1) I'm convinced that Area Council members will think through the implications of an organizational change before they make a final decision.

3. (11) ECWA leaders really do want missionaries for quite a few years.

4. (10) I'm satisfied that the General Council has given the right guidelines for church-mission relationships.

5. (4) I'm satisfied with the way missionary salaries will be handled in the new organizational structure.

6. (17) A missionary Personnel Officer is a good way to take care of missionary needs.

7. (22) I feel that I understand the main points of the proposed structure.

8. (9) ECWA is trying hard to improve its financial policies.

9. (25) We should try hard to preserve the SIM "family spirit" in the new structure.

10. (12) I feel that closer integration with ECWA will help solve some SIM problems.

11. (18) I have confidence in the leadership ability of ECWA headquarter executive.

12. (2) I feel secure with the probable method of stationing missionaries.

13. (29) The long-range prospects of the church will improve when all the work is under ECWA.

14. (28) We in SIM will be better able to help the church when we are under ECWA.

15. (14) I'm satisfied that missionary health needs will be taken care of under the new organizational structure.

16. (19) I'm impressed with the spiritual maturity of most ECWA leaders.

17. (13) The schooling of M.K.'s will be taken care of when we are working under ECWA.

18. (24) The vision for reaching unreached areas will be just as strong under ECWA as it has been under SIM.

Neutral

19. (16) I feel confident that my needs and ideas will be well represented in the new organizational structure.

20. (15) I'm satisfied that we missionaries will have adequate voice or input in formulating policies when we are under ECWA leadership.

21. (8) I feel we should have had closer organizational ties with ECWA several years ago.

22. (21) I'm satisfied with the present D.S. system of representation.

23. (3) The D.S. job has worked fairly well in the past and we should keep it similar to what it is presently.

24. (20) I have confidence in the leadership at the local church level.

25. (7) I have confidence in ECWA's ability to handle finance.

26. (26) The personal needs of the missionary will not be cared for under the new system as much as now.

Disagree

27. (27) Turning the work over to ECWA is going to make the work deteriorate.

28. (6) The mission is capitulating to the demands of the church.

29. (5) I don't see the need for closer integration with ECWA. Things are working with the present structures.

CHURCH AND MISSION ORGANIZATIONAL CHARTS
BEFORE AND AFTER TRANSFER OF RESPONSIBILITY

BEFORE (1954-1976)

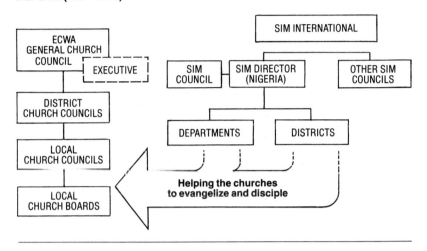

AFTER (1976 onwards)

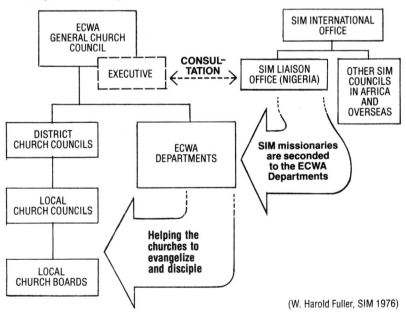

(W. Harold Fuller, SIM 1976)

APPENDIX M

Memo to ECWA Executive

From Area Director, SIM

September 29, 1976

STATIONING OF MISSIONARIES

In the past, the stationing of missionaries has been done by the Ghana-Nigeria Council of SIM. Under the new organizational structure, the stationing will be done by the Joint ECWA-SIM Executive upon the recommendations of the department heads meetings. It is suggested that at the next department heads meeting, the department heads have a practice session for the stationing of missionaries. As we are still under the old organizational structure, the final ratification and stationing this year will be done by the Ghana-Nigeria Council, but that may be the last time the Council will perform this duty.

I would like to list here some of the guidelines used in the past for stationing. We feel these are very important for the good morale of our missionaries so they can do an effective work for the Lord Jesus Christ.

Procedures for stationing -- matters to be considered:

1. Qualifications and jobs where these can be used.

2. Experience both outside and inside Nigeria.

3. Personal desires of the missionary and his sense of the Lord's call in his life. (A nurse may have come to Nigeria with a definite call from God to teach Religious Knowledge (Bible) classes, or else she would not have come.)

4. Health. (A person may need to be stationed in a dry or wet climate, or on the Plateau, for medical reasons.)

5. Whether married or single.

6. Family considerations. (Some children cannot be separated from parents for psychological reasons, and therefore the parents must be stationed near a school.)

7. Compatibility with other workers.

Preparations for stationing:

1. The department head, with his colleagues, will consider departmental needs and missionaries who may be available for stationing.

2. If a missionary is to be changed from his present stationing, this should be discussed with him or her and the Local Personnel Officer. If the change is within the department, the department head will discuss it. If a department is requesting a missionary from another department, this must be discussed with the other department head and a decision mutually made as to who will approach the missionary. If there is disagreement on the part of the department heads, this should be referred to the Area Personnel Officer, who must be informed on all stationing changes, and must concur with them before they are made.

3. A meeting of the department heads with the Area Personnel Officer will make the final recommendations to the Joint ECWA-SIM Executive for ratification.

4. Any change should be communicated to the missionary involved before any public announcement is made.

5. Confidentiality. All the discussions in the department heads meeting and all considerations regarding the restationing of the missionary should be treated as highly confidential to ensure frank discussion of all possible problems without harming the people involved.

These guidelines and procedures have developed in SIM over the past years from a great deal of experience, and we feel they are essential to the good morale and effective use of our missionaries, as well as the continuing confidence of the missionaries and their supporters overseas, in SIM overseas and ECWA in Nigeria. If you or others feel that any of these guidelines should be modified in view of our organizational changes, I shall be happy to discuss further.

Sincerely,
W. Harold Fuller
Area Director

STATIONING PROCEDURE

Approved by the Ghana-Nigeria Council November 1976

1. Each SIM missionary will be appointed to a department of ECWA.

2. Transfers within a department can be made by the department head with the agreement of the missionary involved and the APO (Area Personnel Officer). The institution head will be consulted where applicable.

3. Inter-departmental transfers can be made by the department heads involved with the agreement of the missionary and the APO. Institution heads will be consulted where one is involved.

4. In the case of disagreement between any of the people involved, the decision will be made by ECWA Executive with the Liaison Officer and his staff.

5. Advice from department heads meeting may be sought at any of the stages.

6. The APO in each case may confer with the Local Personnel Counselor as necessary.

CONDITIONS OF SECONDMENT

Personnel recruited by SIM International will be seconded to ECWA as requested for work in Nigeria. The following conditions explain the specific relationship.

1. A position description with attainable standards of performance and qualifications will be provided by the department head under whom the missionary will be working. Annual appraisals shall be made with a full and frank discussion between the missionary and his immediate superior.

2. Health care will be provided by SIM International.

3. Education of missionary children will be provided by SIM International.

4. Financial income will be paid by and through SIM International. If the missionary receives salaries or allowances as remuneration from Nigerian sources, these will be put into a fund for use in the work in Nigeria.

5. Length of furloughs and holidays shall follow the guidelines set by SIM International, but specific times shall be agreed upon in consultation with the department head concerned, taking into account such factors as missionary travel arrangements, economic factors, personal needs, etc., along with the needs of the work.

6. Appointments and transfers will follow guidelines and procedures set by the Joint Executive. Cost of transfer will be paid by the receiving department or institution.

7. Housing shall be provided by ECWA under conditions agreed upon by the Joint Executive. Standards for housing will be set by the Services Committee.

8. Discipline for doctrinal or moral reasons shall be administered according to the policy of SIM International in consultation with the Joint Executive. Disciplinary action may be initiated by the institution head, the department head, or the Area Personnel Officer, and may result in termination of secondment. Termination of membership in SIM International will be handled by the respective National Council.

9. Termination of a specific secondment other than for doctrinal or moral reasons can arise through such reasons as family needs, medical needs, educational needs, conclusion of ministry, incompatibility, insubordination, redundancy, conclusion of short-term service, transfer of responsibility, or a feeling of the Lord's call to another area of service. Termination of secondment can be initiated by the missionary, the department head, or by the Area Personnel Officer in consultation with SIM International.

APPENDIX P

THE DEVELOPMENT OF ECWA-SIM RELATIONS — Seen in Four Phases

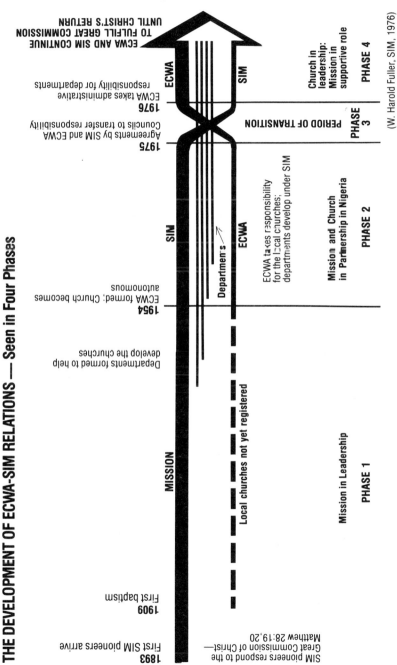

(W. Harold Fuller, SIM, 1976)

ECWA AND SIM CONTINUE TO FULFILL GREAT COMMISSION UNTIL CHRIST'S RETURN

ECWA takes administrative responsibility for departments

1976

Agreements by SIM and ECWA Councils to transfer responsibility

1975

ECWA takes responsibility for the local churches; departments develop under SIM

Departments formed to help develop the churches

ECWA formed; Church becomes autonomous

1954

Local churches not yet registered

First baptism

1909

First SIM pioneers arrive

1893

SIM pioneers respond to the Great Commission of Christ—Matthew 28:19,20

Church in leadership; Mission in supportive role

PHASE 4

PERIOD OF TRANSITION

PHASE 3

Mission and Church in Partnership in Nigeria

PHASE 2

Mission in Leadership

PHASE 1

ECWA / SIM / MISSION

APPENDIX Q

THE VISION OF SIM

by Dr. Ian M. Hay, General Director, SIM

The Sudan Interior Mission began with a vision -- a vision shared by only a very few people -- a vision for evangelism in the interior region of the geographic area then known as the Soudan, the broad expanse across the continent of Africa south of the Sahara Desert. Nigeria became the first objective.

This vision was not achieved easily. It was fraught with difficulties. During the first 14 years, the graves of the missionaries cast a shadow which blurred the vision. In fact, there were more graves than there were Christians.

They persevered, however, and by the grace of God that initial vision has been wonderfully fulfilled until today there are thousands of Christians in Nigeria. For this we are profoundly thankful to God.

In October 1909 the first baptism took place, at Ogga, and thus the church came into existence. Immediately our pioneers caught a new vision -- they had a dream. It was to teach these new Christians and organize them into local indigenous churches. From the beginning SIM's vision had been precisely that -- the establishment of an indigenous church. Through the years the numbers of these local churches grew throughout Nigeria. By 1925 there were 50,000 Christians in the areas where SIM was working, with 100 Nigerians ministering to them.

By 1954 this second vision was partially realized with the establishment of the Evangelical Churches of West Africa. The individual local congregations scattered through many ethnic groups were brought together in ECWA, which, by 1956, was duly recognized by the Nigerian Government. This church has now grown to over 1300 churches with a Christian community of around 500,000. Nine hundred Nigerian pastors are ministering in these churches.

Today that organizational objective is achieved. SIM by action of its General Council, an international body, determined in 1975 that the time had come to hand over its remaining program in Nigeria to ECWA, this indigenous church which has grown out of SIM's work in this nation. SIM comes to this day with great joy. Vision has become reality.

SIM, however, has not stopped dreaming. Now we have a new vision -- a vision of a responsible church in Nigeria growing in every sector, one that is itself aggressive in evangelism and church planting, and we are happy to assist ECWA in the achievement of these goals. I would like to

leave to ECWA a passage of Scripture. In doing so, SIM asks ECWA to share
this vision with us. The passage is Isaiah 60:1-3:

> Arise, shine; for thy light is come, and the glory of the Lord
> is risen upon thee. For, behold, the darkness shall cover the
> earth, and gross darkness the people: but the Lord shall arise
> upon thee, and His glory shall be seen upon thee. And the
> Gentiles shall come to thy light, and kings to the brightness
> of thy rising.

Verse 1 says that the light belongs to Zion because it shines upon her.
Verse 3 says it belongs to her because it shines from her. Verse 1 says
the glory of the Lord is risen on her. Verse 3 says the nations will come
to the brightness of His glory.

So, our vision is that ECWA will stand in the center of the radiance of
the light of the glory of God, and standing in that light, she will become
light. So that, as a sunlit, sun-like church, she will arise and shine in
a world that is increasingly darkened through ignorance concerning God and
His love.

And so, with great gratitude to God, I am happy to share a vision which
began long ago in 1893. Now we have come to an historic moment. On behalf
of SIM International and on behalf of all the SIM missionaries both past
and present, I wish to ECWA in the name of our Lord Jesus Christ, God's
richest blessings. May He through the Holy Spirit grant to ECWA the joy
of seeing these goals and visions accomplished to His glory.

*A message given at ceremony marking turnover of responsibility
from SIM to ECWA, November 19, 1976.*

TRANSFER OF RESPONSIBILITY

November 19, 1976

The Executive
The Association of Evangelical Churches of West Africa
Jos, Nigeria

Dear brothers in Christ:

On behalf of the Sudan Interior Mission, I herewith turn over to ECWA the responsibility for the work of SIM in Nigeria, as per the attached Motion of our Area Council.

We give thanks to God that He has raised up an indigenous sister organization, ECWA, which can take over this responsibility, with the goal of continuing the objectives with which the work was begun -- the evangelization of the nation, and the discipling of believers into the body of Christ through local churches.

We also note with thanksgiving that this is the continuation of a turning-over process which began with the establishment of ECWA as a fully autonomous and indigenous church in 1954 (registered with the government in 1956), and the transfer to ECWA of academic schools, Bible schools, dispensaries, SIM bookshops, Publication Department, Christian Education Department, and other institutions, as well as many properties in the intervening years.

In turning over responsibility for the remaining work today, we assure ECWA that SIM will continue as strong an interest in the work as before. By God's enabling power, we shall pray for ECWA and shall work together with her, to His glory.

May God give to you and all who have leadership in ECWA, His divine wisdom, strength, and grace as you take on this responsibility.

In the name of our Lord and Savior,
W. Harold Fuller
Area Director

ACCEPTANCE OF RESPONSIBILITY

*The address of acceptance of responsibility of turnover
to the Association of Evangelical Churches of West
Africa (ECWA) by SIM, November 19, 1976*

by Rev. D.M. Olusiyi, ECWA President

The SIM International Director, ECWA Trustees, Honorable Commissioners,
Fellow Christians, Ladies and Gentlemen:

It is with much gratitude to God on behalf of the Association of
Evangelical Churches of West Africa (ECWA) that I am accepting the responsibility for the work of SIM in Nigeria for God's glory and the progress
of His sacred ministry in our land. From now on ECWA assumes the responsibility for all SIM work and personnel in Nigeria.

We are making history today in the life of ECWA. It will be 82 years
on December 4th this year since the first three SIM missionaries arrived
in Lagos in answer to the Great Commission of our Lord Jesus Christ to "go
and preach the gospel to all the nations." When they arrived in Lagos,
they were welcomed by words of discouragement from a missionary leader of
another mission in the coastal area by telling them that they were at-
tempting an impossibility. But with strong faith in Christ they knelt on
their knees, praying to God, and with a mighty faith they rose up, and
with full joy and hope, they said, "It will be done!" Today we are grateful to God that we are living witnesses of what the living God has done
through them, and what He continues to do through the three pioneers'
successors.

We are grateful to God that the baby born by SIM through the gospel of
Jesus Christ has today become matured. This will be a great joy to our
parent, SIM, that her baby has grown to the state of manhood to take up
her full responsibilities. We are sure that the mission will not stand
aloof as we struggle to carry the old and the newly added responsibilities.
But both of us will, with the spirit of Christ, continue to labor together
as one body.

I will appeal to all of us that, in order to carry out the heavy responsibility successfully, we should detach ourselves from everything that
can hinder us from fully enjoying the progress of the ministry. Let us
replace hatred, petty jealousies, tribalism, and sectionalism, with love,
unity, self-discipline, dedication, and self-sacrifice.

By the grace of God we shall not deviate from the mighty and living faith in the Lord Jesus as has been passed to us, ECWA, by you, SIM, through God's Word. We shall ever continue to keep our pledge to keep flying the banner of our Master, Jesus Christ, through sound proclamation of the gospel, living the gospel, and by teaching the Word of God.

Brethren, I want to say again that this is a happy occasion for ECWA, and by the faith of our fathers, would challenge all ECWA members, both black and white, in the words of a hymn:

> "Onward, Christian soldiers! marching as to war,
> Looking unto Jesus, who is gone before.
> Hell's foundations quiver at the shout of praise;
> Brothers, lift your voices, loud your anthems raise!
> Like a mighty army moves the church of God;
> Brothers, we are treading where the saints have trod;
> We are not divided, all one body we,
> One in hope and doctrine, one in charity."

SIM COUNCIL MOTION ON SIM-ECWA RELATIONS IN NIGERIA

The SIM Area Council meeting in Jos, Nigeria, November 16-19, 1976, gives thanks to God that He has raised up a responsible church as a result of the work of the Sudan Interior Mission (SIM) in Nigeria, and that this church, the Association of Evangelical Churches of West Africa (ECWA) in its General Church Council meeting of April 1976, has expressed its readiness to accept responsibility for the work of SIM in Nigeria. This followed the decision of the SIM General Council that the time had come to hand over its remaining program in Nigeria to ECWA, which is the indigenous church which has grown out of SIM's work in this nation.

Council notes that this is the logical sequence of establishing an indigenous church, and is a continuation of the process of transfer of responsibility which has been taking place since ECWA was formed in 1954, and registered by the Nigerian Government as an indigenous church in 1956. Council further notes that this action is in full accord with policy established by SIM General Council in June 1975.

Therefore this Council, with the agreement of the SIM General Director, endorses the structure worked out in consultation with ECWA Executive and approves the following relationship between SIM and ECWA:

1. ECWA will be responsible for the work of the departments formerly under SIM. The departments as agreed upon by ECWA General Council include:

Church Growth
Education (including Theological and Christian Education)
Evangelism
Finance
Media
Medical
Resources and Stewardship (Rural Development)
Services

Each department will operate under its own board which will administer the work and will in turn be responsible to ECWA G.C.C. through ECWA's Executive.

2. All SIM Certificates of Occupancy will be transferred to and registered under the Trustees of ECWA. ECWA Headquarters will be responsible for the use, maintenance, and administration of all such property.

3. SIM is a worldwide body, but in Nigeria all the work will be known as ECWA.

4. SIM International will continue to back up the work of ECWA, being joined in an international partnership with ECWA for the provision of consultation and prayer, and recruitment of personnel and finance for projects including Aviation and other special services mutually agreed upon by this international partnership.

5. SIM International will make a Liaison Officer available to ECWA in Nigeria who will provide consultation with ECWA and representation of the SIM International Office overseas.

6. The Services Department will be responsible for the personal care of SIM missionaries recruited for ECWA and serving under ECWA, including their Conditions of Service, salaries, housing, health care, travel and furlough arrangements, children's education, and other personal matters needed to enable them to serve under ECWA.

7. SIM missionaries will be responsible to ECWA for their work through the following channels:

    ECWA Trustees
    ECWA G.C.C.
    ECWA Executive
    ECWA Department
    Institution
    SIM missionary

8. SIM International will continue to recruit and support missionaries and help financially in projects mutually agreed on by SIM and ECWA. ECWA will provide SIM with audited annual financial statements of funds provided through SIM.

9. All relationships between SIM and ECWA will be through mutual agreement of ECWA G.C.C. and SIM International Office.

10. In all our relationships, we recognize the Lordship of Christ as Head of the Church, of which ECWA and SIM International are co-members. All our dealings with each other will be directed to bring Him glory through evangelism and the discipling of men, women, and children into the body of Christ.

Jos, Nigeria, November 19, 1976

APPENDIX U

ECWA COUNCIL MOTION ON ECWA-SIM RELATIONSHIP

The General Church Council (G.C.C.) of ECWA (Evangelical Churches of West Africa) meeting in Jos, November 19, 1976, gives glory to God Almighty for His faithfulness in saving and sanctifying thousands of Nigerians through the gospel ministry of the Sudan Interior Mission in Nigeria. These Christians in 1954 organized themselves into a body and were registered by the Federal Government of Nigeria as an indigenous church in 1956.

The G.C.C. notes that it is in God's providence that ECWA has grown through the years to assume more and more responsibilities from the Sudan Interior Mission. It is also with gratitude to God that G.C.C. appreciates the steps taken by SIM General Council of June 1975, the Ghana-Nigeria Council of May 1976, and the Ghana-Nigeria Council of November 1976, to bestow such a great honor on and express confidence in ECWA by handing over responsibility for all the work in Nigeria to ECWA.

By the grace of God the G.C.C. accepts and assumes full responsibility for the work of SIM in Nigeria and all its missionaries in Nigeria. Henceforth all SIM missionaries in Nigeria will be known as ECWA personnel and will report to ECWA through their respective departments.

The G.C.C. resolves that the departments will include the following:

        Evangelism
        Church Growth
        Education (including Theological and Christian Education)
        Media
        Medical
        Resources and Stewardship (Rural Development)
        Services
        Finance

Each department will operate under its own board which will administer the work and will in turn be responsible to ECWA G.C.C. through ECWA Executive. All SIM missionaries serving under ECWA will report their work according to the following organizational structure:

ECWA Trustees
↑
ECWA G.C.C.
↑
ECWA Executive
↑
ECWA Department Head
↑
ECWA Institution Head
↑
SIM Missionary

All SIM Certificates of Occupancy will be transferred and registered under the Trustees of ECWA and ECWA headquarters will be responsible for the use, maintenance, and administration of all such property.

Being joined in international partnership, ECWA and SIM International will work together in recruitment of personnel and raising of funds overseas for projects mutually agreed upon for the furtherance of the gospel. ECWA will provide SIM International with audited annual financial statements of funds provided through SIM International. A Liaison Officer will be made available to ECWA in Nigeria by SIM International to provide consultation with ECWA and representation of the SIM International office overseas.

Services Department will be responsible for Aviation, personal care of SIM missionaries recruited for ECWA and serving under ECWA, and similar essential services which will be required to ensure the effectiveness of ECWA in its responsibility of gospel propagation.

All relationships between SIM and ECWA will be through mutual agreement of ECWA G.C.C. and SIM International Liaison Officer. All relationships will be based on the authority of the Bible and determined by the goal of ECWA in evangelism and the discipling of men, women, and children into the body of Christ unto full maturity, recognizing that the power to do the work comes from Christ himself through the Holy Spirit.

Draft motion on the property turned over to ECWA:

That all property transferred to and registered under the trustees of ECWA will be controlled by ECWA Headquarters, who will be responsible for the use, maintenance, and administration of such property. SIM personnel will be assured the use of such buildings and sites as are required for them to carry out their services under ECWA. The Local Church Council or District Church Council may be allowed use of such property after:

1. obtaining clearance from ECWA Headquarters that the property is not needed for Headquarters or missionary use;

2. agreeing to the conditions of occupancy.

Headquarters will reserve the right to ask for the re-use of such property if and when the need arises.

CHURCH GROWTH CHANNELS showing relation of ministries to evangelism and church growth of SIM-ECWA in Nigeria

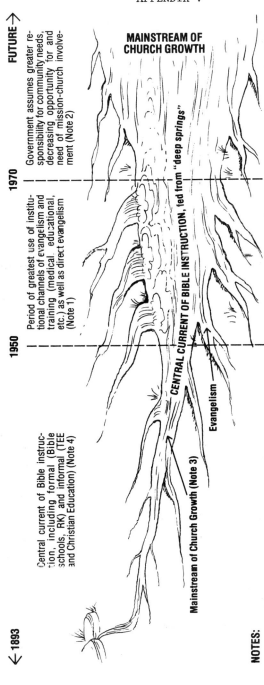

←1893   1950   1970   FUTURE →

MAINSTREAM OF CHURCH GROWTH

CENTRAL CURRENT OF BIBLE INSTRUCTION, fed from "deep springs"

Central current of Bible instruction, including formal (Bible schools, RK) and informal (TEE and Christian Education) (Note 4)

Period of greatest use of institutional channels of evangelism and training (medical, educational, etc.) as well as direct evangelism (Note 1)

Government assumes greater responsibility for community needs, decreasing opportunity for and need of mission-church involvement (Note 2)

Evangelism

Mainstream of Church Growth (Note 3)

(W. Harold Fuller, SIM 1975)

NOTES:

1. Missionary and church evangelistic methods change as opportunities change. Institutional channels of evangelism, such as schools and hospitals, may be needed more in early stages of development of church and community. It is important to identify the gospel with the needs of the community.

2. As governments take increasing responsibility for the needs of their citizens, the opportunity and the need change. This should not be seen as a loss to the work.

3. Throughout, the church should have been growing as believers have been added to it. Even though the channels of evangelism such as hospitals and schools may decrease, the early impetus given to the church through their ministry and training programs should help the church continue to grow.

4. Growth should increase steadily as a result of the central core of Bible teaching, regardless of the changes in the external institutional channels. The investment of personnel and finance in Bible instruction of the members and Bible training of church leaders will need to increase in proportion to the rate of increase in churches and adherents.

ATTITUDE GRID: CHURCH/MISSION CENTRICITY

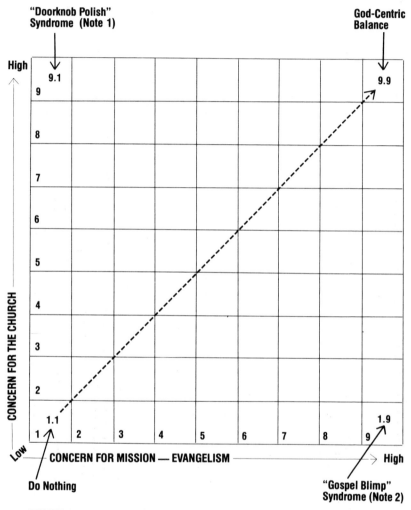

NOTES:

1. "Doorknob Polish" Syndrome — preserving a church institution as an end in itself; no missionary outreach concern.

2. "Gospel Blimp" Syndrome — grandiose outreach projects without regard for establishing a responsible church.

(Ian M. Hay, SIM, 1979)

LIST OF ABBREVIATIONS OF NAMES OF ORGANIZATIONS

USED IN THIS VOLUME

AACC   All Africa Conference of Churches

AEAM   Association of Evangelicals of Africa and Madagascar

AIC   Africa Inland Church

AIM   Africa Inland Mission

AMA   Asia Missions Association

CAMEO   Committee to Assist Missionary Education Overseas

CIM   China Inland Mission

C&MA   Christian & Missionary Alliance

CMS   Church Missionary Society

ECWA   Evangelical Churches of West Africa

EMS   Evangelical Missionary Society

GCC   General Church Council (of ECWA)

IFES   International Fellowship of Evangelical Students

ILO   International Liaison Officer

IMC   International Missionary Council

LAM   Latin America Mission

OMF   Overseas Missionary Fellowship

PACLA   Pan Africa Christian Leadership Assembly

SIC   Sudan Interior Church

SIM   Sudan Interior Mission

TEE   Theological Education by Extension

WCC   World Council of Churches

Bibliography

ABUN-NASR, Jamil M. *A History of the Maghrib*. Cambridge: Cambridge University Press, 1971.

ADEYEMO, Tokunboh. *Salvation in African Tradition* Nairobi: Evangel Publishing House, 1979.

AJAYI, J.F. Ade, ESPIE, Ian (Eds.). *A Thousand Years of West African History* -- A Handbook for Teachers and Students. Ibadan: Ibadan University Press, 1965; London: Thomas Nelson, 1965.

AJAYI, J.F.A. *Christian Missions in Nigeria 1841-1891* -- The Making of a New Elite. Ibadan History Series, General Ed., K. O. Dike. London: Longmans, Green and Co., 1965.

ALLEN, Roland. *The Spontaneous Expansion of the Church*. London: World Dominion Press, 1960.

ANDERSEN, Wilhelm. *Towards a Theology of Missions* -- A Study of the Encounter between the Missionary Enterprise and the Church and Its Theology. I.M.C. Research Pamphlet No. 2. London: SCM Press, 1955.

AYANDELE, E.A. *The Missionary Impact on Modern Nigeria 1842-1914* -- A Political and Social Analysis. Ibadan History Series, Gen. Ed., K.O. Dike. London: Longmans, Green and Co., 1966.

BARRETT, David B. *Schism and Renewal in Africa* -- An Analysis of Six Thousand Contemporary Religious Movements. London: Oxford University Press, 1968.

BARRETT, David B., MAMBO, George K., McLAUGHLIN, Janice, McVEIGH, Malcolm J. (Eds.). *Kenya Churches Handbook* -- The Development of Kenyan Christianity 1498-1973. Kisumu, Kenya: Evangel Publishing House, 1973.

BAVINCK, J.H. *An Introduction to the Science of Missions* (trans. by David H. Freeman). Grand Rapids: Baker Book House, 1960.

BEAVER, R. Pierce. *All Loves Excelling*. Grand Rapids: Wm. B. Eerdmans Publishing Co., 1968.

BEAVER, R. Pierce. (Ed.). *Christianity and African Education* -- The Papers of a Conference at the University of Chicago. Grand Rapids: Wm. B. Eerdmans Publishing Co., 1966.

BEAVER, R. Pierce. (Ed.). *The Gospel and Frontier People* -- A Report of a Consultation, December 1972. South Pasadena: William Carey Library, 1973.

BEAVER, R. Pierce. *To Advance the Gospel.* Grand Rapids: Wm. B. Eerdmans Publishing Co., 1967.

BELLAMY, Wilfred A. (Ed.). *West African Congress on Evangelism* -- Detailed Report of Congress proceedings as they took place at the University of Ibadan, Nigeria from the 5th to 15th July, 1968. Nigerian Evangelical Fellowship, New Life for All.

BEYERHAUS, Peter, LEFEVER, Henry. *The Responsible Church and the Foreign Mission.* Grand Rapids: Wm. B. Eerdmans Publishing Co., 1964.

BOVILL, E.W. *The Golden Trade of the Moors.* Second Edition. London: Oxford University Press, 1970.

CLARK, Dennis E. *The Third World Mission.* Waco, Texas: Word Books, 1971.

COGGINS, Wade T., FRIZEN, E.L. Jr. *Evangelical Missions Tomorrow.* South Pasadena: William Carey Library, 1977.

COOK, Harold R. *Strategy of Missions* -- An Evangelical View. Chicago: Moody Press, 1963.

COOK, Harold R. *An Introduction to the Study of Christian Missions.* Chicago: Moody Press, 1954.

COOK, Harold R. *Missionary Life and Work* -- A Discussion of Principles and Practices of Missions. Chicago: Moody Press, 1959.

COSTAS, Orlando E. *The Church and Its Mission.* Wheaton: Tyndale House Publishers, Inc., 1974.

COTTERELL, F. Peter. *Born at Midnight.* Chicago: Moody Press, 1973.

CRAMPTON, E.P.T. *Christianity in Northern Nigeria.* Zaria, Nigeria: Gaskiya Corporation Ltd., 1975.

Crossroads in Missions. (Key Reprints of the Last Decade). South Pasadena: William Carey Library.

DAVIDSON, Basil. *The African Past* -- Chronicles from Antiquity to Modern Times. Penguin African Library. Harmondsworth, Middlesex: Penguin Books, 1966 (First Published Longmans 1964).

DAVIS, Raymond J. *Fire on the Mountains.* Grand Rapids: Zondervan Publishing House, 1966.

DE LA HAYE, Sophie. *Tread upon the Lion* -- The Story of Tommie Titcombe. Toronto: Sudan Interior Mission, 1974.

DODGE, Ralph E. *The Unpopular Missionary.* Westwood: Fleming H. Revell Co., 1964.

DOUGLAS, J.D. (Ed.). *Let the Earth Hear His Voice* -- International Congress on World Evangelization, Lausanne, Switzerland. Minneapolis: World Wide Publications, 1975.

ENAHORO, Peter. *How To Be a Nigerian. Daily Times*, Nigeria, 1966.

ENGEL, James F., NORTON, H. Wilbert. *What's Gone Wrong With The Harvest?* Grand Rapids: Zondervan Publishing House, 1975.

ENGEL, James F. *Contemporary Christian Communication*. New York: Thomas Nelson, 1979.

Facing Facts in Modern Missions -- A Symposium. Chicago: Moody Press, 1963.

FAGE, J.D. (Ed.). *Africa Discovers Her Past*. London: Oxford University Press, 1970.

FASHOLE-LUKE, Edward, GRAY, Richard, HASTINGS, Adrian, TASIE, Godwin. *Christianity in Independent Africa*. Bloomington: Indiana University Press, 1978.

FIFE, Eric S., GLASSER, Arthur F. *Missions in Crisis* -- Rethinking Missionary Strategy. Chicago: InterVarsity Press, 1961.

FORSBERG, Malcolm. *Dry Season*. Toronto: Sudan Interior Mission, 1964.

FULLER, W. Harold. *Run While the Sun Is Hot*. Toronto: Sudan Interior Mission, 1967.

GERBER, Vergil. *God's Way to Keep a Church Going and Growing*. Regal Books Division, G/L Publications, Glendale, South Pasadena: William Carey Library, 1973.

GERBER, Vergil (Ed.). *Missions in Creative Tension* -- The Green Lake '71 Compendium. South Pasadena: William Carey Library, 1971.

GRIMLEY, John B., ROBINSON, Gordon E. *Church Growth in Central and Southern Nigeria*. Grand Rapids: Wm. B. Eerdmans Publishing Co., 1966.

HALL, Edward T. *The Hidden Dimension*. Garden City, New York: Doubleday and Co., 1969, and *The Silent Language*. Garden City, New York: Doubleday and Co., 1959.

HODGES, Melvin L. *On the Mission Field* -- The Indigenous Church. Chicago: Moody Press, 1953.

HOKE, Donald E. (Ed.). *Evangelicals Face the Future*. Pasadena: William Carey Library, 1978.

HORNER, Norman A. (Ed.). *Protestant Crosscurrents in Mission* -- The Ecumenical-Conservative Encounter. Nashville: Abingdon Press, 1968.

HUNTER, J.H. *A Flame of Fire* -- The Life and Work of R.V. Bingham, Toronto: Sudan Interior Mission, 1961.

IDOWU, Bolaji. *Towards an Indigenous Church*. Nigeria: Literature Department, Methodist Church, 1973. (First published OUP, 1965.)

ISAIAS, Juan. *The Other Side of the Coin*. Grand Rapids: Wm. B. Eerdmans Publishing Co., 1966.

JOHNSTON, Arthur. *The Battle for World Evangelism*. Wheaton: Tyndale House Publishers, Inc., 1978.

JOHNSTONE, P. J. *Operation World*. Bromley: STL Publications, 1978.

KANE, J. Herbert. *A Global View of Christian Missions* -- From Pentecost to the Present. Grand Rapids: Baker Book House, 1971.

KATO, B.H. *African Cultural Revolution and the Christian Faith*. Jos: Challenge, 1975.

KATO, B.H. *Theological Pitfalls in Africa*. Kisumu, Kenya: Evangel Publishing House, 1975.

KENDALL, Elliott. *The End of an Era*. London: SPCK, 1978.

KRAFT, C. H., and WISLEY, T. N. *Readings in Dynamic Indigeneity*. South Pasadena: William Carey Library, 1979.

LAGEER, Eileen. *New Life for All*. London: Oliphants, 1969.

LINDSELL, Harold (Ed.). *The Church's Worldwide Mission*. Waco, Texas: Word Books, 1966.

LOEWEN, Jacob A. *Culture and Human Values* -- Christian Intervention in Anthropological Perspective. South Pasadena: William Carey Library, 1975.

LOEWEN, Jacob A. *The Christian Encounter with Culture*. Monrovia, CA: World Vision, 1967.

LUZBETAK, Louis. *The Church and Cultures* -- An Applied Anthropology for the Religious Worker. South Pasadena: William Carey Library, 1970.

MBITI, John S. *The Crisis of Missions in Africa*. Uganda Church Press, 1971.

McGAVRAN, Donald A. (Ed.). *Crucial Issues in Missions Tomorrow*. Chicago: Moody Press, 1972.

McGAVRAN, Donald A. *Understanding Church Growth*. Grand Rapids: Wm. B. Eerdmans Publishing Co., 1970.

McGAVRAN, Donald A. *The Clash between Christianity and Cultures*. Washington: Canon Press, 1974.

McGAVRAN, Donald A. *How Churches Grow* -- The New Frontiers of Mission. London: World Dominion Press, 1959.

McGAVRAN, Donald A. *The Bridges of God* -- A Study in the Strategy of Missions. London: World Dominion Press, 1955.

McGAVRAN, Donald A. *Church Growth and Christian Mission*. New York: Harper & Row, 1965.

MELLIS, Charles J. *Committed Communities*. South Pasadena: William Carey Library, 1976.

MOORHOUSE, Geoffrey, *The Missionaries*. New York: J. B. Lippincott, 1973.

NEILL, Stephen. *A History of Christian Missions*. The Pelican History of the Church: 6. Baltimore: Penguin Books, 1964.

NEILL, Stephen. *Colonialism and Christian Missions*. New York: McGraw-Hill, 1966.

NEILL, Stephen, ANDERSON, Gerald H., GOODWIN, John (Eds.). *Concise Dictionary of the Christian World Mission.* World Christian Books. United Society for Christian Literature, London: Lutterworth Press, 1970.

NEILL, Stephen. *Salvation Tomorrow.* London: Lutterworth Press, 1976.

NEVIUS, John L. *The Planting and Development of Missionary Churches.* Philadelphia: The Presbyterian and Reformed Publishing Company, 1958.

NIDA, Eugene. *Customs and Cultures.* New York: Harper & Row, 1954.

NIDA, Eugene. *Religion Across Cultures* -- A Study in the Communication of Christian Faith. New York: Harper & Row, 1968.

NILES, D.T. *Upon the Earth.* New York: McGraw-Hill, 1962.

NORTHCOTT, Cecil. *Christianity in Africa.* London: SCM Press, 1963.

OLIVER, Dennis Mackintosh. *Make Disciples,* the Nature and Scope of the Great Commission. An unpublished thesis submitted to Fuller Theological Seminary, May 15, 1973.

One World, One Task. Report of the Evangelical Alliance Commission on World Mission. London: Scripture Union, 1971.

ORR, J. Edwin. *Evangelical Awakenings in Africa.* Minneapolis: Bethany Fellowship, 1975.

PADEN, John N. *Religion and Political Culture in Kano.* Los Angeles: University of California, 1973.

PALMER, Donald C. *Explosion of People Evangelism.* Chicago: Moody Press, 1974.

PAN AFRICAN CHRISTIAN LEADERSHIP ASSEMBLY. *Facing the New Challenges.* Kisumu, Kenya: Evangel Publishing House, 1977.

PARRINDER, Geoffrey. *Religion in Africa.* Penguin African Library, Harmondsworth, Middlesex: Penguin Books, 1969.

PAYNE, Denis (Ed.). *African Independence and Christian Freedom* -- Addresses delivered at Makerere University College, Uganda, 1962. London: Oxford University Press, 1965.

PETERS, George W. *Saturation Evangelism.* Grand Rapids: Zondervan, 1970.

PETERS, George W. *A Biblical Theology of Missions.* Chicago: Moody Press, 1972.

PICKETT, J. Waskom. *The Dynamics of Church Growth.* New York: Abingdon Press, 1972.

READ, William R., INESON, Frank A. *Brazil 1980: The Protestant Handbook* -- The Dynamics of Church Growth in the 1950s and 60s and the Tremendous Potential for the 70s. Monrovia, CA: World Vision, 1973.

SCHERER, James A. *Missionary Go Home!* A Reappraisal of the Christian World Mission. Englewood Cliffs: Prentice-Hall, 1964.

SHORTER, Aylward. *African ·Culture and the Christian Church* -- An
  Introduction to Social and Pastoral Anthropology. New York:
  Orbis Books, 1974. (First published Geoffrey Chapman Publishers.)

SMALLEY, William. *Readings in Missionary Anthropology.* Tarrytown,
  New York: *Practical Anthropology,* 1967.

SNYDER, Howard A. *The Community of the King.* Downers Grove: Inter-
  Varsity Press, 1977.

SOLTAU, T. Stanley. *Missions at the Crossroads* -- The Indigenous Church --
  A Solution for the Unfinished Task. Grand Rapids: Baker Book House,
  1955.

STOTT, John R.W. *Christian Mission in the Modern World.* Downers Grove,
  IL: InterVarsity Press, 1975.

SUDAN INTERIOR MISSION. *Root from Dry Ground* The Story of the Sudan
  Interior Mission. Toronto: Sudan Interior Mission, 1966.

SWANK, Gerald O. *Frontier Peoples of Central Nigeria.* South Pasadena:
  William Carey Library, 1977.

TABER, Charles R. *The Church in Africa 1977.* South Pasadena: William
  Carey Library, 1977.

THIESSEN, John Caldwell. *A Survey of World Missions.* Third Edition.
  Chicago: Moody Press, 1961.

TIPPETT, A.R. (Ed.). *God, Man and Church Growth.* Grand Rapids:
  Wm. B. Eerdmans Publishing Co., 1973.

TRIMINGHAM, J. Spencer. *The Christian Church and Islam in West Africa.*
  IMC Research Pamphlets #3. London: SCM Press, 1955.

VERKUYL, J. *Contemporary Missiology, an Introduction.* Grand Rapids:
  Wm. B. Eerdmans Publishing Co., 1978.

WAGNER, Peter. *Look Out! The Pentecostals Are Coming.* Carol Stream,
  IL: Creation House, 1973.

WAGNER, C. Peter. *Frontiers in Missionary Strategy.* Chicago: Moody
  Press, 1971.

WAGNER, C. Peter. *Church/Mission Tensions Today.* Chicago: Moody
  Press, 1972.

WAGNER, C. Peter. DAYTON, Edward R. *Unreached Peoples '79.* Elgin,
  IL: David C. Cook Publishing Co., 1978.

WAKATAMA, Pius. *Independence for the Third World Church.* Downers Grove:
  InterVarsity Press, 1976.

WARREN, Max. *Problems and Promises in Africa Today* -- The Lichfield
  Lectures in Divinity for 1963. London: Hodder and Stoughton, 1964.

WARREN, Max. *Perspective in Mission.* London: Hodder and Stoughton, 1964.

WARREN, Max. *I Believe in the Great Commission.* London: Hodder and
  Stoughton, 1976.

WINTER, Ralph. *The Evangelical Response to Bangkok*. South Pasadena: William Carey Library, 1973.

WINTER, Ralph. *The Two Structures of God's Redemptive Mission*. South Pasadena: William Carey Library, 1974.

WINTER, Ralph. *1980 and That Certain Elite*. South Pasadena: William Carey Library, 1976.

WINTER, Ralph. *The Grounds for a New Thrust in World Mission*. South Pasadena: William Carey Library, 1977.

WINTER, Ralph. *The New Macedonia: A Revolutionary New Era in Mission Begins*. South Pasadena: William Carey Library, 1975.

WOLD, Joseph Conrad. *God's Impatience in Liberia*. Grand Rapids: Wm. B. Eerdmans Publishing Co., 1968.

WORLD EVANGELICAL FELLOWSHIP. *Evangelical Review of Theology*. Vol. 2. No. 2. New Delhi: October 1978.

INDEX

Born in Canada of missionary parents, W. Harold Fuller first
went to Africa in 1951 with the Sudan Interior Mission.
After serving as editor-in-chief of Africa's second largest
monthly, <u>African Challenge</u>, Fuller entered mission administration in 1965 and currently is Deputy General Director of
the Sudan Interior Mission. Author, administrator, and
guest lecturer, Fuller combines his wide mission experience
and journalism to bring new insights to a topic of great
current concern.